VMware vSphere 5.1 Clustering Deepdive

VMware vSphere 5.1 Clustering Deepdive

International Standard Book Number (ISBN:) 978-1478183419

All terms mentioned in this book that are known to be trademarks or service marks have been appropriately capitalized.

Use of a term in this book should not be regarded as affecting the validity of any trademark or service mark.

Version: 1.0

About the Authors

Duncan Epping is a Principal Architect working for VMware as part of Technical Marketing. Duncan specializes in vSphere HA and VMware vCloud infrastructure architecture. Duncan was among the first VMware Certified Design Experts (VCDX 007). Duncan is the owner of Yellow-Bricks.com, one of the leading VMware/virtualization blogs worldwide (Voted number 1 virtualization blog for the 5th consecutive time on vsphere-land.com.) and lead-author of the "vSphere Quick Start Guide" and co-author of "Foundation for Cloud Computing with VMware vSphere 4", "Cloud Computing with VMware vCloud Director", "VMware vSphere 4.1 HA and DRS technical Deepdive" and best seller "VMware vSphere 5.0 Clustering Technical Deepdive".

He can be followed on twitter **@DuncanYB.**

Frank Denneman is a Senior Architect working for VMware as part of Technical Marketing. Frank specializes in resource management and down time avoidance including vSphere DRS, Storage DRS, vMotion and Storage vMotion. Frank is among the first VMware Certified Design Experts (VCDX 029). Frank is the owner of FrankDenneman.nl which has recently been voted number 5 worldwide on vsphere-land.com and co-author of "VMware vSphere 4.1 HA and DRS technical deepdive" and best seller "VMware vSphere 5.0 Clustering Technical Deepdive".

He can be followed on twitter **@FrankDenneman.**

Acknowledgements

The authors of this book work for VMware. The opinions expressed here are the authors' personal opinions. Content published was not approved in advance by VMware and does not necessarily reflect the views and opinions of VMware. This is the authors' book, not a VMware book.

First of all we would like to thank our VMware management team (Kaushik Banerjee, Jim Senicka, Bogomil Balkansky and Raghu Raghuram) for supporting us on this and other projects.

A special thanks goes out to our editor Doug Baer and our technical reviewers Keith Farkas, Marc Sevigny and Elisha Ziskind (HA Engineering), Ken Werneburg (Technical Marketing), Anne Holler, Mustafa Uysal, Ali Mashtizadeh and Gabriel Tarasuk-Levin (vMotion and Storage vMotion Engineering), Lee Dilworth and Stuart Hardman (Systems Engineering), and Daniel Conde (PSO). Thanks for keeping us honest and contributing to this book.

A very special thanks to our families for supporting this project. Without your support we could not have done this.

We would like to dedicate this book to everyone who made VMware to what it is today. You have not only changed our lives but also revolutionized a complete industry.

Duncan Epping and Frank Denneman

Foreword

Datacenters have traditionally required careful configuration, design, monitoring and other operational tasks to run application workloads effectively. However, these activities are fundamentally geared towards "keeping the lights on", and do not add a tremendous amount of value for enabling IT organizations to serve the core goals of the business. Many of these tasks are performed manually to implement policies associated with the running of application workloads. What if application owners defines business requirements at a high level, and the IT organization translates that into system level policies, and the underlying infrastructure interprets those policies and automatically configures, manages and operates the underlying system to meet those policy goals? That's the goal of VMware and the solutions based on the technology to create a new generation of datacenters.

This datacenter is separated into two layers – which we can consider as the "what" and the "how". The upper layer is the area where the owners of the applications rely upon to run their workloads while meeting their business goals – which is the "what". VMware's goal is to make that as autonomic as possible. An owner of an application is not concerned with precisely which physical hosts the virtual machines run on, or how the availability policies for the virtual machines are implemented. The application owners instead specify the requirements and expect the underlying vSphere substrate that is appropriately designed and configured, to deliver services to meet those needs.

The lower layer is concerned with the "how", and this is where core policies such as high availability and distributed resource scheduling are defined at a cluster level and are controlled programmatically. The cluster becomes the unit of management, and policies are defined at the cluster level, and we no longer need to work at the granularity of individual servers. That is the topic of this book and why it is important for successful vSphere deployments. VMware vSphere needs to be configured appropriately at a cluster level to manage resources in order to meet the high level service needs, and by controlling the cluster, a large pool of servers work in a coordinated manner to deliver the resources required by the workloads. These workload requirements may include availability levels, storage I/O requirements and other specifications relevant to the application owners.

Therefore, the new age datacenter is more than just a hypervisor or a virtualization layer. It combines many elements of a traditional datacenter including the compute, storage and network components and enables them to be managed programmatically. This means that elements that previously required manual configuration, rewiring, provisioning or "racking or stacking" are now under programmatic control, and in some cases are instantiated as virtualized software constructs. This provides for the flexibility and operational efficiencies demanded by modern applications. As workload demands change, the underlying infrastructure can adapt or scale-out to meet its needs.

On the long term, we expect more and more elements to be under programmatic control. Higher level constructs such as patching, and app-centric services will start to be part of the standard services. The expansion will also occur on the system side as well. Networking will be become more programmatic; as an example, security policies will be assigned to applications, as opposed to specific devices such as network ports. Similar innovations are occurring in the storage area as well, as we start to consider virtual machines to be unit where data resides, and we will move away from associating data with physical storage, such as LUNs or file systems.

The goals of cloud computing demand that all of these elements continue to be managed in a dynamic manner, and careful design of the underlying infrastructure with the type of knowledge, provided by books such as the one you are reading, will help make the applications run in an environment where IT managers can concentrate foremost on meeting business requirements, as opposed to maintaining IT plumbing to keep the lights on.

We hope you will find this book both useful and educational.

Raghu Raghuram
Executive Vice President, Cloud Infrastructure and Management
VMware

Part I

vSphere High Availability

Chapter 1

Introduction to vSphere High Availability

Availability has traditionally been one of the most important aspects when providing services. When providing services on a shared platform like VMware vSphere, the impact of downtime exponentially grows and as such VMware engineered a feature called VMware vSphere High Availability. VMware vSphere High Availability, hereafter simply referred to as HA, provides a simple and cost effective solution to increase availability for any application running in a virtual machine regardless of its operating system. It is configured using a couple of simple steps through vCenter Server (vCenter) and as such provides a uniform and simple interface. HA enables you to create a cluster out of multiple ESXi or ESX servers. We will use ESXi in this book when referring to either, as ESXi is the standard going forward. This will enable you to protect virtual machines and hence their workloads. In the event of a failure of one of the hosts in the cluster, impacted virtual machines are automatically restarted on other ESXi hosts within that same VMware vSphere Cluster (cluster).

Figure 1: High Availability in action

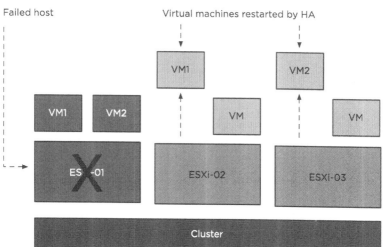

On top of that, in the case of a Guest OS level failure, HA can restart the failed Guest OS. This feature is called VM Monitoring, but is sometimes also referred to as VM-HA. This might sound fairly complex but again can be implemented with a single click.

Figure 2: OS Level HA just a single click

Unlike many other clustering solutions, HA is a fairly simple solution to implement and literally enabled within 5 clicks. On top of that, HA is widely adopted and used in all situations. However, HA is not a 1:1 replacement for solutions like Microsoft Clustering Services (MSCS). The main difference between MSCS and HA being that MSCS was designed to protect stateful cluster-aware applications while HA was designed to protect any virtual machine regardless of the type of application within, but also can be extended to the application layer through the use of VM and Application Monitoring.

In the case of HA, a failover incurs downtime as the virtual machine is literally restarted on one of the remaining nodes in the cluster. Whereas MSCS transitions the service to one of the remaining nodes in the cluster when a failure occurs. In contrary to what many believe, MSCS does not guarantee that there is no downtime during a transition. On top of that, your application needs to be cluster-aware and stateful in order to get the most out of this mechanism, which limits the number of workloads that could really benefit from this type of clustering.

One might ask why would you want to use HA when a virtual machine is restarted and service is temporarily lost. The answer is simple; not all virtual machines (or services) need 99.999% uptime. For many services the type of availability HA provides is more than sufficient. On top of that, many applications were never designed to run on top of an MSCS cluster. This means that there is no guarantee of availability or data consistency if an application is clustered with MSCS but is not cluster-aware.

In addition, MSCS clustering can be complex and requires special skills and training. One example is managing patches and updates/upgrades in a MSCS environment; this could even lead to more downtime if not operated correctly and definitely complicates operational procedures. HA however reduces complexity, costs (associated with downtime and MSCS), resource overhead and unplanned downtime for minimal additional costs. It is important to note that HA, contrary to MSCS, does not require any changes to the guest as HA is provided on the hypervisor level. Also, VM Monitoring does not require any additional software or OS modifications except for VMware Tools, which should be installed anyway as a best practice. In case even higher availability is required, VMware also provides a level of application awareness through Application Monitoring, which has been leveraged by partners like Symantec to enable application level resiliency and could be used by in-house development teams to increase resiliency for their application.

HA has proven itself over and over again and is widely adopted within the industry; if you are not using it today, hopefully you will be convinced after reading this section of the book.

vSphere 5.1

Before we dive into the main constructs of HA and describe all the choices one has to make when configuring HA, we will first briefly touch on what's new in vSphere 5.0 and 5.1 and describe the basic requirements and steps needed to enable HA. The focus of this book is vSphere 5.1 and the enhancements made to increase stability of your virtualized infrastructure. We will also emphasize the changes made with vSphere 5.0 as we recognize that many of you might not be familiar with vSphere 5.0 yet. We will, where applicable, still discuss features and concepts that have been around since vCenter 2.x to ensure that reading this book provides understanding of every aspect of HA.

What's New in 5.x?

Those who have used HA in the past and have not played around with vSphere 5.0 will spot the enhancements which vSphere 5.0 brought quickly. Those who have played around with vSphere 5.0 will probably not see any major changes between 5.0 and 5.1, but there are some and these are highlighted below.

In vSphere 5.0 HA was completely redesigned and developed from the ground up. This is the reason enabling or reconfiguring HA literally takes seconds in 5.x instead of minutes with previous versions.

With the redesign of the HA stack in vSphere 5.0, some very welcome changes were introduced to compliment the already extensive capabilities of HA. Some of the key components of HA changed completely and new functionality was added. We have listed some of these changes below for your convenience and we will discuss them in more detail in the appropriate chapters. All the changes below were introduced in vSphere 5.0

- New HA Agent - Fault Domain Manager (FDM) is the name of the agent. HA has been rewritten from the ground up and FDM replaces the legacy AAM agent.
- No dependency on DNS – HA has been written to use IP only to avoid any dependency on DNS.
- Primary node concept – The primary/secondary node mechanism has been completely removed to lift all limitations (maximum of 5 primary nodes with vSphere 4.1 and before) associated with it.

- Supports management network partitions – Capable of having multiple "master nodes" when multiple network partitions exist.
- Enhanced isolation validation - Avoids false positives when the complete management network has failed.
- Datastore heartbeating – This additional level of heartbeating reduces chances of false positives by using the storage layer to validate the state of the host and to avoid unnecessary downtime when there's a management network interruption.
- Enhanced Admission Control Policies:
  - o The Host Failures based admission control allows for more than 4 hosts to be specified (31 is the maximum).
  - o The Percentage based admission control policy allows you to specify percentages for both CPU and memory separately.
  - o The Failover Host based admission control policy allows you to specify multiple designated failover hosts.

vSphere 5.1 introduced several enhancements. Although compared to vSphere 5.0 these appear to be minor they are important to understand in order to create a highly resilient environment.

- Ability to set slot size for "Host failures tolerated" through the vSphere Web Client
- Ability to retrieve a list of the virtual machines that span multiple slots
- Enhancements to the handling of Permanent Device Loss situations (introduced in 5.0 Update 1)
- Support for Guest OS Sleep mode
- Including the Application Monitoring SDK in the Guest SDK (VMware Tools SDK)
- vSphere HA (FDM) VIB is automatically added to Auto-Deploy image profile
- Ability to delay isolation response through the use of "das.config.fdm.isolationPolicyDelaySec"

What is required for HA to Work?

Each feature or product has very specific requirements and HA is no different. Knowing the requirements of HA is part of the basics we have to cover before diving into some of the more complex concepts. For those who are completely new to HA, we will also show you how to configure it.

Prerequisites

Before enabling HA it is highly recommend validating that the environment meets all the prerequisites. We have also included recommendations from an infrastructure perspective that will enhance resiliency.

Requirements:

- Minimum of two ESXi hosts
- Minimum of 3GB memory per host to install ESXi and enable HA
- VMware vCenter Server
- Shared Storage for virtual machines
- Pingable gateway or other reliable address

Recommendation:

- Redundant Management Network (not a requirement, but highly recommended)
- Multiple shared datastores

Firewall Requirements

The following table contains the ports that are used by HA for communication. If your environment contains firewalls external to the host, ensure these ports are opened for HA to function correctly. HA will open the required ports on the ESX or ESXi firewall. Please note that this is the first substantial difference as HA as of vSphere 5 only uses a single port compared to multiple ports pre-vSphere 5.0 and ESXi 5.0 is enhanced with a firewall.

Table 1: High Availability port settings

Port	Protocol	Direction
8182	UDP	Inbound
8182	TCP	Inbound
8182	UDP	Outbound
8182	TCP	Outbound

Configuring vSphere High Availability

HA can be configured with the default settings within a couple of clicks. The following steps will show you how to create a cluster and enable HA, including VM Monitoring, using the vSphere Web Client. Each of the settings and the design decisions associated with these steps will be described in more depth in the following chapters.

1. Click "Hosts & Clusters" on the Solutions tab..
2. Right-click the Datacenter in the Inventory tree and click New Cluster.
3. Give the new cluster an appropriate name. We recommend at a minimum including the location of the cluster and a sequence number ie. ams-hadrs-001.
4. Select Turn On vSphere HA.
5. Ensure "Enable host monitoring" and "Enable admission control" is selected.
6. Select "Percentage of cluster resources…" under Policy.
7. Enable VM Monitoring Status by selecting "VM and Application Monitoring".
8. Click "OK" to complete the creation of the cluster.

Figure 3: Ready to complete the New Cluster Wizard

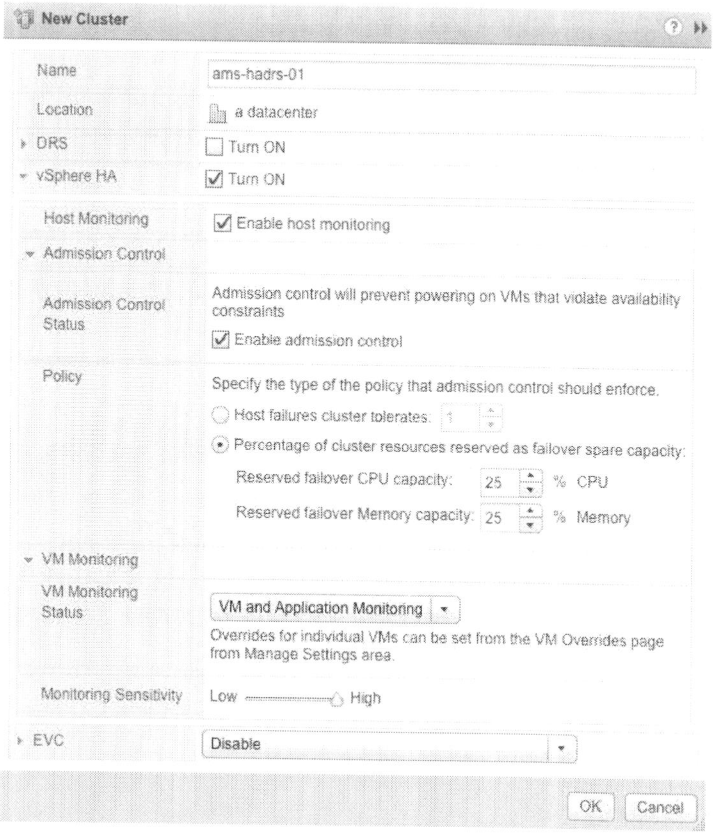

New Cluster   ? ▸▸

Name	ams-hadrs-01
Location	a datacenter
▸ DRS	☐ Turn ON
▾ vSphere HA	☑ Turn ON
Host Monitoring	☑ Enable host monitoring
▾ Admission Control	
Admission Control Status	Admission control will prevent powering on VMs that violate availability constraints ☑ Enable admission control
Policy	Specify the type of the policy that admission control should enforce. ◯ Host failures cluster tolerates: 1 ◉ Percentage of cluster resources reserved as failover spare capacity: Reserved failover CPU capacity: 25 % CPU Reserved failover Memory capacity: 25 % Memory
▾ VM Monitoring	
VM Monitoring Status	VM and Application Monitoring ▾ Overrides for individual VMs can be set from the VM Overrides page from Manage Settings area.
Monitoring Sensitivity	Low ⎯⎯⎯⎯⎯ High
▸ EVC	Disable ▾

OK   Cancel

When the HA cluster has been created, the ESXi hosts can be added to the cluster simply by right clicking the cluster and selecting "Move Hosts into Cluster", if they were already added to vCenter, or by right clicking the cluster and selecting "Add Host".

When an ESXi host is added to the newly-created cluster, the HA agent will be loaded and configured. Once this has completed, HA will enable protection of the workloads running on this ESXi host.

As we have clearly demonstrated, HA is a simple clustering solution that will allow you to protect virtual machines against host failure and operating system failure in literally minutes. Understanding the architecture of HA will enable you to reach that extra 9 when it comes to availability. The following chapters will discuss the architecture and fundamental concepts of HA. We will also discuss all decision-making moments to ensure you will configure HA in such a way that it meets the requirements of your or your customer's environment.

Chapter 2

Components of High Availability

Now that we know what the pre-requisites are and how to configure HA the next steps will be describing which components form HA. Keep in mind that this is still a "high level" overview. There is more under the cover that we will explain in following chapters. The following diagram depicts a two-host cluster and shows the key HA components.

Figure 4: Components of High Availability

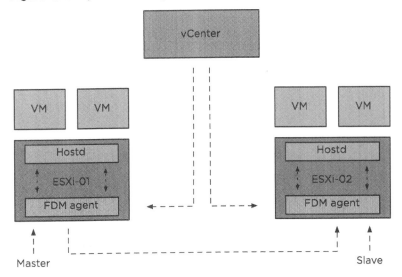

As you can clearly see, there are three major components that form the foundation for HA as of vSphere 5.0:

- FDM
- HOSTD
- vCenter

The first and probably the most important component that forms HA is FDM (Fault Domain Manager). This is the HA agent, and has replaced what was once known as AAM (Legato's Automated Availability Manager).
The FDM Agent is responsible for many tasks such as communicating host resource information, virtual machine states and HA properties to other hosts in the cluster. FDM also handles heartbeat mechanisms, virtual machine placement, virtual machine restarts, logging and much more. We are not going to discuss all of this in-depth separately as we feel that this will complicate things too much.

FDM, in our opinion, is one of the most important agents on an ESXi host, when HA is enabled, of course, and we are assuming this is the case. The engineers recognized this importance and added an extra level of resiliency to HA. Contrary to AAM, FDM uses a single-process agent. However, FDM spawns a watchdog process. In the unlikely event of an agent failure, the watchdog functionality will pick up on this and restart the agent to ensure HA functionality remains without anyone ever noticing it failed. The agent is also resilient to network interruptions and "all paths down" (APD) conditions. Inter-host communication automatically uses another communication path (if the host is configured with redundant management networks) in the case of a network failure.

As of vSphere 5.0, HA is no longer dependent on DNS as it works with IP addresses only. This is one of the major improvements that FDM brought. This also means that the character limit that HA imposed on the hostname has been lifted. (Pre-vSphere 5.0, FQDNs were limited to 26 characters.) This does not mean that ESXi hosts need to be registered with their IP addresses in vCenter; it is still a best practice to register ESXi hosts by FQDN in vCenter. Although HA does not depend on DNS anymore, remember that many other services do. On top of that, monitoring and troubleshooting will be much easier when hosts are correctly registered within vCenter and have a valid FQDN.

Basic design principle
Although HA is not dependent on DNS anymore, it is still recommended to register the hosts with their FQDN.

Another major change that FDM brings is logging. Some of you might have never realized this and some of you might have discovered it the hard way: prior to vSphere 5.0, the HA log files were not sent to syslog.

vSphere 5.0 brings a standardized logging mechanism where a single log file has been created for all operational log messages; it is called fdm.log. This log file is stored under /var/log/ as depicted in Figure 5.

Figure 5: HA log file

Basic design principle

Ensure syslog is correctly configured and log files are offloaded to a safe location to offer the possibility of performing a root cause analysis in case disaster strikes.

HOSTD Agent

One of the most crucial agents on a host is HOSTD. This agent is responsible for many of the tasks we take for granted like powering on virtual machines. FDM talks directly to HOSTD and vCenter, so it is not dependent on VPXA, like in previous releases. This is, of course, to avoid any unnecessary overhead and dependencies, making HA more reliable than ever before and enabling HA to respond faster to power-on requests. That ultimately results in higher VM uptime.

When, for whatever reason, HOSTD is unavailable or not yet running after a restart, the host will not participate in any FDM-related processes. FDM relies on HOSTD for information about the virtual machines that are registered to the host, and manages the virtual machines using HOSTD APIs. In short, FDM is dependent on HOSTD and if HOSTD is not operational, FDM halts all functions and waits for HOSTD to become operational.

vCenter

That brings us to our final component, the vCenter Server. vCenter is the core of every vSphere Cluster and is responsible for many tasks these days. For our purposes, the following are the most important and the ones we will discuss in more detail:

- Deploying and configuring HA Agents
- Communication of cluster configuration changes
- Protection of virtual machines

vCenter is responsible for pushing out the FDM agent to the ESXi hosts when applicable. Prior to vSphere 5, the push of these agents would be done in a serial fashion. With vSphere 5.0, this is done in parallel to allow for faster deployment and configuration of multiple hosts in a cluster. vCenter is also responsible for communicating configuration changes in the cluster to the host which is elected as the master. We will discuss this concept of master and slaves in the following chapter. Examples of configuration changes are modification or addition of an advanced setting or the introduction of a new host into the cluster.

As of vSphere 5.0, HA also leverages vCenter to retrieve information about the status of virtual machines and, of course, vCenter is used to display the protection status (Figure 6) of virtual machines. (What "virtual machine protection" actually means will be discussed in chapter 3.) On top of that, vCenter is responsible for the protection and unprotection of virtual machines. This not only applies to user initiated power-offs or power-ons of virtual machines, but also in the case where an ESXi host is disconnected from vCenter at which point vCenter will request the master HA agent to unprotect the affected virtual machines.

Figure 6: Virtual machine protection state

Although HA is configured by vCenter and exchanges virtual machine state information with HA, vCenter is not involved when HA responds to failure. It is comforting to know that in case of a host failure containing the virtualized vCenter Server, HA takes care of the failure and restarts the vCenter Server on another host, including all other configured virtual machines from that failed host.

There is a corner case scenario with regards to vCenter failure: if the ESXi hosts are so called "stateless hosts" and Distributed vSwitches are used for the management network, virtual machine restarts will not be attempted until vCenter is restarted. For stateless environments, vCenter and Auto Deploy availability is key as the ESXi hosts literally depend on them. If vCenter is unavailable, it will not be possible to make changes to the configuration of the cluster. vCenter is the source of truth for the set of virtual machines that are protected, the cluster configuration, the virtual machine-to-host compatibility information, and the host membership. So, while HA, by design, will respond to failures without vCenter, HA relies on vCenter to be available to configure or monitor the cluster.

When a virtual vCenter Server, or the vCenter Server Appliance, has been implemented, we recommend setting the correct HA restart priorities for it. Although vCenter Server is not required to restart virtual machines, there are multiple components that rely on vCenter and, as such, a speedy recovery is desired. When configuring your vCenter virtual machine with a high priority for restarts, remember to include all services on which your vCenter server depends for a successful restart: DNS, MS AD and MS SQL (or any other database server you are using).

Basic design principles

In stateless environments, ensure vCenter and Auto Deploy are highly available as recovery time of your virtual machines might be dependent on them.

Understand the impact of virtualizing vCenter. Ensure it has high priority for restarts and ensure that services which vCenter Server depends on are available: DNS, AD and database.

Chapter 3

Fundamental Concepts

Now that you know about the components of HA, it is time to start talking about some of the fundamental concepts of HA clusters:

- Master / Slave agents
- Heartbeating
- Isolated vs Network partitioned
- Virtual Machine Protection

Everyone who has implemented vSphere knows that multiple hosts can be configured into a cluster. A cluster can best be seen as a collection of resources. These resources can be carved up with the use of vSphere Distributed Resource Scheduler (DRS) into separate pools of resources or used to increase availability by enabling HA.

With vSphere 5.0, a lot has changed when it comes to HA. For example, an HA cluster used to consist of two types of nodes. A node could either be a primary or a secondary node. This concept was introduced due to the dependency on AAM and allowed scaling up to 32 hosts per cluster. FDM has changed this game completely and removed the whole concept of primary and secondary nodes. (For more details about the legacy (AAM) node mechanism we would like to refer you to the *vSphere 4.1 HA and DRS Technical Deepdive*.)

One of the most crucial parts of an HA design used to be the design considerations around HA primary nodes and the maximum of 5 per cluster. These nodes became the core of every HA implementation and literally were responsible for restarting virtual machines. Without at least one primary node surviving the failure, a restart of virtual machines was not possible. This led to some limitations from an architectural perspective and was also one of the drivers for VMware to rewrite vSphere HA.

The vSphere 5.0 architecture introduces the concept of master and slave HA agents. Except during network partitions, which are discussed later, there is only one master HA agent in a cluster. Any agent can serve as a master, and all others are considered its slaves. A master agent is in charge of monitoring the health of virtual machines for which it is responsible and restarting any that fail. The slaves are responsible for forwarding information to the master agents and restarting any virtual machines at the direction of the master. Another thing that has changed is that the HA agent, regardless of its role as master or slave, implements the VM/App monitoring feature; with AAM, this feature was part of VPXA.

Master Agent

As stated, one of the primary tasks of the master is to keep track of the state of the virtual machines it is responsible for and to take action when appropriate. In a normal situation there is only a single master in a cluster. We will discuss the scenario where multiple masters can exist in a single cluster in one of the following sections, but for now let's talk about a cluster with a single master. A master will claim responsibility for a virtual machine by taking "ownership" of the datastore on which the virtual machine's configuration file is stored.

Basic design principle

To maximize the chance of restarting virtual machines after a failure we recommend masking datastores on a cluster basis. Although sharing of datastores across clusters will work, it will increase complexity from an administrative perspective.

That is not all, of course. The HA master is also responsible for exchanging state information with vCenter. This means that it will not only receive but also send information to vCenter when required. The HA master is also the host that initiates the restart of virtual machines when a host has failed. You may immediately want to ask what happens when the master is the one that fails, or, more generically, which of the hosts can become the master and when is it elected?

Election

A master is elected by a set of HA agents whenever the agents are not in network contact with a master. A master election thus occurs when HA is first enabled on a cluster and when the host on which the master is running:

- fails,
- becomes network partitioned or isolated,
- is disconnected from vCenter Server,
- is put into maintenance or standby mode,
- or when HA is reconfigured on the host.

The HA master election takes approximately 15 seconds and is conducted using UDP. While HA won't react to failures during the election, once a master is elected, failures detected before and during the election will be handled. The election process is simple but robust. The host that is participating in the election with the greatest number of connected datastores will be elected master. If two or more hosts have the same number of datastores connected, the one with the highest Managed Object Id will be chosen. This however is done lexically; meaning that 99 beats 100 as 9 is larger than 1. For each host, the HA State of the host will be shown on the Summary tab. This includes the role as depicted in Figure 7 where the host is a master host.

After a master is elected, each slave that has management network connectivity with it will setup a single secure, encrypted, TCP connection to the master. This secure connection is SSL-based. One thing to stress here though is that slaves do not communicate with each other after the master has been elected unless a re-election of the master needs to take place.

Figure 7: Master Agent

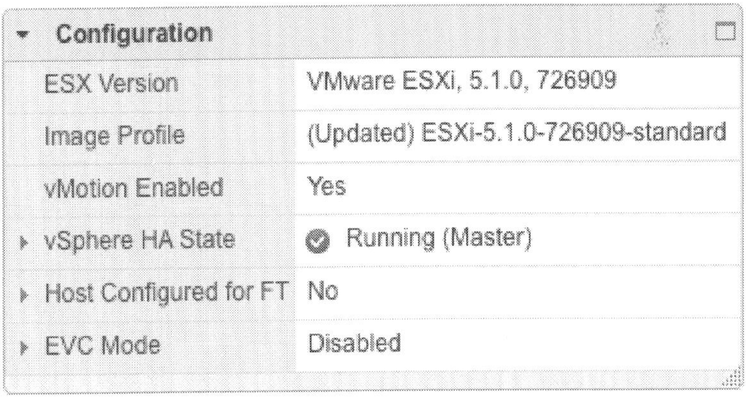

Configuration	
ESX Version	VMware ESXi, 5.1.0, 726909
Image Profile	(Updated) ESXi-5.1.0-726909-standard
vMotion Enabled	Yes
▸ vSphere HA State	⊘ Running (Master)
▸ Host Configured for FT	No
▸ EVC Mode	Disabled

As stated earlier, when a master is elected it will try to acquire ownership of all of the datastores it can directly access or access by proxying requests to one of the slaves connected to it using the management network. It does this by locking a file called "protectedlist" that is stored on the datastores in an existing cluster. The master will also attempt to take ownership of any datastores it discovers along the way, and it will periodically retry any it could not take ownership of previously.

The naming format and location of this file is as follows:

/<root of datastore>/.vSphere-HA/<cluster-specific-directory>/protectedlist

For those wondering how "<cluster-specific-directory>" is constructed:

<uuid of vCenter Server>-<number part of the MoID of the cluster>-<random 8 char string>-<name of the host running vCenter Server>

The master uses this protectedlist file to store the inventory. It keeps track of which virtual machines are protected by HA. Calling it an inventory might be slightly overstating: it is a list of protected virtual machines and it includes information around virtual machine CPU reservation and memory overhead. The master distributes this inventory across all datastores in use by the virtual machines in the cluster. Figure 8 shows an example of this file on one of the datastores.

Figure 8: Protectedlist file

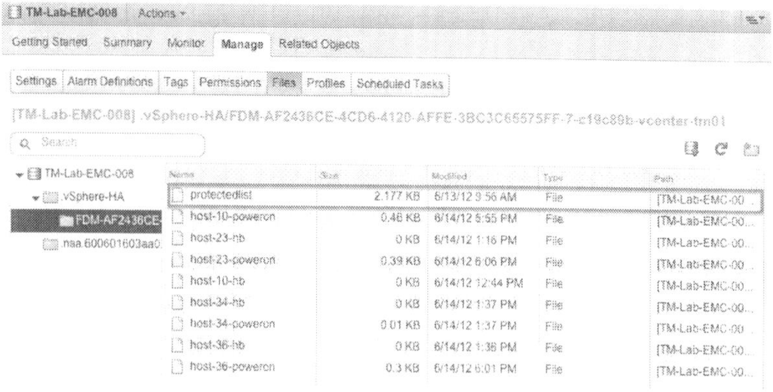

Now that we know the master locks a file on the datastore and that this file stores inventory details, what happens when the master is isolated or fails? If the master fails, the answer is simple: the lock will expire and the new master will relock the file if the datastore is accessible to it.

In the case of isolation, this scenario is slightly different, although the result is similar. The master will release the lock it has on the file on the datastore to ensure that when a new master is elected it can determine the set of virtual machines that are protected by HA by reading the file. If, by any chance, a master should fail right at the moment that it became isolated, the restart of the virtual machines will be delayed until a new master has been elected. In a scenario like this, accuracy and the fact that virtual machines are restarted is more important than a short delay.

Let's assume for a second that your master has just failed. What will happen and how do the slaves know that the master has failed? vSphere 5.0 uses a point-to-point network heartbeat mechanism. If the slaves have received no network heartbeats from the master, the slaves will try to elect a new master. This new master will read the required information and will initiate the restart of the virtual machines within roughly 10 seconds. There is more to this process but we will discuss that in Chapter 4.

Restarting virtual machines is not the only responsibility of the master. It is also responsible for monitoring the state of the slave hosts and reporting this state to vCenter Server. If a slave fails or becomes isolated from the management network, the master will determine which virtual machines must be restarted. When virtual machines need to be restarted, the master is also responsible for determining the placement of those virtual machines. It uses a placement engine that will try to distribute the virtual machines to be restarted evenly across all available hosts.

All of these responsibilities are really important, but without a mechanism to detect a slave has failed, the master would be useless. Just like the slaves receive heartbeats from the master, the master receives heartbeats from the slaves so it knows they are alive.

Slaves
A slave has substantially fewer responsibilities than a master: a slave monitors the state of the virtual machines it is running and informs the master about any changes to this state.

The slave also monitors the health of the master by monitoring heartbeats. If the master becomes unavailable, the slaves initiate and participate in the election process. Last but not least, the slaves send heartbeats to the master so that the master can detect outages. Like the master to slave communication, all slave to master communication is point to point. HA does not use multicast.

Figure 9: Slave Agent

Configuration	
ESX Version	VMware ESXi, 5.1.0, 726909
Image Profile	(Updated) ESXi-5.1.0-726909-standard
vMotion Enabled	Yes
▶ vSphere HA State	⊘ Connected (Slave)
▶ Host Configured for FT	No
▶ EVC Mode	Disabled

Files for both Slave and Master

Both the master and slave use files not only to store state, but also as a communication mechanism. We've already seen the protectedlist file (Figure 8) used by the master to store the list of protected virtual machines. We will now discuss the files that are created by both the master and the slaves. Remote files are files stored on a shared datastore and local files are files that are stored in a location only directly accessible to that host.

Remote Files

The set of powered on virtual machines is stored in a per-host "poweron" file. (See Figure 8 for an example of these files.) It should be noted that, because a master also hosts virtual machines, it also creates a "poweron" file.

The naming scheme for this file is as follows:

```
host-<number>-poweron
```

Tracking virtual machine power-on state is not the only thing the "poweron" file is used for. This file is also used by the slaves to inform the master that it is isolated from the management network: the top line of the file will either contain a 0 or a 1. A 0 means not-isolated and a 1 means isolated. The master will inform vCenter about the isolation of the host.

Local Files

As mentioned before, when HA is configured on a host, the host will store specific information about its cluster locally.

Figure 10: Locally stored files

```
~ # cd /etc/opt/vmware/fdm/
/etc/opt/vmware/fdm # ls
clusterconfig   fdm.cfg          hostlist        vmmetadata
/etc/opt/vmware/fdm # ls -lah
drwxr-xr-x   1 root     root         512 Jun 14 16:00 .
-r--------T   1 root     root           0 May 13 17:00 .#clusterconfig
-r--------T   1 root     root           0 May 13 17:00 .#hostlist
-r--------T   1 root     root           0 May 13 17:00 .#vmmetadata
drwxr-xr-x   1 root     root         512 Jun 14 11:28 ..
-rw-------T   1 root     root         653 Jun 14 11:36 clusterconfig
-rw-------T   1 root     root        2.2K May 13 17:00 fdm.cfg
-rw-------T   1 root     root        2.6K Jun 14 11:36 hostlist
-rw-------T   1 root     root         589 Jun 14 16:00 vmmetadata
/etc/opt/vmware/fdm #
```

Each host, including the master, will store data locally. The data that is locally stored is important state information. Namely, the VM-to-host compatibility matrix, cluster configuration, and host membership list. This information is persisted locally on each host. Updates to this information is sent to the master by vCenter and propagated by the master to the slaves. Although we expect that most of you will never touch these files – and we highly recommend against modifying them – we do want to explain how they are used:

- **clusterconfig**
  This file is not human-readable. It contains the configuration details of the cluster.
- **vmmetadata (5.1 and higher)**
  compatlist (5.0)
  This file is not human-readable. It contains the actual compatibility info matrix for every HA protected virtual machine and lists all the hosts with which it is compatible plus a vm/host dictionary

- **fdm.cfg**
  This file contains the configuration settings around logging. For instance, the level of logging and syslog details are stored in here.
- **hostlist**
  A list of hosts participating in the cluster, including hostname, IP addresses, MAC addresses and heartbeat datastores.

Heartbeating

We mentioned it a couple of times already in this chapter, and it is an important mechanism that deserves its own section: heartbeating. Heartbeating is the mechanism used by HA to validate whether a host is alive. With the introduction of vSphere 5.0, not only did the heartbeating mechanism slightly change, an additional heartbeating mechanism was introduced. Let's discuss traditional network heartbeating first.

Network Heartbeating

vSphere 5.0 introduced some changes to the well-known heartbeat mechanism. vSphere 5.0 doesn't use the concept of primary and secondary nodes, there was no reason for hundreds of heartbeat combinations. As of vSphere 5.0, each slave will send a heartbeat to its master and the master sends a heartbeat to each of the slaves, this is point to point communications and in contrary to 4.1 and earlier multicast is no longer used. These heartbeats are sent by default every second.

When a slave isn't receiving any heartbeats from the master, it will try to determine whether it is Isolated– we will discuss "states" in more detail later on in this chapter.

Basic design principle

Network heartbeating is key for determining the state of a host. Ensure the management network is highly resilient to enable proper state determination.

Datastore Heartbeating

Those familiar with HA prior to vSphere 5.0 hopefully know that virtual machine restarts were always attempted, even if only the heartbeat network was isolated and the virtual machines were still running on the host. As you can imagine, this added an unnecessary level of stress to the host. This has been mitigated by the introduction of the datastore heartbeating mechanism. Datastore heartbeating adds a new level of resiliency and prevents unnecessary restart attempts from occurring.

Datastore heartbeating enables a master to more correctly determine the state of a host that is not reachable via the management network. The new datastore heartbeat mechanism is only used in case the master has lost network connectivity with the slaves. The datastore heartbeat mechanism is then used to validate whether a host has failed or is merely isolated/network partitioned. Isolation will be validated through the "poweron" file which, as mentioned earlier, will be updated by the host when it is isolated. Without the "poweron" file, there is no way for the master to validate isolation. Let that be clear! Based on the results of checks of both files, the master will determine the appropriate action to take. If the master determines that a host has failed (no datastore heartbeats), the master will restart the failed host's virtual machines. If the master determines that the slave is Isolated or Partitioned, it will only take action when it is appropriate to take action. With that meaning that the master will only initiate restarts when virtual machines are down or powered down / shut down by a triggered isolation response, but we will discuss this in more detail in Chapter 4.

By default, HA selects 2 heartbeat datastores – it will select datastores that are available on all hosts, or as many as possible. Although it is possible to configure an advanced setting (*das.heartbeatDsPerHost*) to allow for more datastores for datastore heartbeating we do not recommend configuring this option as the default should be sufficient for most scenarios, except for stretched cluster environments which is described in part IV.

The selection process gives preference to VMFS datastores over NFS ones, and seeks to choose datastores that are backed by different LUNs or NFS servers. If desired, you can also select the heartbeat datastores yourself. We, however, recommend letting vCenter deal with this operational "burden" as vCenter uses a selection algorithm to select heartbeat datastores that are presented to all hosts. This however is not a guarantee that vCenter can select datastores which are connected to all hosts. It should be noted that vCenter is not site-aware. In scenarios where hosts are geographically dispersed it is recommend to manually select heartbeat datastores to ensure each site has one site-local heartbeat datastore at minimum. This scenario is described in-depth in Part IV of this book.

Basic design principle

In a metro-cluster / geographically dispersed cluster we recommend setting the minimum number of heartbeat datastores to four. It is recommended to manually select site local datastores, two for each site.

Figure 11: Selecting the heartbeat datastores

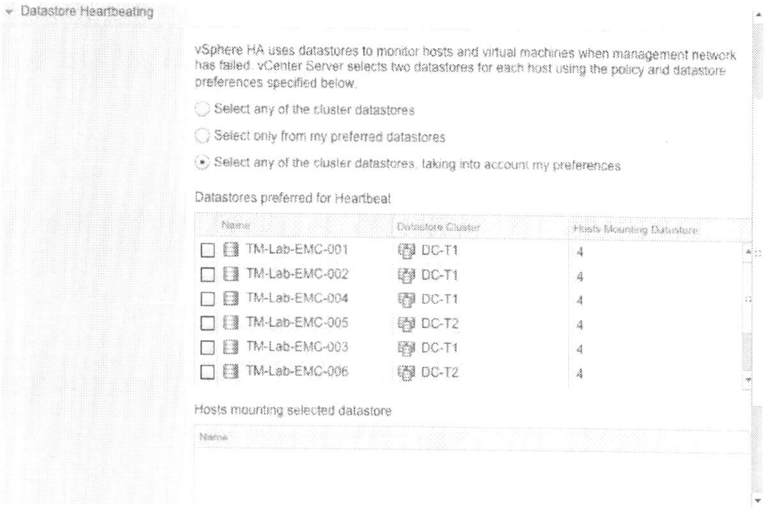

The question now arises: what, exactly, is this datastore heartbeating and which datastore is used for this heartbeating? Let's answer which datastore is used for datastore heartbeating first as we can simply show that with a screenshot, Figure 12. vSphere 5.1 displays extensive details around the "Cluster Status" on the Cluster's Monitor tab. This for instance shows you which datastores are being used for heartbeating and which hosts are using which specific datastore(s). In addition, it displays how many virtual machines are protected and how many hosts are connected to the master.

Figure 12: Validating the heartbeat datastores

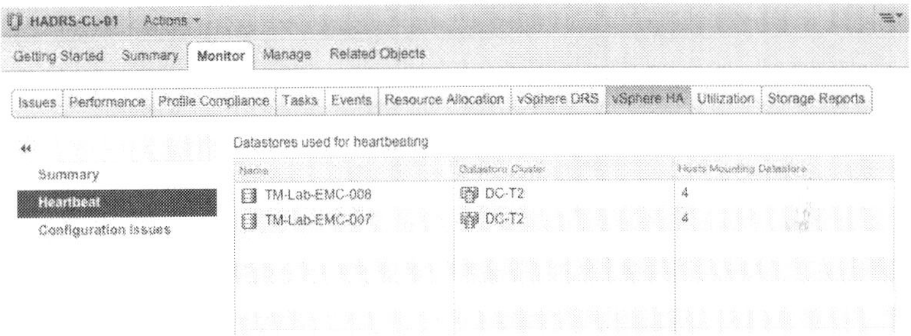

How does this heartbeating mechanism work? In block based storage environments HA leverages an existing VMFS file system mechanism. The mechanism uses a so called "heartbeat region" which is updated as long as the file is open. On VMFS datastores, HA will simply check whether the heartbeat region has been updated. In order to update a datastore heartbeat region, a host needs to have at least one open file on the volume. HA ensures there is at least one file open on this volume by creating a file specifically for datastore heartbeating. In other words, a per-host file is created on the designated heartbeating datastores, as shown in Figure 13. The naming scheme for this file is as follows:

host-<number>-hb

Figure 13: Heartbeat file

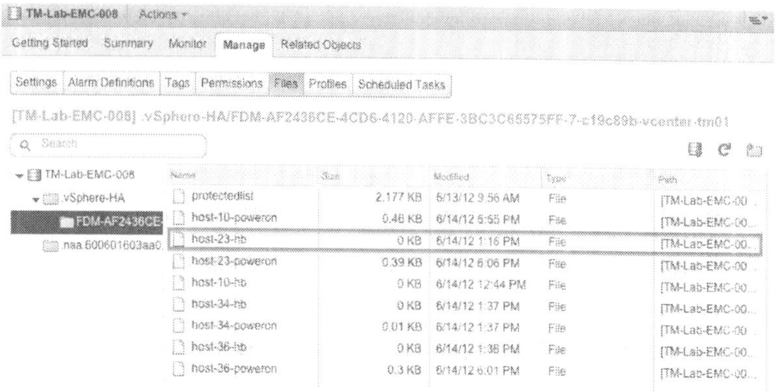

On NFS datastores, each host will write to its heartbeat file once every 5 seconds, ensuring that the master will be able to check host state. The master will simply validate this by checking that the time-stamp of the file changed.

Realize that in the case of a converged network environment, the effectiveness of datastore heartbeating will vary depending on the type of failure. For instance, a NIC failure could impact both network and datastore heartbeating. If, for whatever reason, the datastore or NFS share becomes unavailable or is removed from the cluster, HA will detect this and select a new datastore or NFS share to use for the heartbeating mechanism.

Basic design principle

Datastore heartbeating adds a new level of resiliency but is not the be-all end-all. In converged networking environments, the use of datastore heartbeating adds little value due to the fact that a NIC failure may result in both the network and storage becoming unavailable.

Isolated versus Partitioned

We've already briefly touched on it and it is time to have a closer look. As of vSphere 5.0 HA, a new cluster node state called Partitioned exists. What is this exactly and when is a host Partitioned rather than Isolated? Before we will explain this we want to point out that there is the state as reported by the master and the state as observed by an administrator and the characteristics these have.

First, consider the administrator's perspective. Two hosts are considered partitioned if they are operational but cannot reach each other over the management network. Further, a host is isolated if it does not observe any HA management traffic on the management network and it can't ping the configured isolation addresses. It is possible for multiple hosts to be isolated at the same time. We call the set of hosts that are partitioned but can communicate with each other a management network partition. Network partitions involving more than two partitions are possible but not likely.

Now, consider the FDM perspective. When any FDMs are not in network contact with a master, they will elect a new master. So, when a network partition exists, a master election will occur so that a host failure or network isolation within this partition will result in appropriate action on the impacted virtual machine(s). Figure 14 shows possible ways in which an Isolation or a Partition can occur.

Figure 14: Isolated versus Partitioned

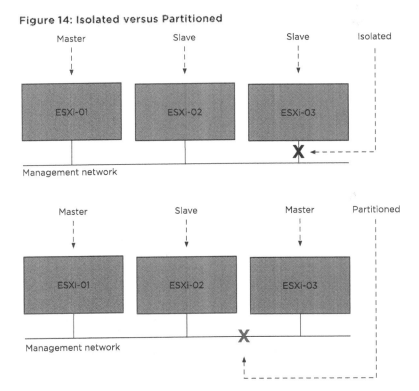

If a cluster is partitioned in multiple segments, each partition will elect its own master, meaning that if you have 4 partitions your cluster will have 4 masters. When the network partition is corrected, any of the four masters will take over the role and be responsible for the cluster again. It should be noted that a master could claim responsibility for a virtual machine that lives in a different partition. If this occurs and the virtual machine happens to fail, the master will be notified through the datastore communication mechanism.

In the HA architecture, whether a host is partitioned is determined by the master reporting the condition. So, in the above example, the master on host ESXi-01 will report ESXi-03 and 04 partitioned while the master on host 04 will report 01 and 02 partitioned. When a partition occurs, vCenter reports the perspective of one master.

A master reports a host as partitioned or isolated when it can't communicate with the host over the management network, it can observe the host's datastore heartbeats via the heartbeat datastores. The master cannot alone differentiate between these two states – a host is reported as isolated only if the host informs the master via the datastores that is isolated.

This still leaves the question open how the master differentiates between a Failed, Partitioned, or Isolated host.

When the master stops receiving network heartbeats from a slave, it will check for host "liveness" for the next 15 seconds. Before the host is declared failed, the master will validate if it has actually failed or not by doing additional liveness checks. First, the master will validate if the host is still heartbeating to the datastore. Second, the master will ping the management IP address of the host. If both are negative, the host will be declared Failed. This doesn't necessarily mean the host has PSOD'ed; it could be the network is unavailable, including the storage network, which would make this host Isolated from an administrator's perspective but Failed from an HA perspective. As you can imagine, however, there are a various combinations possible. The following table depicts these combinations including the "state".

Table 2: Host states

State	Network Heartbeat	Storage Heartbeat	Host Live- ness Ping	Isolation Criteria Met
Running	Yes	N/A	N/A	N/A
Isolated	No	Yes	No	Yes
Partitioned	No	Yes	No	No
Failed	No	No	No	N/A
FDM Agent Down	N/A	N/A	Yes	N/A

HA will trigger an action based on the state of the host. When the host is marked as Failed, a restart of the virtual machines will be initiated. When the host is marked as Isolated, the master might initiate the restarts. As mentioned earlier, this is a substantial change compared to HA prior to vSphere 5.0 when restarts were always initiated, regardless of the state of the virtual machines or hosts. The one thing to keep in mind when it comes to isolation response is that a virtual machine will only be shut down or powered off when the isolated host knows there is a master out there that has taken ownership for the virtual machine or when the isolated host loses access to the home datastore of the virtual machine.

For example, if a host is isolated and runs two virtual machines, stored on separate datastores, the host will validate if it can access each of the home datastores of those virtual machines. If it can, the host will validate whether a master owns these datastores. If no master owns the datastores, the isolation response will not be triggered and restarts will not be initiated. If the host does not have access to the datastore, for instance, during an "All Paths Down" condition, HA will trigger the isolation response to ensure the "original" virtual machine is powered down and will be safely restarted. This to avoid so-called "split-brain" scenarios.

To reiterate, as this is a major change compared to all previous versions of HA, the remaining hosts in the cluster will only be requested to restart virtual machines when the master has detected that either the host has failed or has become isolated and the isolation response was triggered. If the term isolation response is not clear yet, don't worry as we will discuss it in more depth in chapter 4.

Virtual Machine Protection

The way virtual machines are protected has changed substantially in vSphere 5.0. Prior to vSphere 5.0, virtual machine protection was handled by vpxd which notified AAM through a VPXA module called vmap. With vSphere 5.0, virtual machine protection happens on several layers but is ultimately the responsibility of vCenter. We have explained this briefly but want to expand on it a bit more to make sure everyone understands the dependency on vCenter when it comes to protecting virtual machines. We do want to stress that this only applies to protecting virtual machines; virtual machine restarts in no way require vCenter to be available at the time.

When the state of a virtual machine changes, vCenter will direct the master to enable or disable HA protection for that virtual machine. Protection, however, is only guaranteed when the master has committed the change of state to disk. The reason for this, of course, is that a failure of the master would result in the loss of any state changes that exist only in memory. As pointed out earlier, this state is distributed across the datastores and stored in the *"protectedlist"* file.

When the power state change of a virtual machine has been committed to disk, the master will inform vCenter Server so that the change in status is visible both for the user in vCenter and for other processes like monitoring tools.

To clarify the process, we have created a workflow diagram (Figure 15) of the protection of a virtual machine from the point it is powered on through vCenter:

Figure 15: Virtual Machine protection workflow

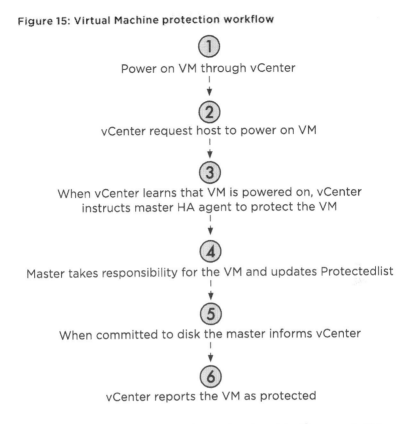

① Power on VM through vCenter

② vCenter request host to power on VM

③ When vCenter learns that VM is powered on, vCenter instructs master HA agent to protect the VM

④ Master takes responsibility for the VM and updates Protectedlist

⑤ When committed to disk the master informs vCenter

⑥ vCenter reports the VM as protected

But what about "unprotection?" When a virtual machine is powered off, it must be removed from the protectedlist. We have documented this workflow in Figure 16 for the situation where the power off is invoked from vCenter.

Figure 16: Virtual Machine Unprotection workflow

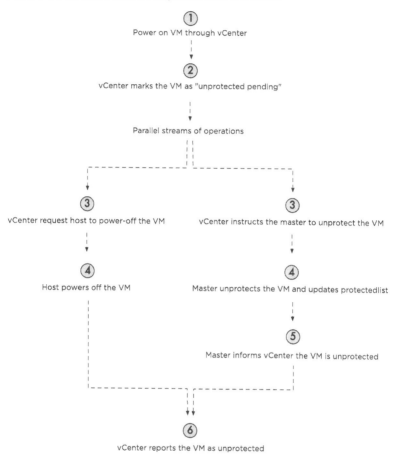

Chapter 4

Restarting Virtual Machines

In the previous chapter, we have described most of the lower level fundamental concepts of HA. We have shown you that multiple mechanisms were introduced in vSphere 5.0 to increase resiliency and reliability of HA. Reliability of HA in this case mostly refers to restarting (or resetting) virtual machines, as that remains HA's primary task.

HA will respond when the state of a host has changed, or, better said, when the state of one or more virtual machines has changed. There are multiple scenarios in which HA will respond to a virtual machine failure, the most common of which are listed below:

- Failed host
- Isolated host
- Failed guest operating system

Depending on the type of failure, but also depending on the role of the host, the process will differ slightly. Changing the process results in slightly different recovery timelines. There are many different scenarios and there is no point in covering all of them, so we will try to describe the most common scenario and include timelines where possible.

Before we dive into the different failure scenarios, we want to emphasize a couple of very substantial changes compared to vSphere pre-5.0 with regards to restart priority and retries. These apply to every situation we will describe.

Restart Priority and Order

Prior to vSphere 5.0, HA would take the priority of the virtual machine into account when a restart of multiple virtual machines was required. This, by itself, has not changed; HA will still take the configured priority of the virtual machine into account. However, with vSphere 5.0, new types of virtual machines have been introduced: Agent Virtual Machines. These virtual machines typically offer a "service" to other virtual machines and, as such, take precedence during the restart procedure as the "regular" virtual machines may rely on them. A good example of an agent virtual machine is a vShield Endpoint virtual machine which offers anti-virus services. These agent virtual machines are considered top priority virtual machines.

Prioritization is done by each host and not globally. Each host that has been requested to initiate restart attempts will attempt to restart all top priority virtual machines before attempting to start any other virtual machines. If the restart of a top priority virtual machine fails, it will be retried after a delay. In the meantime, however, HA will continue powering on the remaining virtual machines. Keep in mind that some virtual machines might be dependent on the agent virtual machines. You should document which virtual machines are dependent on which agent virtual machines and document the process to start up these services in the right order in the case the automatic restart of an agent virtual machine fails.

Basic design principle

Virtual machines can be dependent on the availability of agent virtual machines or other virtual machines. Although HA will do its best to ensure all virtual machines are started in the correct order, this is not guaranteed. Document the proper recovery process.

Besides agent virtual machines, HA also prioritizes FT secondary machines. We have listed the full order in which virtual machines will be restarted below:

- Agent virtual machines
- FT secondary virtual machines
- Virtual Machines configured with a restart priority of high
- Virtual Machines configured with a medium restart priority
- Virtual Machines configured with a low restart priority

It should be noted that HA will not place any virtual machines on a host if the required number of agent virtual machines are not running on the host at the time placement is done.

Now that we have briefly touched on it, we would also like to address "restart retries" and parallelization of restarts as that more or less dictates how long it could take before all virtual machines of a failed or isolated host are restarted.

Restart Retries

The number of retries is configurable as of vCenter 2.5 U4 with the advanced option *"das.maxvmrestartcount"*. The default value is 5. Prior to vCenter 2.5 U4, HA would keep retrying forever which could lead to serious problems. This scenario is described in KB article 1009625 where multiple virtual machines would be registered on multiple hosts simultaneously, leading to a confusing and an inconsistent state. (http://kb.vmware.com/kb/1009625)

Note

Prior to vSphere 5.0 "das.maxvmrestartcount" did not include the initial restart. Meaning that the total amount of restarts was 6. As of vSphere 5.0 the initial restart is included in the value.

HA will try to start the virtual machine on one of your hosts in the affected cluster; if this is unsuccessful on that host, the restart count will be increased by 1. Before we go into the exact timeline, let it be clear that T0 is the point at which the master initiates the first restart attempt. This by itself could be 30 seconds after the virtual machine has failed. The elapsed time between the failure of the virtual machine and the restart, though, will depend on the scenario of the failure, which we will discuss in this chapter.

As said, prior to vSphere 5, the actual number of restart attempts was 6, as it excluded the initial attempt. With vSphere 5.0 the default is 5. There are specific times associated with each of these attempts. The following bullet list will clarify this concept. The 'm' stands for "minutes" in this list.

- T0 – Initial Restart
- T2m – Restart retry 1
- T6m – Restart retry 2
- T14m – Restart retry 3
- T30m – Restart retry 4

Figure 17: High Availability restart timeline

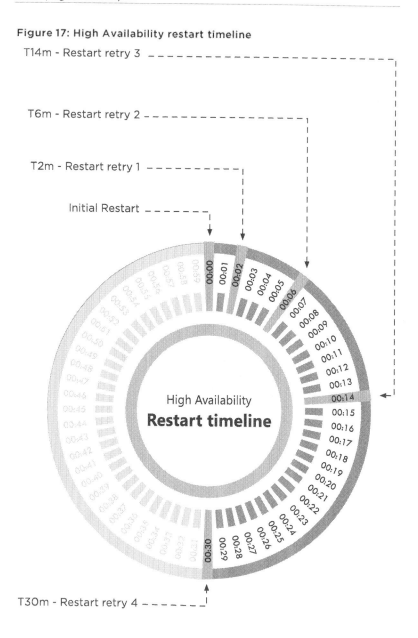

T14m - Restart retry 3

T6m - Restart retry 2

T2m - Restart retry 1

Initial Restart

High Availability
Restart timeline

T30m - Restart retry 4

As clearly depicted in Figure 17, a successful power-on attempt could take up to ~30 minutes in the case where multiple power-on attempts are unsuccessful. This is, however, not exact science. For instance, there is a 2-minute waiting period between the initial restart and the first restart retry. HA will start the 2-minute wait as soon as it has detected that the initial attempt has failed. So, in reality, T2 could be T2 plus 8 seconds. Another important fact that we want emphasize is that there is no coordination between masters, and so if multiple ones are involved in trying to restart the virtual machine, each will retain their own sequence. As of vSphere 5.0 Update 1 multiple masters could attempt to restart a virtual machine. Although only one will succeed, it might change some of the timelines.

Let's give an example to clarify the scenario in which a master fails during a restart sequence:

Cluster: 4 Host (esxi01, esxi02, esxi03, esxi04)
Master: esxi01

The host "esxi02" is running a single virtual machine called "vm01" and it fails. The master, esxi01, will try to restart it but the attempt fails. It will try restarting "vm01" up to 5 times but, unfortunately, on the 4th try, the master also fails. An election occurs and "esxi03" becomes the new master. It will now initiate the restart of "vm01", and if that restart would fail it will retry it up to 4 times again for a total including the initial restart of 5.

Be aware, though, that a successful restart might never occur if the restart count is reached and all five restart attempts (the default value) were unsuccessful.

When it comes to restarts, one thing that is very important to realize is that HA will not issue more than 32 concurrent power-on tasks on a given host. To make that more clear, let's use the example of a two host cluster: if a host fails which contained 33 virtual machines and all of these had the same restart priority, 32 power on attempts would be initiated. The 33rd power on attempt will only be initiated when one of those 32 attempts has completed regardless of success or failure of one of those attempts.

Now, here comes the gotcha. If there are 32 low-priority virtual machines to be powered on and a single high-priority virtual machine, the power on attempt for the low-priority virtual machines will not be issued until the power on attempt for the high priority virtual machine has completed. Let it be absolutely clear that HA does not wait to restart the low-priority virtual machines until the high-priority virtual machines are started, it waits for the issued power on attempt to be reported as "completed". In theory, this means that if the power on attempt fails, the low-priority virtual machines could be powered on before the high priority virtual machine.

The restart priority however does guarantee that when a placement is done, the higher priority virtual machines get first right to any available resources.

Basic design principle

Configuring restart priority of a virtual machine is not a guarantee that virtual machines will actually be restarted in this order. Ensure proper operational procedures are in place for restarting services or virtual machines in the appropriate order in the event of a failure.

Now that we know how virtual machine restart priority and restart retries are handled, it is time to look at the different scenarios.

- Failed host
  - Failure of a master
  - Failure of a slave
- Isolated host and response

Failed Host

Prior to vSphere 5.0, the restart of virtual machines from a failed host was straightforward. With the introduction of master/slave hosts and heartbeat datastores in vSphere 5.0, the restart procedure has also changed, and with it the associated timelines. There is a clear distinction between the failure of a master versus the failure of a slave. We want to emphasize this because the time it takes before a restart attempt is initiated differs between these two scenarios. Let's start with the most common failure, that of a host failing, but note that failures generally occur infrequently. In most environments, hardware failures are very uncommon to begin with. Just in case it happens, it doesn't hurt to understand the process and its associated timelines.

The Failure of a Slave

This is a fairly complex scenario compared to how HA handled host failures prior to vSphere 5.0. Part of this complexity comes from the introduction of a new heartbeat mechanism. Actually, there are two different scenarios: one where heartbeat datastores are configured and one where heartbeat datastores are not configured. Keeping in mind that this is an actual failure of the host, the timeline is as follows:

- T0 – Slave failure.
- T3s – Master begins monitoring datastore heartbeats for 15 seconds.
- T10s – The host is declared unreachable and the master will ping the management network of the failed host. This is a continuous ping for 5 seconds.
- T15s – If **no** heartbeat datastores are configured, the host will be declared dead.
- T18s – If heartbeat datastores are configured, the host will be declared dead.

The master monitors the network heartbeats of a slave. When the slave fails, these heartbeats will no longer be received by the master. We have defined this as T0. After 3 seconds (T3s), the master will start monitoring for datastore heartbeats and it will do this for 15 seconds. On the 10th second (T10s), when no network or datastore heartbeats have been detected, the host will be declared as "unreachable". The master will also start pinging the management network of the failed host at the 10th second and it will do so for 5 seconds. If no heartbeat datastores were configured, the host will be declared "dead" at the 15th second (T15s) and virtual machine restarts will be initiated by the master. If heartbeat datastores have been configured, the host will be declared dead at the 18th second (T18s) and restarts will be initiated. We realize that this can be confusing and hope the timeline depicted in Figure 18 makes it easier to digest.

Figure 18: Restart timeline slave failure

No Datastore heartbeats configured

Datastore heartbeats configured

Slave failure

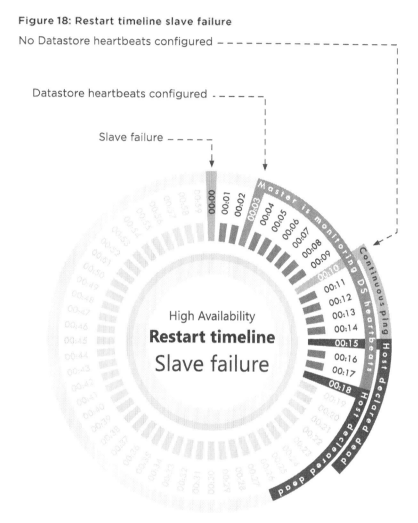

The master filters the virtual machines it thinks failed before initiating restarts. Prior to vSphere 5.0 Update 1, a master used the protectedlist. If the master did not know the on-disk protection state for the virtual machine, the master did not try to restart it. And, the on-disk state could be obtained only by one master at a time since it required opening the protectedlist file in exclusive mode. As of vSphere 5.0 Update 1 (and above) this behavior has been changed. If there is a network partition multiple masters could try to restart the same virtual machine as vCenter Server also provided the necessary details for a restart. As an example, it could happen that a master has locked a virtual machine's home datastore while the other master is in contact with vCenter Server and as such is aware of the current desired protected state. In this scenario it could happen that the master which does not own the home datastore of the virtual machine will restart the virtual machine based on the information provided by vCenter Server.

This change in behavior was introduced to avoid the scenario where a restart of a virtual machine would fail due to insufficient resources in the partition which was responsible for the virtual machine. With this change, there is less chance of such a situation occurring as the master in the other partition would be using the information provided by vCenter Server to initiate the restart.

That leaves us with the question of what happens in the case of the failure of a master.

The Failure of a Master

In the case of a master failure, the process and the associated timeline are slightly different. The reason being that there needs to be a master before any restart can be initiated. This means that an election will need to take place amongst the slaves. The timeline is as follows:

- T0 – Master failure.
- T10s – Master election process initiated.
- T25s – New master elected and reads the protectedlist.
- T35s – New master initiates restarts for all virtual machines on the protectedlist which are not running.

Slaves receive network heartbeats from their master. If the master fails, let's define this as To, the slaves detect this when the network heartbeats cease to be received. As every cluster needs a master, the slaves will initiate an election at T10s. The election process takes 15s to complete, which brings us to T25s. At T25s, the new master reads the protectedlist. This list contains all the virtual machines which are protected by HA. At T35s, the master initiates the restart of all virtual machines that are protected but not currently running. The timeline depicted in Figure 19 hopefully clarifies the process.

Figure 19: Restart timeline master failure

Besides the failure of a host, there is another reason for restarting virtual machines: an isolation event.

Isolation Response and Detection

Before we will discuss the timeline and the process around the restart of virtual machines after an isolation event, we will discuss Isolation Response and Isolation Detection. One of the first decisions that will need to be made when configuring HA is the "Isolation Response".

Isolation Response

The Isolation Response refers to the action that HA takes for its virtual machines when the host has lost its connection with the network and the remaining nodes in the cluster. This does not necessarily mean that the whole network is down; it could just be the management network ports of this specific host. Today there are three isolation responses: "Power off", "Leave powered on" and "Shut down". This isolation response answers the question, "what should a host do with the virtual machines it manages when it detects that it is isolated from the network?" Let's discuss these three options more in-depth:

- **Power off** – When isolation occurs, all virtual machines are powered off. It is a hard stop, or to put it bluntly, the "virtual" power cable of the virtual machine will be pulled out!

- **Shut down** – When isolation occurs, all virtual machines running on the host will be shut down using a guest-initiated shutdown through VMware Tools. If this is not successful within 5 minutes, a "power off" will be executed. This time out value can be adjusted by setting the advanced option *das.isolationShutdownTimeout*. If VMware Tools is not installed, a "power off" will be initiated immediately.

- **Leave powered on** – When isolation occurs on the host, the state of the virtual machines remains unchanged.

This setting can be changed on the cluster settings under virtual machine options (Figure 20).

Figure 20: Cluster default settings

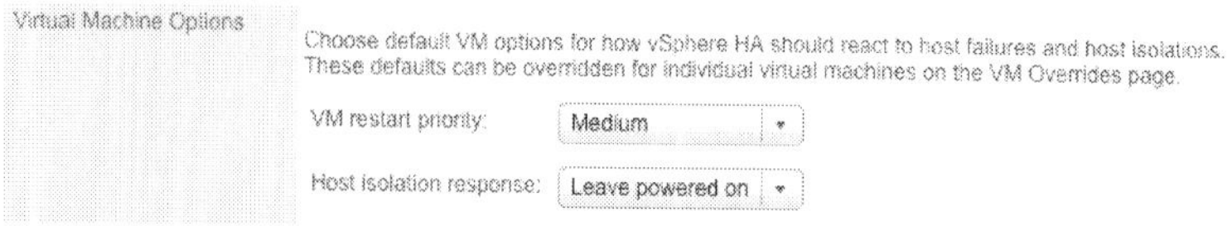

Virtual Machine Options

Choose default VM options for how vSphere HA should react to host failures and host isolations. These defaults can be overridden for individual virtual machines on the VM Overrides page.

VM restart priority: Medium ▾

Host isolation response: Leave powered on ▾

The default setting for the isolation response has changed multiple times over the last couple of years and this has caused some confusion.

- Up to ESXi3.5 U2 / vCenter 2.5 U2 the default isolation response was "Power off"
- With ESXi3.5 U3 / vCenter 2.5 U3 this was changed to "Leave powered on"
- With vSphere 4.0 it was changed to "Shut down".
- With vSphere 5.0 it has been changed to "Leave powered on".

Keep in mind that these changes are only applicable to newly created clusters. When creating a new cluster, it may be required to change the default isolation response based on the configuration of existing clusters and/or your customer's requirements, constraints and expectations. When upgrading an existing cluster, it might be wise to apply the latest default values. You might wonder why the default has changed once again. There was a lot of feedback from customers that "Leave powered on" was the desired default value.

Basic design principle

Before upgrading an environment to later versions, ensure you validate the best practices and default settings. Document them, including justification, to ensure all people involved understand your reasons.

The question remains, which setting should be used? The obvious answer applies here; it depends. We prefer "Leave powered on" because it eliminates the chances of having a false positive and its associated down time. One of the problems that people have experienced in the past is that HA triggered its isolation response when the full management network went down. Basically resulting in the power off (or shutdown) of every single virtual machine and none being restarted. With vSphere 5.0, this problem has been mitigated. HA will validate if virtual machines restarts can be attempted – there is no reason to incur any down time unless absolutely necessary. It does this by validating that a master owns the datastore the virtual machine is stored on. Of course, the isolated host can only validate this if it has access to the datastores. In a converged network environment with iSCSI storage, for instance, it would be impossible to validate this during a full isolation as the validation would fail due to the inaccessible datastore from the perspective of the isolated host.

We feel that changing the isolation response is most useful in environments where a failure of the management network is likely correlated with a failure of the virtual machine network(s). If the failure of the management network won't likely correspond with the failure of the virtual machine networks, isolation response would cause unnecessary downtime as the virtual machines can continue to run without management network connectivity to the host.

A second use for power off/shutdown is in scenarios where the virtual machine retains access to the virtual machine network but loses access to its storage, leaving the virtual machine powered-on could result in two virtual machines on the network with the same IP address.

It is still difficult to decide which isolation response should be used. The following table was created to provide some more guidelines.

Table 3: Isolation response guidance

Likelihood that host will retain access to VM datastore	Likelihood VMs will retain access to VM network	Recommended Isolation Policy	Rationale
Likely	Likely	Leave Powered On	Virtual machine is running fine, no reason to power it off
Likely	Unlikely	Either Leave Powered On or Shutdown.	Choose shutdown to allow HA to restart virtual machines on hosts that are not isolated and hence are likely to have access to storage
Unlikely	Likely	Power Off	Use Power Off to avoid having two instances of the same virtual machine on the virtual machine network
Unlikely	Unlikely	Leave Powered On or Power Off	Leave Powered on if the virtual machine can recover from the network/datastore outage if it is not restarted because of the isolation, and Power Off if it likely can't.

The question that we haven't answered yet is how HA knows which virtual machines have been powered-off due to the triggered isolation response and why the isolation response is more reliable than with previous versions of HA. Previously, HA did not care and would always try to restart the virtual machines according to the last known state of the host. That is no longer the case with vSphere 5.0. Before the isolation response is triggered, the isolated host will verify whether a master is responsible for the virtual machine.

As mentioned earlier, it does this by validating if a master owns the home datastore of the virtual machine. When isolation response is triggered, the isolated host removes the virtual machines which are powered off or shutdown from the "poweron" file. The master will recognize that the virtual machines have disappeared and initiate a restart. On top of that, when the isolation response is triggered, it will create a per-virtual machine file under a "poweredoff" directory which indicates for the master that this virtual machine was powered down as a result of a triggered isolation response. This information will be read by the master node when it initiates the restart attempt in order to guarantee that only virtual machines that were powered off / shut down by HA will be restarted by HA.

This is, however, only one part of the increased reliability of HA. Reliability has also been improved with respect to "isolation detection," which will be described in the following section.

Isolation Detection

We have explained what the options are to respond to an isolation event and what happens when the selected response is triggered. However, we have not extensively discussed how isolation is detected. The mechanism is fairly straightforward and works with heartbeats, as earlier explained. There are, however, two scenarios again, and the process and associated timelines differ for each of them:

- Isolation of a slave
- Isolation of a master

Before we explain the differences in process between both scenarios, we want to make sure it is clear that a change in state will result in the isolation response not being triggered in either scenario. Meaning that if a single ping is successful or the host observes election traffic and is elected a master or slave, the isolation response will not be triggered, which is exactly what you want as avoiding down time is at least as important as recovering from down time. When a host has declared itself isolated and observes election traffic it will declare itself no longer isolated.

Isolation of a Slave

The isolation detection mechanism has changed substantially since previous versions of vSphere. The main difference is the fact that HA triggers a master election process before it will declare a host is isolated. In this timeline, "s" refers to seconds. The following timeline is the timeline for a vSphere 5.0 host:

- T0 – Isolation of the host (slave)
- T10s – Slave enters "election state"
- T25s – Slave elects itself as master
- T25s – Slave pings "isolation addresses"
- T30s – Slave declares itself isolated and "triggers" isolation response

For a vSphere 5.1 host this timeline slightly differs due the insertion of a minimum 30s delay after the host declares itself isolated before it applies the configured isolation response. This delay can be increased using the advanced option:

- T0 – Isolation of the host (slave)
- T10s – Slave enters "election state"
- T25s – Slave elects itself as master
- T25s – Slave pings "isolation addresses"
- T30s – Slave declares itself isolated
- T60s – Slave "triggers" isolation response

When the isolation response is triggered, with both 5.0 and 5.1, HA creates a "power-off" file for any virtual machine HA powers off whose home datastore is accessible. Next it powers off the virtual machine (or shuts down) and updates the host's poweron file. The power-off file is used to record that HA powered off the virtual machine and so HA should restart it. These power-off files are deleted when a virtual machine is powered back on or HA is disabled.

After the completion of this sequence, the master will learn the slave was isolated through the "poweron" file as mentioned earlier, and will restart virtual machines based on the information provided by the slave.

Figure 21: Isolation of a slave timeline

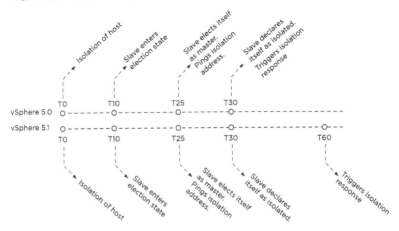

Isolation of a Master

In the case of the isolation of a master, this timeline is a bit less complicated because there is no need to go through an election process. In this timeline, "s" refers to seconds.

- To – Isolation of the host (master)
- To – Master pings "isolation addresses"
- T5s – Master declares itself isolated
- T35s – Master "triggers" isolation response

Additional Checks

Before a host declares itself isolated, it will ping the default isolation address which is the gateway specified for the management network, and will continue to ping the address until it becomes unisolated. HA gives you the option to define one or multiple additional isolation addresses using an advanced setting. This advanced setting is called *das.isolationaddress* and could be used to reduce the chances of having a false positive. We recommend setting an additional isolation address. If a secondary management network is configured, this additional address should be part of the same network as the secondary management network. If required, you can configure up to 10 additional isolation addresses. A secondary management network will more than likely be on a different subnet and it is recommended to specify an additional isolation address which is part of the subnet. (Figure 22)

Figure 22: Isolation Address

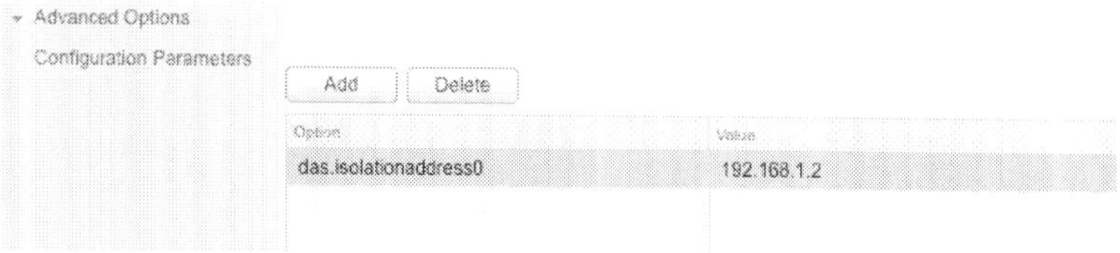

Advanced Options

Configuration Parameters

| Add | Delete |

Option	Value
das.isolationaddress0	192.168.1.2

Selecting an Additional Isolation Address

A question asked by many people is which address should be specified for this additional isolation verification. We generally recommend an isolation address close to the hosts to avoid too many network hops and an address that would correlate with the liveness of the virtual machine network. In many cases, the most logical choice is the physical switch to which the host is directly connected. Basically, use the gateway for whatever subnet your management network is on. Another usual suspect would be a router or any other reliable and pingable device on the same subnet. However, when you are using IP-based shared storage like NFS or iSCSI, the IP-address of the storage device can also be a good choice.

Basic design principle

Select a reliable secondary isolation address. Try to minimize the number of "hops" between the host and this address.

Failure Detection Time

Those who are familiar with vSphere 4.x or VI 3.x will probably wonder by now what happened to the concept of "Failure Detection Time". Prior to vSphere 5.0, "*das.failuredetectiontime*" was probably the most used advanced setting within vSphere. As of vSphere 5.0, it is no longer possible to configure this advanced setting. This setting was completely removed when HA was rewritten. However with vSphere 5.1 a similar concept is introduced again as many customers desired to have this advanced option to allow tweaking to network service level agreements.

"das.config.fdm.isolationPolicyDelaySec" is introduced in vSphere 5.1 and is an advanced setting which allows changing the number of seconds to wait before the isolation policy is executed is. The minimum value is 30. If set to a value less than 30, the delay will be 30 seconds. We do not recommend changing this advanced setting unless there is a specific requirement to do so. In almost all scenarios 30 seconds should suffice.

Restarting Virtual Machines

The most important procedure has not yet been explained: restarting virtual machines. We have dedicated a full section to this concept as, again, substantial changes have been introduced in vSphere 5.0.

We have explained the difference in behavior from a timing perspective for restarting virtual machines in the case of a both master node and slave node failures. For now, let's assume that a slave node has failed. When the master node declares the slave node as Partitioned or Isolated, it determines which virtual machines were running on using the information it previously read from the host's "poweron" file. These files are asynchronously read approximately every 30s. If the host was not Partitioned or Isolated before the failure, the master uses cached data to determine the virtual machines that were last running on the host before the failure occurred.

Before it will initiate the restart attempts, though, the master will first validate that the virtual machine should be restarted. This validation uses the protection information vCenter Server provides to each master, or if the master is not in contact with vCenter Server, the information saved in the protectedlist files. If the master is not in contact with vCenter Server or has not locked the file, the virtual machine is filtered out. At this point, all virtual machines having a restart priority of "disabled" are also filtered out.

Now that HA knows which virtual machines it should restart, it is time to decide where the virtual machines are placed. HA will take multiple things in to account:

- CPU and memory reservation, including the memory overhead of the virtual machine
- Unreserved capacity of the hosts in the cluster
- Restart priority of the virtual machine relative to the other virtual machines that need to be restarted
- Virtual-machine-to-host compatibility set

- The number of dvPorts required by a virtual machine and the number available on the candidate hosts
- The maximum number of vCPUs and virtual machines that can be run on a given host
- Restart latency
- Whether the active hosts are running the required number of agent virtual machines.

Restart latency refers to the amount of time it takes to initiate virtual machine restarts. This means that virtual machine restarts will be distributed by the master across multiple hosts to avoid a boot storm, and thus a delay, on a single host.

If a placement is found, the master will send each target host the set of virtual machines it needs to restart. If this list exceeds 32 virtual machines, HA will limit the number of concurrent power on attempts to 32. If a virtual machine successfully powers on, the node on which the virtual machine was powered on will inform the master of the change in power state. The master will then remove the virtual machine from the restart list.

If a placement cannot be found, the master will place the virtual machine on a "pending placement list" and will retry placement of the virtual machine when one of the following conditions changes:

- A new virtual-machine-to-host compatibility list is provided by vCenter.
- A host reports that its unreserved capacity has increased.
- A host (re)joins the cluster (For instance, when a host is taken out of maintenance mode, a host is added to a cluster, etc.)
- A new failure is detected and virtual machines have to be failed over.
- A failure occurred when failing over a virtual machine.

But what about DRS? Wouldn't DRS be able to help during the placement of virtual machines when all else fails? It does. The master node will report to vCenter the set of virtual machines that were not placed due to insufficient resources, as is the case today. If DRS is enabled, this information will be used in an attempt to have DRS make capacity available. This is described more in-depth in Chapter 8.

Corner Case Scenario: Split-Brain

In the past (pre-vSphere 4.1), split-brain scenarios could occur. A split brain in this case meaning that a virtual machine would be powered up simultaneously on two different hosts. That would be possible in the scenario where the isolation response was set to "leave powered on" and network based storage, like NFS or iSCSI, was used. This situation could occur during a full network isolation, which may result in the lock on the virtual machine's VMDK being lost, enabling HA to actually power up the virtual machine. As the virtual machine was not powered off on its original host (isolation response set to "leave powered on"), it would exist in memory on the isolated host and in memory with a disk lock on the host that was requested to restart the virtual machine.

vSphere 4.1 and vSphere 5.0 brought multiple enhancements to avoid scenarios like these. Keep in mind that they truly are corner case scenarios which are very unlikely to occur in most environments. In case it does happen, HA relies on the "lost lock detection" mechanism to mitigate this scenario. In short, as of version 4.0 Update 2, ESXi detects that the lock on the VMDK has been lost and, when the datastore becomes accessible again and the lock cannot be reacquired, issues a question whether the virtual machine should be powered off; HA automatically answers the question with Yes. However, you will only see this question if you directly connect to the ESXi host during the failure. HA will generate an event for this auto-answered question though.

As stated above, as of ESXi 4 update 2, the question will be auto-answered and the virtual machine will be powered off to recover from the split brain scenario.

The question still remains: in the case of an isolation with iSCSI or NFS, should you power off virtual machines or leave them powered on?

As just explained, HA will automatically power off your original virtual machine when it detects a split-brain scenario. This process however is not instantaneous and as such it is recommended to use use the isolation response of "Power Off" or "Leave powered on. We also recommend increasing heartbeat network resiliency to avoid getting in to this situation. We will discuss the options you have for enhancing Management Network resiliency in the next chapter.

Permanent Device Loss

As of vSphere 5.0 Update 1, enhancements have been introduced to allow for an automated fail-over of virtual machines residing on a datastore that has a "Permanent Device Loss" (PDL) condition. A PDL condition, is a condition that is communicated by the array controller to ESXi via a SCSI sense code. This condition indicates that a device (LUN) has become unavailable and is likely permanently unavailable. An example scenario in which this condition would be communicated by the array would be when a LUN is set offline. This condition is used in non-uniform models during a failure scenario to ensure ESXi takes appropriate action when access to a LUN is revoked. It should be noted that when a full storage failure occurs it is impossible to generate the Permanent Device Loss condition as there is no communication possible between the array and the ESXi host. This state will be identified by the ESXi host as an All Paths Down (APD) condition.

It is important to recognize that the following settings only apply to a PDL condition and not to an APD condition. In the failure scenarios we will demonstrate the difference in behavior for these two conditions. In order to allow vSphere HA to respond to a PDL condition two advanced settings have been introduced in vSphere 5.0 U1. The first setting is configured on a host level and is *disk.terminateVMOnPDLDefault*. This setting can be configured in /etc/vmware/settings and is should be set to "True" by default, note that this is a per host setting. This setting ensures that a virtual machine is killed when the datastore on which it resides enters a PDL state. The virtual machine is killed as soon as it initiates disk I/O on a datastore which is in a PDL condition. With vSphere 5.0 Update 1 virtual machines whose files spanned multiple datastores were explicitly not supported. As of vSphere 5.1, we do support such virtual machines.

We recommend setting *diskterminateVMonPDLDefault* to true. Please note that virtual machines are only killed when issuing I/O to the datastore. If the virtual machine is not issuing I/O to the datastore the virtual machine remains alive. Virtual machines that are running memory intensive workloads without issuing I/O to the datastore may remain active in such situations. Note that this can lead to two instances of the same virtual machine being on the virtual machine network.

The second setting is a vSphere HA advanced setting called
das.maskCleanShutdownEnabled. This setting was introduced in vSphere 5.0
Update 1 and is not enabled by default: It will need to be set to "True". This
setting allows HA to trigger a restart response for a virtual machine which
has been killed automatically due to a PDL condition. This setting was
introduced because HA cannot differentiate between a virtual machine that
was killed due to the PDL state and a virtual machine that has been powered
off by an administrator. By setting it to true, you are telling HA to assume
such power offs were due to the virtual machine being killed during a PDL. If
you set it to true, note that any virtual machine powered off during an APD
will also be assumed by HA to have failed and will be restarted.

Figure 23: PDL Advanced Setting

Chapter 5

Adding Resiliency to HA (Network Redundancy)

In the previous chapter we extensively covered both Isolation Detection which triggers the selected Isolation Response and the impact of a false positive. The Isolation Response enables HA to restart virtual machines when "Power off" or "Shut down" has been selected and the host becomes isolated from the network. However, this also means that it is possible that, without proper redundancy, the Isolation Response may be unnecessarily triggered. This leads to downtime and should be prevented.

To increase resiliency for networking, VMware implemented the concept of NIC teaming in the hypervisor for both VMkernel and virtual machine networking. When discussing HA, this is especially important for the Management Network.

Quote

"NIC teaming is the process of grouping together several physical NICs into one single logical NIC, which can be used for network fault tolerance and load balancing."

Using this mechanism, it is possible to add redundancy to the Management Network to decrease the chances of an isolation event. This is, of course, also possible for other "Portgroups" but that is not the topic of this chapter or book. Another option is configuring an additional Management Network by enabling the "management network" tick box on another VMkernel port. A little understood fact is that if there are multiple VMkernel networks on the same subnet, HA will use all of them for management traffic, even if only one is specified for management traffic!
Although there are many configurations possible and supported, we recommend a simple but highly resilient configuration. We have included the vMotion (VMkernel) network in our example as combining the Management Network and the vMotion network on a single vSwitch is the most commonly used configuration and an industry accepted best practice.

Requirements:

- 2 physical NICs
- VLAN trunking

Recommended:

- 2 physical switches
- If available, enable "link state tracking" to ensure link failures are reported

The vSwitch should be configured as follows:

- vSwitch0: 2 Physical NICs (vmnic0 and vmnic1).
- 2 Portgroups (Management Network and vMotion VMkernel).
- Management Network active on vmnic0 and standby on vmnic1.
- vMotion VMkernel active on vmnic1 and standby on vmnic0.
- Failback set to No.

Each portgroup has a VLAN ID assigned and runs dedicated on its own physical NIC; only in the case of a failure it is switched over to the standby NIC. We highly recommend setting failback to "No" to avoid chances of an unwanted isolation event, which can occur when a physical switch routes no traffic during boot but the ports are reported as "up". (NIC Teaming Tab)

Pros: Only 2 NICs in total are needed for the Management Network and vMotion VMkernel, especially useful in blade server environments. Easy to configure.

Cons: Just a single active path for heartbeats.
The following diagram depicts this active/standby scenario:

Figure 24: Active-Standby Management Network design

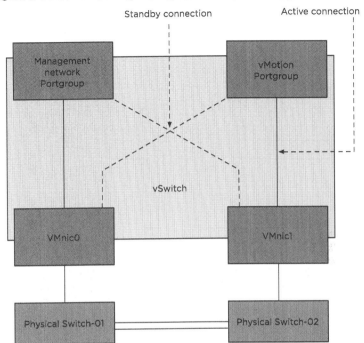

To increase resiliency, we also recommend implementing the following advanced settings and using NIC ports on different PCI busses – preferably NICs of a different make and model. When using a different make and model, even a driver failure could be mitigated.

Advanced Settings:

- *das.isolationaddressX* = <ip-address>

The isolation address setting is discussed in more detail in chapter 4. In short; it is the IP address that the HA agent pings to identify if the host is completely isolated from the network or just not receiving any heartbeats. If multiple VMkernel networks on different subnets are used, it is recommended to set an isolation address per network to ensure that each of these will be able to validate isolation of the host.

Basic design principle

Take advantage of some of the basic features vSphere has to offer like NIC teaming. Combining different physical NICs will increase overall resiliency of your solution.

Link State Tracking

This was already briefly mentioned in the list of recommendations, but this feature is something we would like to emphasize. We have noticed that people often forget about this even though many switches offer this capability, especially in blade server environments.

Link state tracking will mirror the state of an upstream link to a downstream link. Let's clarify that with a diagram.

Figure 25: Link State tracking mechanism

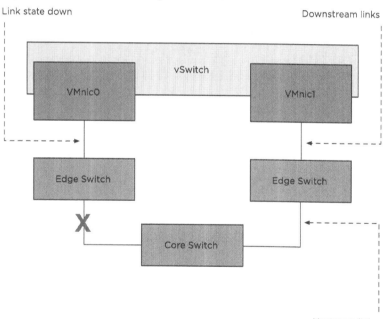

Figure 25 depicts a scenario where an uplink of a "Core Switch" has failed. Without Link State Tracking, the connection from the "Edge Switch" to vmnic0 will be reported as up. With Link State Tracking enabled, the state of the link on the "Edge Switch" will reflect the state of the link of the "Core Switch" and as such be marked as "down". You might wonder why this is important but think about it for a second. Many features that vSphere offer rely on networking and so do your virtual machines. In the case where the state is not reflected, some functionality might just fail, for instance network heartbeating could fail if it needs to flow through the core switch. We call this a 'black hole' scenario: the host sends traffic down a path that it believes is up, but the traffic never reaches its destination due to the failed upstream link.

Basic design principle

Know your network environment, talk to the network administrators and ensure advanced features like Link State Tracking are used when possible to increase resiliency.

Chapter 6

Admission Control

Admission Control is more than likely the most misunderstood concept vSphere holds today and because of this it is often disabled. However, Admission Control is a must when availability needs to be guaranteed and isn't that the reason for enabling HA in the first place?

What is HA Admission Control about? Why does HA contain this concept called Admission Control? The "Availability Guide" a.k.a HA bible states the following:

Quote

"vCenter Server uses admission control to ensure that sufficient resources are available in a cluster to provide failover protection and to ensure that virtual machine resource reservations are respected."

Please read that quote again and especially the first two words. Indeed it is vCenter that is responsible for Admission Control, contrary to what many believe. Although this might seem like a trivial fact it is important to understand that this implies that Admission Control will not disallow HA initiated restarts. HA initiated restarts are done on a host level and not through vCenter.

As said, Admission Control guarantees that capacity is available for an HA initiated failover by reserving resources within a cluster. It calculates the capacity required for a failover based on available resources. In other words, if a host is placed into maintenance mode or disconnected, it is taken out of the equation. This also implies that if a host has failed or is not responding but has not been removed from the cluster, it is still included in the equation. "Available Resources" indicates that the virtualization overhead has already been subtracted from the total amount.

To give an example; VMkernel memory is subtracted from the total amount of memory to obtain the memory available memory for virtual machines. There is one gotcha with Admission Control that we want to bring to your attention before drilling into the different policies. When Admission Control is enabled, HA will in no way violate availability constraints. This means that it will always ensure multiple hosts are up and running and this applies for manual maintenance mode actions and, for instance, to VMware Distributed Power Management. So, if a host is stuck trying to enter Maintenance Mode, remember that it might be HA which is not allowing Maintenance Mode to proceed as it would violate the Admission Control Policy. In this situation, users can manually vMotion virtual machines off the host or temporarily disable admission control to allow the operation to proceed.

With vSphere 4.1 and prior when you disable Admission Control and enabled DPM it could lead to a serious impact on availability. When Admission Control was disabled, DPM could place all hosts except for 1 in standby mode to reduce total power consumption. This could lead to issues in the event that this single host would fail. As of vSphere 5.0, this behavior has changed: when DPM is enabled, HA will ensure that there are always at least two hosts powered up for failover purposes.

As of vSphere 4.1, DPM is also smart enough to take hosts out of standby mode to ensure enough resources are available to provide for HA initiated failovers. If by any chance the resources are not available, HA will wait for these resources to be made available by DPM and then attempt the restart of the virtual machines. In other words, the retry count (5 retries by default) is not wasted in scenarios like these.

If you are still using an older version of vSphere or, god forbid, VI3, please understand that you could end up with all but one ESXi host placed in standby mode, which could lead to potential issues when that particular host fails or resources are scarce as there will be no host available to power on your virtual machines. This situation is described in the following knowledge base article: http://kb.vmware.com/kb/1007006.

Admission Control Policy

The Admission Control Policy dictates the mechanism that HA uses to guarantee enough resources are available for an HA initiated failover. This section gives a general overview of the available Admission Control Policies. The impact of each policy is described in the following section, including our recommendation. HA has three mechanisms to guarantee enough capacity is available to respect virtual machine resource reservations.

Figure 26: Admission control policy

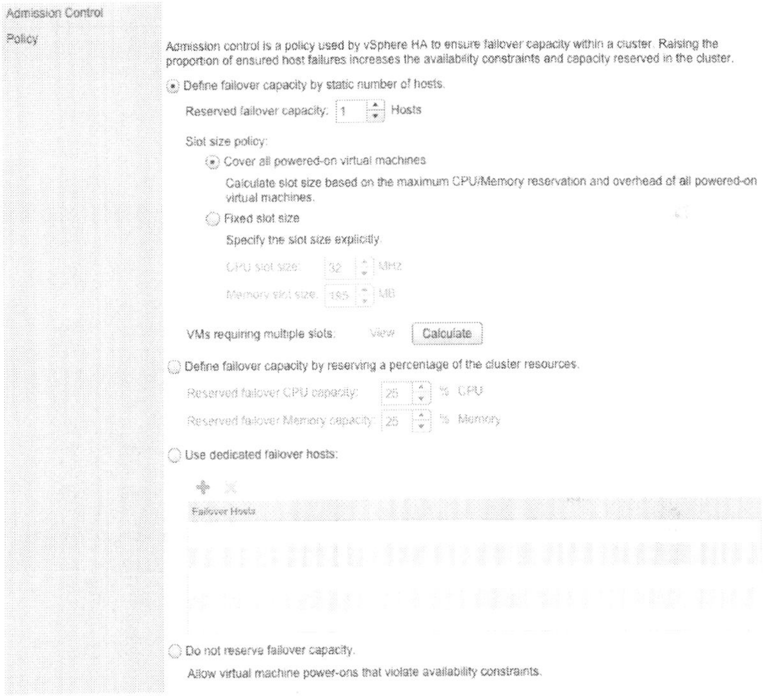

Below we have listed all three options currently available as the Admission Control Policy. Each option has a different mechanism to ensure resources are available for a failover and each option has its caveats.

Admission Control Mechanisms

Each Admission Control Policy has its own Admission Control mechanism. Understanding each of these Admission Control mechanisms is important to appreciate the impact each one has on your cluster design. For instance, setting a reservation on a specific virtual machine can have an impact on the achieved consolidation ratio. This section will take you on a journey through the trenches of Admission Control Policies and their respective mechanisms and algorithms.

Host Failures Cluster Tolerates

The Admission Control Policy that has been around the longest is the "Host Failures Cluster Tolerates" policy. It is also historically the least understood Admission Control Policy due to its complex admission control mechanism.

Although the "Host Failures Tolerates" Admission Control Policy mechanism itself hasn't changed, a limitation has been removed. Pre-vSphere 5.0, the maximum host failures that could be tolerated was 4, due to the primary/secondary node mechanism. As of vSphere 5.0, this mechanism has been replaced with a master/slave node mechanism and it is possible to plan for N-1 host failures. In the case of a 32 host cluster, you could potentially set "Host failures the cluster tolerates" to 31.

A new feature only available in the vSphere 5.1 Web Client is the ability to manually specify the slot size as can be seen in the below figure. The vSphere 5.1 Web Client also allows you to view which virtual machines span multiple slots. This can be very useful in scenarios where the slot size has been explicitly specified, we will explain why in just a second.

Figure 27: Host Failures

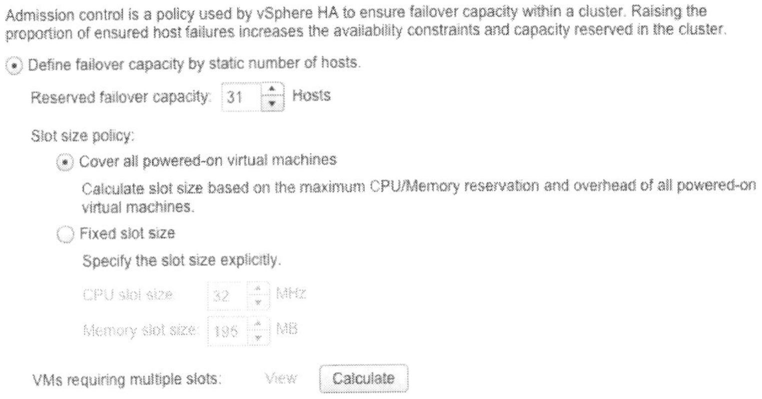

Admission control is a policy used by vSphere HA to ensure failover capacity within a cluster. Raising the proportion of ensured host failures increases the availability constraints and capacity reserved in the cluster.

⦿ Define failover capacity by static number of hosts.

    Reserved failover capacity: [31 ⬍] Hosts

    Slot size policy:

       ⦿ Cover all powered-on virtual machines

          Calculate slot size based on the maximum CPU/Memory reservation and overhead of all powered-on virtual machines.

       ◯ Fixed slot size

          Specify the slot size explicitly.

          CPU slot size   [32 ⬍] MHz

          Memory slot size [195 ⬍] MB

    VMs requiring multiple slots: View   [Calculate]

The so-called "slots" mechanism is used when the "Host failures cluster tolerates" has been selected as the Admission Control Policy. The details of this mechanism have changed several times in the past and it is one of the most restrictive policies; more than likely, it is also the least understood.

Slots dictate how many virtual machines can be powered on before vCenter starts yelling "Out Of Resources!" Normally, a slot represents one virtual machine. Admission Control does not limit HA in restarting virtual machines, it ensures enough unfragmented resources are available to power on all virtual machines in the cluster by preventing "over-commitment". Technically speaking "over-commitment" is not the correct terminology as Admission Control ensures virtual machine reservations can be satisfied and that all virtual machines' initial memory overhead requirements are met. Although we have already touched on this, it doesn't hurt repeating it as it is one of those myths that keeps coming back; **HA initiated failovers are not prone to the Admission Control Policy**. Admission Control is done by vCenter. HA initiated restarts, in a normal scenario, are executed directly on the ESXi host without the use of vCenter. The corner-case is where HA requests DRS (DRS is a vCenter task!) to defragment resources but that is beside the point. Even if resources are low and vCenter would complain, it couldn't stop the restart from happening.

Let's dig in to this concept we have just introduced, slots.

Quote

"A slot is defined as a logical representation of the memory and CPU resources that satisfy the reservation requirements for any powered-on virtual machine in the cluster."

In other words a slot is the worst case CPU and memory **reservation** scenario in a cluster. This directly leads to the first "gotcha."

HA uses the highest CPU reservation of any given powered-on virtual machine and the highest memory reservation of any given powered-on virtual machine in the cluster. If no reservation of higher than 32 MHz is set, HA will use a default of 32 MHz for CPU. Note that this behavior has changed: pre-vSphere 5.0 the default value was 256 MHz. This has changed as some felt that 256 MHz was too aggressive. If no memory reservation is set, HA will use a default of 0 MB+memory overhead for memory. (See the VMware vSphere Resource Management Guide for more details on memory overhead per virtual machine configuration.) The following example will clarify what "worst-case" actually means.

Example: If virtual machine "VM1" has 2 GHz of CPU reserved and 1024 MB of memory reserved and virtual machine "VM2" has 1 GHz of CPU reserved and 2048 MB of memory reserved the slot size for memory will be 2048 MB (+ its memory overhead) and the slot size for CPU will be 2 GHz. It is a combination of the highest reservation of both virtual machines that leads to the total slot size. Reservations defined at the Resource Pool level however, will not affect HA slot size calculations.

Basic design principle

Be really careful with reservations, if there's no need to have them on a per virtual machine basis; don't configure them, especially when using host failures cluster tolerates. If reservations are needed, resort to resource pool based reservations.

Now that we know the worst-case scenario is always taken into account when it comes to slot size calculations, we will describe what dictates the amount of available slots per cluster as that ultimately dictates how many virtual machines can be powered on in your cluster.

First, we will need to know the slot size for memory and CPU, next we will divide the total available CPU resources of a host by the CPU slot size and the total available memory resources of a host by the memory slot size. This leaves us with a total number of slots for both memory and CPU for a host. The most restrictive number (worst-case scenario) is the number of slots for this host. In other words, when you have 25 CPU slots but only 5 memory slots, the amount of available slots for this host will be 5 as HA always takes the worst case scenario into account to "guarantee" all virtual machines can be powered on in case of a failure or isolation.

The question we receive a lot is how do I know what my slot size is? The details around slot sizes can be monitored on the HA section of the Cluster's Monitor tab by checking the the "Advanced Runtime Info" section when the "Host Failures" Admission Control Policy is configured.

Figure 28: High Availability cluster monitor section

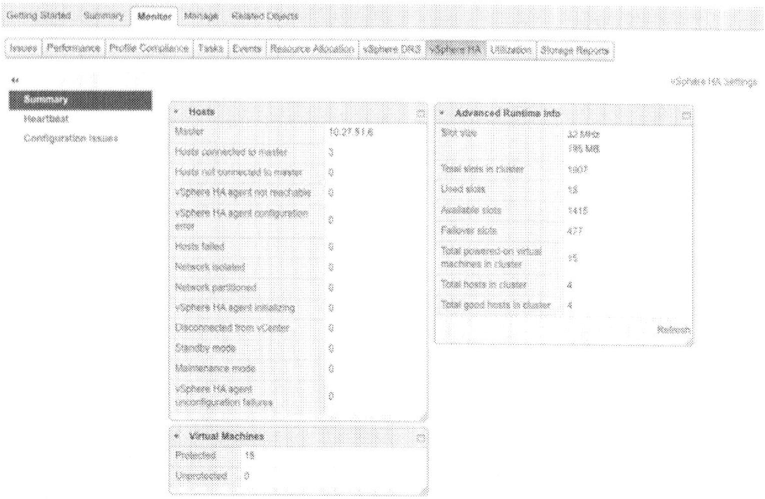

Advanced Runtime Info will show the specifics the slot size and more useful details such as the number of slots available as depicted in Figure 28.

Figure 29: High Availability advanced runtime info

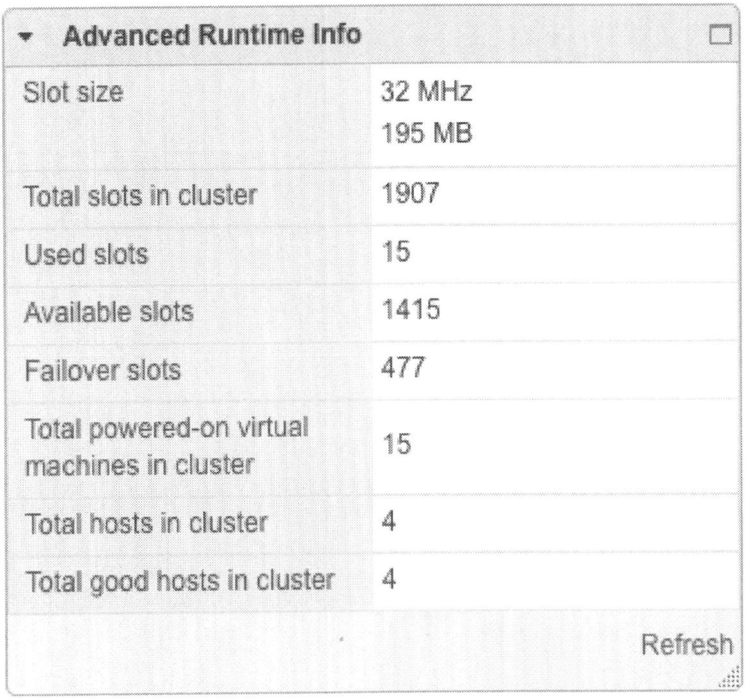

Advanced Runtime Info	
Slot size	32 MHz 195 MB
Total slots in cluster	1907
Used slots	15
Available slots	1415
Failover slots	477
Total powered-on virtual machines in cluster	15
Total hosts in cluster	4
Total good hosts in cluster	4

Refresh

As you can imagine, using reservations on a per virtual machine basis can lead to very conservative consolidation ratios. However, with vSphere 5.1, this is something that is configurable through the Web Client. If you have just one virtual machine with a really high reservation, you can set an explicit slot size by going to "Edit Cluster Services" and specifying them under the Admission Control Policy section as shown in Figure 27.

If one of these advanced settings is used, HA will ensure that the virtual machine that skewed the numbers can be restarted by "assigning" multiple slots to it. However, when you are low on resources, this could mean that you are not able to power on the virtual machine with this reservation because resources may be fragmented throughout the cluster instead of available on a single host. As of vSphere 4.1, HA will notify DRS that a power-on attempt was unsuccessful and a request will be made to defragment the resources to accommodate the remaining virtual machines that need to be powered on. In order for this to be successful DRS will need to be enabled and configured to fully automated. When not configured to fully automated user action is required to execute DRS recommendations.

Figure 30 depicts a scenario where a virtual machine spans multiple slots:

Figure 30: Virtual machine spanning multiple HA slots

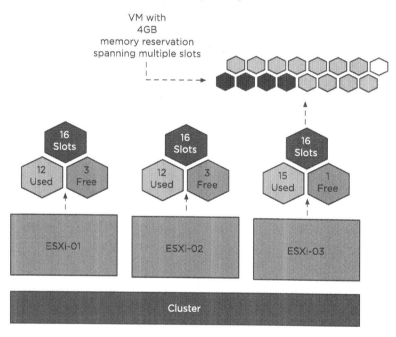

Notice that because the memory slot size has been manually set to 1024 MB, one of the virtual machines (grouped with dotted lines) spans multiple slots due to a 4 GB memory reservation. As you might have noticed, none of the hosts has enough resources available to satisfy the reservation of the virtual machine that needs to failover. Although in total there are enough resources available, they are fragmented and HA will not be able to power-on this particular virtual machine directly but will request DRS to defragment the resources to accommodate this virtual machine's resource requirements.

Admission Control does not take fragmentation of slots into account when slot sizes are manually defined with advanced settings. It will take the number of slots this virtual machine will consume into account by subtracting them from the total number of available slots, but it will not verify the amount of available slots per host to ensure failover. As stated earlier, though, HA will request DRS to defragment the resources. This is by no means a guarantee of a successful power-on attempt.

Basic design principle

Avoid using advanced settings to decrease the slot size as it could lead to more down time and adds an extra layer of complexity. If there is a large discrepancy in size and reservations we recommend using the percentage based admission control policy.

vSphere 5.1 added new functionality around identifying virtual machines which span multiple slots, as shown in Figure 27. We highly recommend monitoring this section on a regular basis to get a better understand of your environment and to identify those virtual machines that might be problematic to restart in case of a host failure.

Unbalanced Configurations and Impact on Slot Calculation

It is an industry best practice to create clusters with similar hardware configurations. However, many companies started out with a small VMware cluster when virtualization was first introduced. When the time has come to expand, chances are fairly large the same hardware configuration is no longer available. The question is will you add the newly bought hosts to the same cluster or create a new cluster?

From a DRS perspective, large clusters are preferred as it increases the load balancing opportunities. However there is a caveat for DRS as well, which is described in the DRS section of this book. For HA, there is a big caveat. When you think about it and understand the internal workings of HA, more specifically the slot algorithm, you probably already know what is coming up.

Let's first define the term "unbalanced cluster."

An unbalanced cluster would, for instance, be a cluster with 3 hosts of which one contains substantially more memory than the other hosts in the cluster. Let's try to clarify that with an example.

Example:

What would happen to the total number of slots in a cluster of the following specifications?

- Three host cluster
- Two hosts have 16 GB of available memory
- One host has 32 GB of available memory

The third host is a brand new host that has just been bought and as prices of memory dropped immensely the decision was made to buy 32 GB instead of 16 GB.

The cluster contains a virtual machine that has 1 vCPU and 4 GB of memory. A 1024 MB memory reservation has been defined on this virtual machine. As explained earlier, a reservation will dictate the slot size, which in this case leads to a memory slot size of 1024 MB + memory overhead. For the sake of simplicity, we will calculate with 1024 MB.

Figure 31 depicts this scenario:

Figure 31: High Availability memory slot size

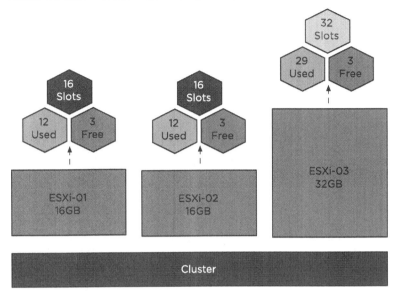

When Admission Control is enabled and the number of host failures has been selected as the Admission Control Policy, the number of slots will be calculated per host and the cluster in total. This will result in:

Table 4: Number of Slots overview

Host	Number of slots
ESXi-01	16 Slots
ESXi-02	16 Slots
ESXi-03	32 Slots

As Admission Control is enabled, **a worst-case scenario is taken into account**. When a single host failure has been specified, this means that the host with the largest number of slots will be taken out of the equation. In other words, for our cluster, this would result in:

ESXi-01 + ESXi-02 = 32 slots available

Although you have doubled the amount of memory in one of your hosts, you are still stuck with only 32 slots in total. As clearly demonstrated, there is absolutely no point in buying additional memory for a single host when your cluster is designed with Admission Control enabled and the number of host failures has been selected as the Admission Control Policy.

In our example, the memory slot size happened to be the most restrictive; however, the same principle applies when CPU slot size is most restrictive.

Basic design principle

When using admission control, balance your clusters and be conservative with reservations as it leads to decreased consolidation ratios.

Now, what would happen in the scenario above when the number of allowed host failures is to 2? In this case ESXi-03 is taken out of the equation and one of any of the remaining hosts in the cluster is also taken out, resulting in 16 slots. This makes sense, doesn't it?

Can you avoid large HA slot sizes due to reservations without resorting to advanced settings? That's the question we get almost daily and the answer is the "Percentage of Cluster Resources Reserved" admission control mechanism.

Percentage of Cluster Resources Reserved

With vSphere 4.0, VMware introduced the ability to specify a percentage next to a number of host failures and a designated failover host. This was a single value for CPU and memory. With vSphere 5.0, this was changed which allows you to select different percentages for CPU and memory as shown in Figure 32.

Figure 32: Setting a different percentage for CPU/Memory

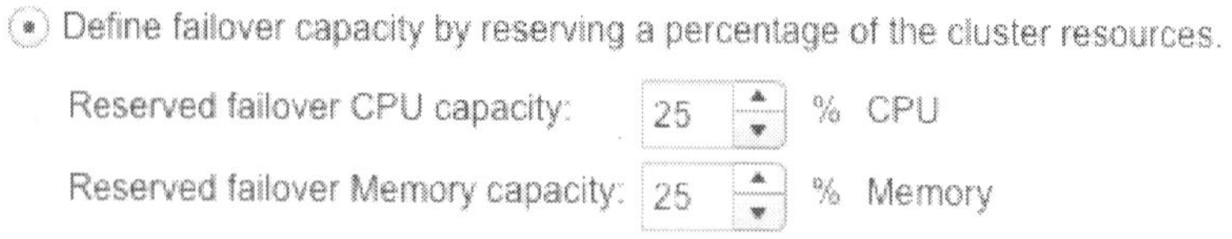

⊙ Define failover capacity by reserving a percentage of the cluster resources.

    Reserved failover CPU capacity: `25` ⬍ % CPU

    Reserved failover Memory capacity: `25` ⬍ % Memory

The main advantage of the percentage based Admission Control Policy is that it avoids the commonly experienced slot size issue where values are skewed due to a large reservation. But if it doesn't use the slot algorithm, what does it use?

When you specify a percentage, and let's assume for now that the percentage for CPU and memory will be configured equally, that percentage of the total amount of available resources will stay reserved for HA purposes. First of all, HA will add up all available resources to see how much it has available (virtualization overhead will be subtracted) in total. Then, HA will calculate how much resources are currently reserved by adding up all reservations for memory and for CPU for all powered on virtual machines.

For those virtual machines that do not have a reservation, a default of 32 MHz will be used for CPU and a default of 0 MB+memory overhead will be used for Memory. (Amount of overhead per configuration type can be found in the "Understanding Memory Overhead" section of the Resource Management guide.)

In other words:

((total amount of available resources – total reserved virtual machine resources)/total amount of available resources) <= (percentage HA should reserve as spare capacity)

Total reserved virtual machine resources includes the default reservation of 32 MHz and the memory overhead of the virtual machine.

Let's use a diagram to make it a bit clearer:

Figure 33: Percentage of cluster resources reserved

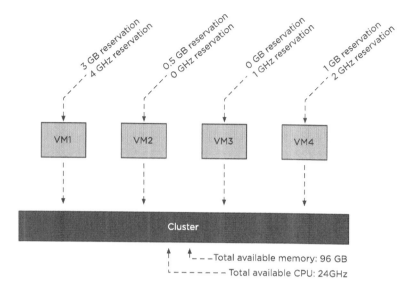

Total cluster resources are 24GHz (CPU) and 96GB (MEM). This would lead to the following calculations:

((24 GHz - (2 GHz + 1 GHz + 32 MHz + 4 GHz)) / 24 GHz) = 69 % available
((96 GB - (1,1 GB + 114 MB + 626 MB + 3,2 GB)/96 GB= 85 % available

As you can see, the amount of memory differs from the diagram. Even if a reservation has been set, the amount of memory overhead is added to the reservation. This example also demonstrates how keeping CPU and memory percentage equal could create an imbalance. Ideally, of course, the hosts are provisioned in such a way that there is no CPU/memory imbalance. Experience over the years has proven, unfortunately, that most environments run out of memory resources first and this might need to be factored in when calculating the correct value for the percentage. However, this trend might be changing as memory is getting cheaper every day.

In order to ensure virtual machines can always be restarted, Admission Control will constantly monitor if the policy has been violated or not. Please note that this Admission Control process is part of vCenter and not of the ESXi host! When one of the thresholds is reached, memory or CPU, Admission Control will disallow powering on any additional virtual machines as that could potentially impact availability. These thresholds can be monitored on the HA section of the Cluster's summary tab.

Figure 34: High Availability summary

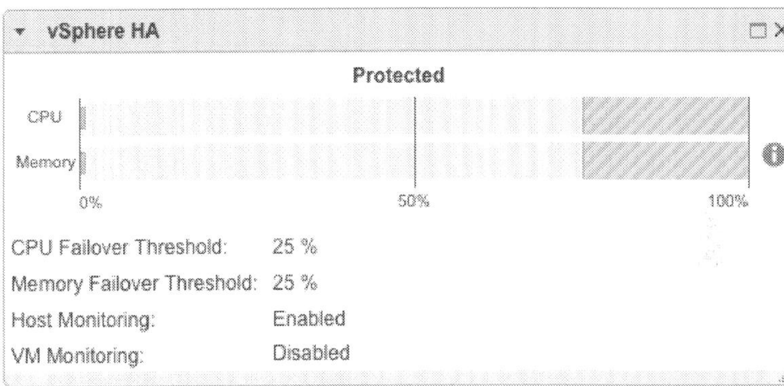

If you have an unbalanced cluster (hosts with different sizes of CPU or memory resources), your percentage should be equal or preferably larger than the percentage of resources provided by the largest host. This way you ensure that all virtual machines residing on this host can be restarted in case of a host failure.

As earlier explained, this Admission Control Policy does not use slots. As such, resources might be fragmented throughout the cluster. Although, as of vSphere 4.1, DRS is notified to rebalance the cluster, if needed, to accommodate these virtual machines resource requirements, a guarantee cannot be given. We recommend selecting the highest restart priority for this virtual machine (of course, depending on the SLA) to ensure it will be able to boot.

The following example and diagram (Figure 35) will make it more obvious: You have 3 hosts, each with roughly 80% memory usage, and you have configured HA to reserve 20% of resources for both CPU and memory. A host fails and all virtual machines will need to failover. One of those virtual machines has a 4 GB memory reservation. As you can imagine, HA will not be able to initiate a power-on attempt, as there are not enough memory resources available to guarantee the reserved capacity. Instead an event will get generated indicating "not enough resources for failover" for this virtual machine.

Figure 35: Available resources

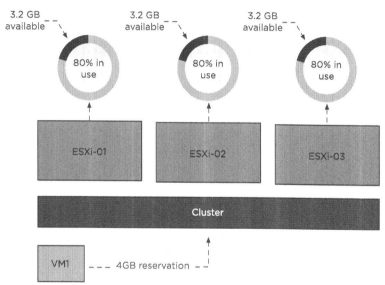

Basic design principle

Although vSphere 5.0 will utilize DRS to try to accommodate for the resource requirements of this virtual machine a guarantee cannot be given. Do the math; verify that any single host has enough resources to power-on your largest virtual machine. Also take restart priority into account for this/these virtual machine(s).

Failover Hosts

The third option one could choose is to select one or multiple designated Failover hosts. This is commonly referred to as a hot standby. Besides the fact that vSphere 5.0 increases the amount of failover hosts you can designate there is actually not much to tell around this mechanism.

Figure 36: Select failover hosts Admission Control Policy

It is "what you see is what you get". When you designate hosts as failover hosts, they will not participate in DRS and you will not be able to run virtual machines on these hosts! These hosts are literally reserved for failover situations. HA will attempt to use these hosts first to failover the virtual machines. If, for whatever reason, this is unsuccessful, it will attempt a failover on any of the other hosts. For example, when three hosts would fail, including the hosts designated as failover hosts, HA will still try to restart the impacted virtual machines on the host that is left. Although this host was not a designated failover host, HA will use it to limit downtime.

Figure 37: Select multiple failover hosts

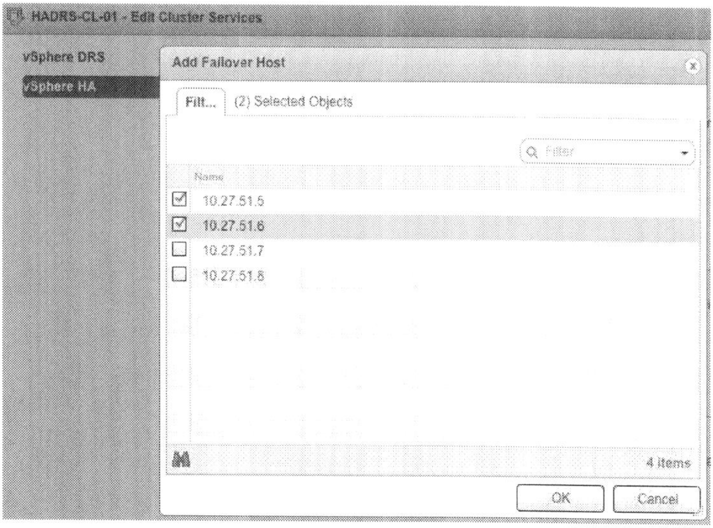

Decision Making Time

As with any decision you make, there is an impact to your environment. This impact could be positive but also, for instance, unexpected. This especially goes for HA Admission Control. Selecting the right Admission Control Policy can lead to a quicker Return On Investment and a lower Total Cost of Ownership. In the previous section, we described all the algorithms and mechanisms that form Admission Control and in this section we will focus more on the design considerations around selecting the appropriate Admission Control Policy for your or your customer's environment.

The first decision that will need to be made is whether Admission Control will be enabled. We generally recommend enabling Admission Control as it is the only way of guaranteeing your virtual machines will be allowed to restart after a failure. It is important, though, that the policy is carefully selected and fits your or your customer's requirements.

Basic design principle

Admission control guarantees enough capacity is available for virtual machine failover. As such we recommend enabling it.

Although we already have explained all the mechanisms that are being used by each of the policies in the previous section, we will give a high level overview and list all the pros and cons in this section. On top of that, we will expand on what we feel is the most flexible Admission Control Policy and how it should be configured and calculated.

Host Failures Cluster Tolerates

This option is historically speaking the most used for Admission Control. Most environments are designed with an N+1 redundancy and N+2 is also not uncommon. This Admission Control Policy uses "slots" to ensure enough capacity is reserved for failover, which is a fairly complex mechanism. Slots are based on VM-level reservations and if reservations are not used a default slot size for CPU of 32 MHz is defined and for memory the largest memory overhead of any given virtual machine is used.

Pros:
- Fully automated (When a host is added to a cluster, HA re-calculates how many slots are available.)
- Guarantees failover by calculating slot sizes.

Cons:
- Can be very conservative and inflexible when reservations are used as the largest reservation dictates slot sizes.
- Unbalanced clusters lead to wastage of resources.
- Complexity for administrator from calculation perspective.

Percentage as Cluster Resources Reserved

The percentage based Admission Control Policy was introduced with vSphere 4.0. The percentage based Admission Control is based on per-reservation calculation instead of the slots mechanism. The percentage based Admission Control Policy is less conservative than "Host Failures" and more flexible than "Failover Hosts".

Pros:
- Accurate as it considers actual reservation per virtual machine to calculate available failover resources.
- Cluster dynamically adjusts when resources are added.

Cons:

- Manual calculations needed when adding additional hosts in a cluster and number of host failures needs to remain unchanged.
- Unbalanced clusters can be a problem when chosen percentage is too low and resources are fragmented, which means failover of a virtual machine can't be guaranteed as the reservation of this virtual machine might not be available as a block of resources on a single host.

Please note that, although a failover cannot be guaranteed, there are few scenarios where a virtual machine will not be able to restart due to the integration HA offers with DRS and the fact that most clusters have spare capacity available to account for virtual machine demand variance. Although this is a corner-case scenario, it needs to be considered in environments where absolute guarantees must be provided.

Specify Failover Hosts

With the "Specify Failover Hosts" Admission Control Policy, when one or multiple hosts fail, HA will attempt to restart all virtual machines on the designated failover hosts. The designated failover hosts are essentially "hot standby" hosts. In other words, DRS will not migrate virtual machines to these hosts when resources are scarce or the cluster is imbalanced.

Pros:

- What you see is what you get.
- No fragmented resources.

Cons:

- What you see is what you get.
- Dedicated failover hosts not utilized during normal operations.

Recommendations

We have been asked many times for our recommendation on Admission Control and it is difficult to answer as each policy has its pros and cons. However, we generally recommend a Percentage based Admission Control Policy. It is the most flexible policy as it uses the actual reservation per virtual machine instead of taking a "worst case" scenario approach like the number of host failures does. However, the number of host failures policy guarantees the failover level under all circumstances. Percentage based is less restrictive, but offers lower guarantees that in all scenarios HA will be able to restart all virtual machines. With the added level of integration between HA and DRS we believe a Percentage based Admission Control Policy will fit most environments.

Basic design principle

Do the math, and take customer requirements into account. We recommend using a "percentage" based admission control policy, as it is the most flexible.

Now that we have recommended which Admission Control Policy to use, the next step is to provide guidance around selecting the correct percentage. We cannot tell you what the ideal percentage is as that totally depends on the size of your cluster and, of course, on your resiliency model (N+1 vs. N+2). We can, however, provide guidelines around calculating how much of your resources should be set aside and how to prevent wasting resources.

Selecting the Right Percentage

It is a common strategy to select a single host as a percentage of resources reserved for failover. We generally recommend selecting a percentage which is the equivalent of a single or multiple hosts, Let's explain why and what the impact is of not using the equivalent of a single or multiple hosts.

Let's start with an example: a cluster exists of 8 ESXi hosts, each containing 70 GB of available RAM. This might sound like an awkward memory configuration but to simplify things we have already subtracted 2 GB as virtualization overhead. Although virtualization overhead is probably less than 2 GB, we have used this number to make calculations easier. This example zooms in on memory but this concept also applies to CPU, of course.

For this cluster we will define the percentage of resources to reserve for both Memory and CPU to 20%. For memory, this leads to a total cluster memory capacity of 448 GB:

$$(70\ GB + 70\ GB + 70\ GB + 70\ GB + 70\ GB + 70\ GB + 70\ GB + 70\ GB) * (1 - 20\%)$$

A total of 112 GB of memory is reserved as failover capacity.

Once a percentage is specified, that percentage of resources will be unavailable for virtual machines, therefore it makes sense to set the percentage as close to the value that equals the resources a single (or multiple) host represents. We will demonstrate why this is important in subsequent examples.

In the example above, 20% was used to be reserved for resources in an 8-host cluster. This configuration reserves more resources than a single host contributes to the cluster. HA's main objective is to provide automatic recovery for virtual machines after a physical server failure. For this reason, it is recommended to reserve resources equal to a single or multiple hosts. When using the per-host level granularity in an 8-host cluster (homogeneous configured hosts), the resource contribution per host to the cluster is 12.5%. However, the percentage used must be an integer (whole number). It is recommended to round up to the value guaranteeing that the full capacity of one host is protected, in this example (Figure 38), the conservative approach would lead to a percentage of 13%.

Figure 38: Setting the correct value

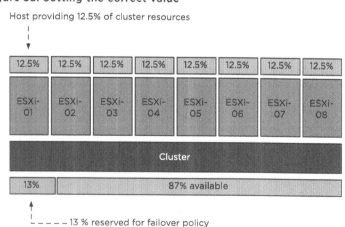

Aggressive Approach

We have seen many environments where the percentage was set to a value that was less than the contribution of a single host to the cluster. Although this approach reduces the amount of resources reserved for accommodating host failures and results in higher consolidation ratios, it also offers a lower guarantee that HA will be able to restart all virtual machines after a failure. One might argue that this approach will more than likely work as most environments will not be fully utilized; however it also does eliminate the guarantee that after a failure all virtual machines will be recovered. Wasn't that the reason for enabling HA in the first place?

Adding Hosts to Your Cluster

Although the percentage is dynamic and calculates capacity at a cluster-level, changes to your selected percentage might be required when expanding the cluster. The reason being that the amount of reserved resources for a fail-over might not correspond with the contribution per host and as a result lead to resource wastage. For example, adding 4 hosts to an 8-host cluster and continuing to use the previously configured admission control policy value of 13% will result in a failover capacity that is equivalent to 1.5 hosts. Figure 39 depicts a scenario where an 8-host cluster is expanded to 12 hosts. Each host holds 8 2 GHz cores and 70 GB of memory. The cluster was originally configured with admission control set to 13%, which equals to 109.2 GB and 24.96 GHz. If the requirement is to allow a single host failure 7.68 Ghz and 33.6 GB is "wasted" as clearly demonstrated in Figure 39.

Figure 39: Avoid wasting resources

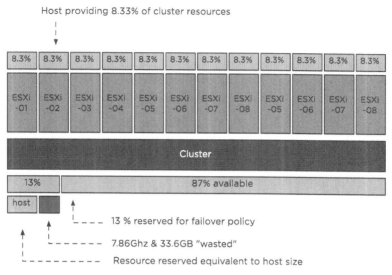

How to Define Your Percentage?

As explained earlier it will fully depend on the N+X model that has been chosen. Based on this model, we recommend selecting a percentage that equals the amount of resources a single host represents. So, in the case of an 8 host cluster and N+2 resiliency, the percentage should be set as follows:

2 / 8 (*100) = 25%

Basic design principle

In order to avoid wasting resources we recommend carefully selecting your N+X resiliency architecture. Calculate the required percentage based on this architecture.

Chapter 7

VM and Application Monitoring

VM and Application Monitoring is an often overlooked but really powerful feature of HA. The reason for this is most likely that it is disabled by default and relatively new compared to HA. We have tried to gather all the information we could around VM and Application Monitoring, but it is a pretty straightforward product that actually does what you expect it would do.

Figure 40: VM and Application Monitoring

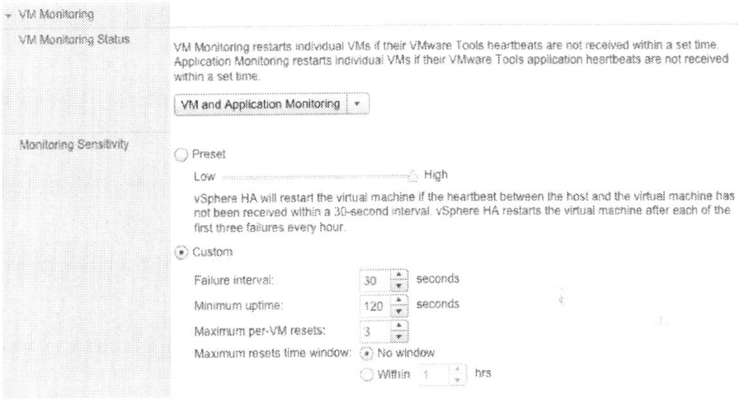

Why Do You Need VM/Application Monitoring?

VM and Application Monitoring acts on a different level from HA. VM/App Monitoring responds to a single virtual machine or application failure as opposed to HA which responds to a host failure. An example of a single virtual machine failure would, for instance, be the infamous "blue screen of death". In the case of App Monitoring the type of failure that triggers a response is defined by the application developer or administrator.

How Does VM/App Monitoring Work?

VM Monitoring resets individual virtual machines when needed. VM/App monitoring uses a heartbeat similar to HA. If heartbeats, and, in this case, VMware Tools heartbeats, are not received for a specific (and configurable) amount of time, the virtual machine will be restarted. These heartbeats are monitored by the HA agent and are not sent over a network, but stay local to the host.

Figure 41: VM Monitoring sensitivity

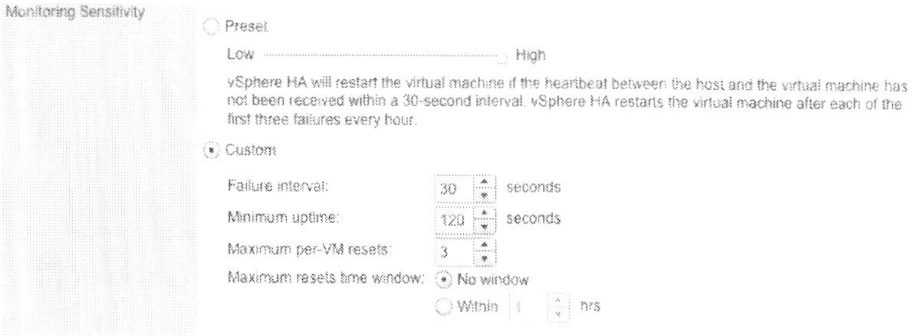

When enabling VM/App Monitoring, the level of sensitivity (Figure 41) can be configured. The default setting should fit most situations. Low sensitivity basically means that the number of allowed "missed" heartbeats is higher and the chances of running into a false positive are lower. However, if a failure occurs and the sensitivity level is set to Low, the experienced downtime will be higher. When quick action is required in the event of a failure, "high sensitivity" can be selected. As expected, this is the opposite of "low sensitivity". Note that the advanced settings mentioned in Table 4 are deprecated and listed for educational purposes.

Table 5: VM monitoring sensitivity

Sensitivity	Failure interval	Max failures	Maxim resets time window
Low	120 Seconds	3	7 Days
Medium	60 Seconds	3	24 Hours
High	30 Seconds	3	1 hour

It is important to remember that VM Monitoring does not infinitely reboot virtual machines unless you specify a custom policy with this requirement. This is to avoid a problem from repeating. By default, when a virtual machine has been rebooted three times within an hour, no further attempts will be taken. Unless the specified time has elapsed. The following advanced settings can be set to change this default behavior or "custom" can be selected as shown in Figure 41.

Although the heartbeat produced by VMware Tools is reliable, VMware added a further verification mechanism. To avoid false positives, VM Monitoring also monitors I/O activity of the virtual machine. When heartbeats are not received AND no disk or network activity has occurred over the last 120 seconds, per default, the virtual machine will be reset. Changing the advanced setting "*das.iostatsInterval*" can modify this 120-second interval.

It is recommended to align the *das.iostatsInterval* with the *failure interval* selected in the VM Monitoring section of vSphere HA within the Web Client or the vSphere Client.

Basic design principle

Align *das.iostatsInterval* with the failure interval.

VM Monitoring Implementation Details

Prior to vSphere 5.0, VM/App Monitoring was implemented by HA code in VPXA. As of vSphere 5.0, it is enabled by the HA agent itself. This means that the "VM/App Monitoring" logic lives within the HA Agent. The agent uses the "Performance Manager" to monitor disk and network I/O; VM/App Monitoring uses the "usage" counters for both disk and network and it requests these counters once enough heartbeats have been missed that the configured policy is triggered.

As stated before, VM/App Monitoring uses heartbeats just like host-level HA. The heartbeats are monitored by the HA agent, which is responsible for the restarts. Of course, this information is also being rolled up into vCenter, but that is done via the Management Network, not using the virtual machine network. This is crucial to know as this means that when a virtual machine network error occurs, the virtual machine heartbeat will still be received. When an error occurs, HA will trigger a restart of the virtual machine when all three conditions are met:

1. No VMware Tools heartbeat received
2. No network I/O over the last 120 seconds
3. No storage I/O over the last 120 seconds

Just like with host-level HA, the HA agent works independently of vCenter when it comes to virtual machine restarts.

Timing

The VM/App monitoring feature monitors the heartbeat(s) issued by a guest and resets the virtual machine if there is a heartbeat failure that satisfies the configured policy for the virtual machine. HA can monitor just the heartbeats issued by the VMware tools process or can monitor these heartbeats plus those issued by an optional in-guest agent.

If the VM monitoring heartbeats stop at time T-o, the minimum time before HA will declare a heartbeat failure is in the range of 81 seconds to 119 seconds, whereas for heartbeats issued by an in-guest application agent, HA will declare a failure in the range of 61 seconds to 89 seconds. Once a heartbeat failure is declared for application heartbeats, HA will attempt to reset the virtual machine. However, for VMware tools heartbeats, HA will first check whether any IO has been issued by the virtual machine for the last 2 minutes (by default) and only if there has been no IO will it issue a reset. Due to how HOSTD publishes the I/O statistics, this check could delay the reset by approximately 20 seconds for virtual machines that were issuing I/O within approximately 1 minute of T-o.

Timing details: the range depends on when the heartbeats stop relative to the HOSTD thread that monitors them. For the lower bound of the VMware tools heartbeats, the heartbeats stop a second before the HOSTD thread runs, which means, at T+31, the FDM agent on the host will be notified of a tools yellow state, and then at T+61 of the red state, which HA reacts to. HA then monitors the heartbeat failure for a minimum of 30 seconds, leading to the min of T+91. The 30 seconds monitoring period done by HA can be increased using the das.failureInterval policy setting. For the upper bound, the FDM is not notified until T+59s (T=0 the failure occurs, T+29 HOSTD notices it and starts the heartbeat failure timer, and at T+59 HOSTD reports a yellow state, and at T+89 reports a red state).

For the heartbeats issued by an in-guest agent, no yellow state is sent, so the there is no additional 30 seconds period.

Screenshots

One of the most useful features as part of VM Monitoring is the fact that it takes screenshots of the virtual machine's console. The screenshots are taken right before VM Monitoring resets a virtual machine. This was added in vCenter 4.0. It is a very useful feature when a virtual machine "freezes" every once in a while for no apparent reason. This screenshot can be used to debug the virtual machine operating system when needed, and is stored in the virtual machine's working directory as logged in the Events view on the Monitor tab of the virtual machine.

Basic design principle

VM and Application monitoring can substantially increase availability. It is part of the HA stack and we strongly recommend using it!

Application Monitoring

With vSphere 4.1, VMware introduced Application Monitoring as part of VM Monitoring. Application Monitoring was a brand new feature that partners could leverage to increase resiliency, as shown in Figure 42. For Application Monitoring in vSphere 4.1, a hidden API was created. As of vSphere 5.0, the SDK has been made available to the general public and with vSphere 5.1 it is part of the guest SDK.

Figure 42: VM and Application Monitoring

The Guest SDK is currently primarily used by application developers from partners like Symantec to develop solutions that increase resilience on a different level than VM Monitoring and HA. In the case of Symantec, a simplified version of Veritas Cluster Server (VCS) is used to enable application availability monitoring, including responding to issues. Note that this is not a multi-node clustering solution like VCS itself, but a single node solution.

Symantec ApplicationHA, as it is called, is triggered to get the application up and running again by restarting it. Symantec's ApplicationHA is aware of dependencies and knows in which order services should be started or stopped. If, however, this fails for a certain number (configurable option within ApplicationHA) of times, VMware HA will be requested to take action. This action will be a restart of the virtual machine.

Although Application Monitoring is relatively new and there are only a few partners currently exploring the capabilities, in our opinion, it does add a whole new level of resiliency. Your in-house development team could leverage functionality offered through the API, or you could use a solution developed by one of VMware's partners. We have tested ApplicationHA by Symantec and personally feel it is the missing link. It enables you as System Admin to integrate your virtualization layer with your application layer. It ensures you as a System Admin that services which are protected are restarted in the correct order and it avoids the common pitfalls associated with restarts and maintenance.

Application Awareness API

Prior to vSphere 5.0, the Application Awareness API was not open for customers and only available to a subset of partners. With vSphere 5.0, the Application Awareness API has been opened up to everyone. We feel that this is not the place to do a full deepdive on how to use it, but we do want to discuss it briefly.

The Application Awareness API allows for anyone to talk to it, including scripts, which makes the possibilities endless. Currently there are 6 functions defined:

- *VMGuestAppMonitor_Enable()*
  - Enables Monitoring
- *VMGuestAppMonitor_MarkActive()*
  - Call every 30 seconds to mark application as active
- *VMGuestAppMonitor_Disable()*
  - Disable Monitoring
- *VMGuestAppMonitor_IsEnabled()*
  - Returns status of Monitoring
- *VMGuestAppMonitor_GetAppStatus()*
  - Returns the current application status recorded for the application
- *VMGuestAppMonitor_Free()*
  - Frees the result of the VMGuestAppMonitor_GetAppStatus() call

These functions can be used by your development team, however App Monitoring also offers a new executable. This allows you to use the functionality App Monitoring offers without the need to compile a full binary. This new command, vmware-appmonitoring.exe, takes the following arguments, which are not coincidentally similar to the functions:

- Enable
- Disable
- markActive
- isEnabled
- getAppStatus

When running the command the following output is presented:

```
C:\VMware-GuestAppMonitorSDK\bin\win32>vmware-appmonitor.exe
Usage: vmware-appmonitor.exe {enable | disable | markActive | isEnabled |
getApp Status}
```

As shown there are multiple ways of leveraging Application Monitoring and to enhance resiliency on an application level.

Chapter 8

Integration

Now that you know how HA works inside out, we want to explain the different integration points between HA, DRS, SDRS and other components or features we feel are worth mentioning. Although we acknowledge that some of the information might be pre-mature we feel it is important enough to include it in this part of the book.

HA and Stateless ESXi

One of the most spectacular features introduced with vSphere 5.0 was most definitely Stateless ESXi. Stateless ESXi basically means that there is no "boot" disk required. That is, no USB/SD, local disks or boot from SAN. ESXi can be PXE booted and directly loaded into memory. This, however, does impose some interesting challenges. What about HA's configuration information that it requires when a host is booted and the HA agent is started? For stateless ESXi hosts, we rely on the Auto Deploy Server to store the configuration information for the HA agent. After a power-on or a reboot, the HA agent will be re-initialized. vSphere 5.1 auto-deploy images contain the HA VIB file by default and as such an install of the agent itself is not needed after a power-on or a reboot of a host.

We described the configuration files in Chapter 2. These files are cached by the Auto Deploy Server as they are required for the configuration of HA. vCenter publishes versions of the files needed for HA as the configuration continues to change so that the correct cached copies of these files are available for the auto-deploy managed hosts.

HA and Storage DRS

vSphere HA informs Storage DRS when a failure has occurred. This to prevent the relocation of any HA protected virtual machine, meaning, a virtual machine that was powered on, but which failed, and has not been restarted yet due to their being insufficient capacity available. Further, Storage DRS is not allowed to Storage vMotion a virtual machine that is owned by a master other than the one vCenter Server is talking to. This is because in such a situation, HA would not be able to reprotect the virtual machine until the master to which vCenter Server is talking is able to lock the datastore again.

Storage vMotion and HA

Storage vMotion is revamped in vSphere 5.0. We have described the enhancements in Chapter 23 but want to discuss the integration with HA in this paragraph. If a virtual machine needs to be restarted by HA and the virtual machine is in the process of being Storage vMotioned and the virtual machine fails, the restart process is not started until vCenter informs the master that the Storage vMotion task has completed or has been rolled back. If the source host fails, however, virtual machine will restart the virtual machine as part of the normal workflow. During a Storage vMotion, the HA agent on the host on which the Storage vMotion was initiated masks the failure state of the virtual machine. If, for whatever reason, vCenter is unavailable, the masking will timeout after 15 minutes to ensure that the virtual machine will be restarted.

Also note that in vSphere 5.0 Update 1 and above, when a Storage vMotion completes, vCenter will report the virtual machine as unprotected until the master reports it protected again under the new path.

HA and DRS

As of vSphere 4.1, HA integrates on multiple levels with DRS. It is a huge improvement and it is something that we wanted to stress as it has changed both the behavior and the reliability of HA.

HA and Resource Fragmentation

When a failover is initiated, HA will first check whether there are resources available on the destination hosts for the failover. If, for instance, a particular virtual machine has a very large reservation and the Admission Control Policy is based on a percentage, for example, it could happen that resources are fragmented across multiple hosts. (For more details on this scenario, see Chapter 7.) HA, as of vSphere 4.1, will ask DRS to defragment the resources to accommodate for this virtual machine's resource requirements. Although HA will request a defragmentation of resources, a guarantee cannot be given. As such, even with this additional integration, you should still be cautious when it comes to resource fragmentation.

Flattened Shares

Pre-vSphere 4.1, an issue could arise when shares had been set custom on a virtual machine. When HA fails over a virtual machine, it will power-on the virtual machine in the Root Resource Pool. However, the virtual machine's shares were those configured by a user for it, and not scaled for it being parented under the Root Resource Pool. This could cause the virtual machine to receive either too many or too few resources relative to its entitlement.

A scenario where and when this can occur would be the following: VM1 has a 1000 shares and Resource Pool A has 2000 shares. However Resource Pool A has 2 virtual machines and both virtual machines will have 50% of those "2000" shares. The following diagram depicts this scenario:

Figure 43: Flatten shares starting point

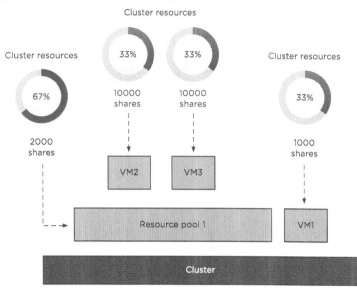

When the host fails, both VM2 and VM3 will end up on the same level as VM1, the Root Resource Pool. However, as a custom shares value of 10,000 was specified on both VM2 and VM3, they will completely blow away VM1 in times of contention. This is depicted in the following diagram:

Figure 44: Flatten shares host failure

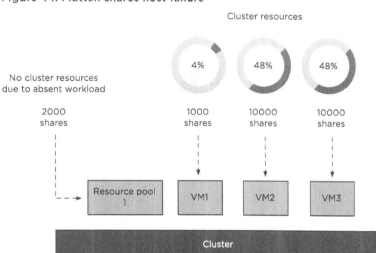

This situation would persist until the next invocation of DRS would re-parent the virtual machines VM2 and VM3 to their original Resource Pool. To address this issue, as of vSphere 4.1, HA calculates a flattened share value before the virtual machine's is failed-over. This flattening process ensures that the virtual machine will get the resources it would have received if it had failed over to the correct Resource Pool. This scenario is depicted in the following diagram. Note that both VM2 and VM3 are placed under the Root Resource Pool with a shares value of 1000.

Figure 45: Flatten shares after host failure before DRS invocation

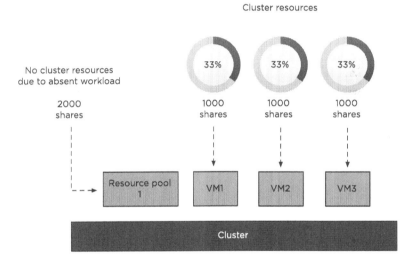

Of course, when DRS is invoked, both VM2 and VM3 will be re-parented under Resource Pool 1 and will again receive the number of shares they had been originally assigned.

DPM and HA

If DPM is enabled and resources are scarce during an HA failover, HA will use DRS to try to adjust the cluster (for example, by bringing hosts out of standby mode or migrating virtual machines to defragment the cluster resources) so that HA can perform the failovers.

If HA strict Admission Control is enabled (default), DPM will maintain the necessary level of powered-on capacity to meet the configured HA failover capacity. HA places a constraint to prevent DPM from powering down too many ESXi hosts if it would violate the Admission Control Policy.

As of vSphere 5.0, when HA admission control is disabled, HA will prevent DPM from powering off all but one host in the cluster. A minimum of two hosts are kept up regardless of the resource consumption. The reason this behavior has changed is that it is impossible to restart virtual machines when the only host left in the cluster has just failed.

In a failure scenario, if HA cannot restart some virtual machines, it asks DRS/DPM to try to defragment resources or bring hosts out of standby to allow HA another opportunity to restart the virtual machines. Another change is that DRS/DPM will power-on or keep on hosts needed to address cluster constraints, even if those host are lightly utilized. Once again, in order for this to be successful DRS will need to be enabled and configured to fully automated. When not configured to fully automated user action is required to execute DRS recommendations and allow the restart of virtual machines to occur.

Chapter 9

Summarizing

Hopefully we have succeeded in giving you a better understanding of the internal workings of HA. We hope that this book has handed you the tools needed to update your vSphere design and ultimately to increase the resiliency and uptime of your environment.

We have tried to simplify some of the concepts to make it easier to understand, still we acknowledge that some concepts are difficult to grasp and the amount of architectural changes that vSphere 5 has brought can be confusing at times. We hope though that after reading this section of the book everyone is confident enough to make the required or recommended changes.

If there are any questions please do not hesitate to reach out to either of the authors via twitter or our blogs. We will we do our best to answer your questions.

Part II

vSphere Distributed Resource Scheduler

Chapter 10

Introduction to vSphere DRS

VMware vSphere Distributed Resource Scheduler (DRS) is an infrastructure service run by VMware vCenter Server (vCenter). DRS aggregates ESXi host resources into clusters and automatically distributes these resources to virtual machines by monitoring utilization and continuously optimizing virtual machine distribution across ESXi hosts.

DRS computes the dynamic (resource) entitlement for each virtual machine based on static resource allocation settings and dynamic metrics such as active usage and level of contention.

DRS attempts to satisfy the virtual machines' dynamic entitlements with the resources available in the cluster by leveraging vMotion. vMotion is used to balance utilization by migrating virtual machines to ESXi hosts that have more available resources. DRS can also use vMotion to 'defragment' resource capacity and make room for larger virtual machines.

Basic design principle
We recommend enabling DRS to achieve higher consolidation ratios.

Cluster Level Resource Management

Clusters group the resources of the various ESXi hosts together and treat them as a pool of resources. DRS presents the aggregated resources as one big host to the virtual machines. Pooling resources allows DRS to create resource pools spanning all hosts in the cluster and apply cluster level resource allocation policies. It is probably unnecessary to point out, but a virtual machine cannot span hosts even when resources are pooled by using DRS. DRS relies on host-local resource schedulers to allocate physical resources. In addition to resource pools and resource allocation policies, DRS offers the following resource management capabilities:

Initial placement: When a virtual machine is powered on in the cluster, DRS places the virtual machine on an appropriate host or generates a recommendation depending on the automation level.

Load balancing: DRS distributes virtual machine workloads across the ESXi hosts inside the cluster. DRS continuously monitors the active workload and the available resources. DRS compares the monitoring results to the ideal resource distribution and performs or recommends virtual machine migrations to ensure workloads receive the resources to which they are entitled, with the goal of maximizing workload performance.

Power management: When Distributed Power Management (DPM) is enabled, DRS compares cluster-level and host-level capacity to the demand of the virtual machines, including recent historical demand. It places, or recommends placing ESXi hosts in standby mode if excessive capacity is detected or it powers hosts on if more capacity is needed.

Cluster Maintenance mode: DRS evaluates a set of hosts that can be put into maintenance mode at the same time in order to speed up the VMware Update Manager remediation process. DRS will take HA, DPM, Fault Tolerance, vMotion compatibility and reservations into account when determining the number of hosts eligible for entering maintenance mode simultaneously.

Constraint correction: DRS redistributes virtual machines across ESXi hosts to evacuate hosts for user requests that the hosts enter maintenance or standby mode, and moves virtual machines as needed to adhere to user-defined affinity and anti-affinity rules.

Support for agent virtual machines: Agent virtual machines are virtual machines that are required to be deployed and active on every host and belong to solutions that use ESX Agent Manager. DRS and DPM fully support ESX agents and respect the requirements of the ESX agent virtual machine. DRS and DPM understands that:

- Agent virtual machines reservations must be respected, even when the virtual machine is not powered on.
- Agent virtual machines do not have to be evacuated for a host to enter maintenance mode or standby.
- Agent virtual machines must be available before virtual machines can complete migration to or be powered up on a host.

Requirements

In order for DRS to function correctly, the virtual infrastructure must meet the following requirements:

- VMware ESXi in a cluster
- VMware vCenter Server
- VMware vSphere Enterprise or Enterprise Plus License
- Meet vMotion requirements (not mandatory, but highly recommended)
  - Shared datastores accessible by all ESXi hosts inside the cluster.
  - Private migration network
  - Gigabit Ethernet
  - Processor compatibility

For DRS to allow automatic load balancing, vMotion is required. For initial placement though, vMotion is not a requirement.

Basic design principle
Configure vMotion to fully benefit from the capabilities of DRS.

DRS Cluster Settings

When DRS is enabled on the cluster, you are required to select the automation level and set the migration threshold. DRS settings can be modified when the cluster is in use and without disruption of service. The following high-level steps will show you how to create a cluster and enable DRS:

1. Select the vCenter view.
2. Select Clusters
3. In the Objects view and click New Cluster.

Figure 46: New Cluster

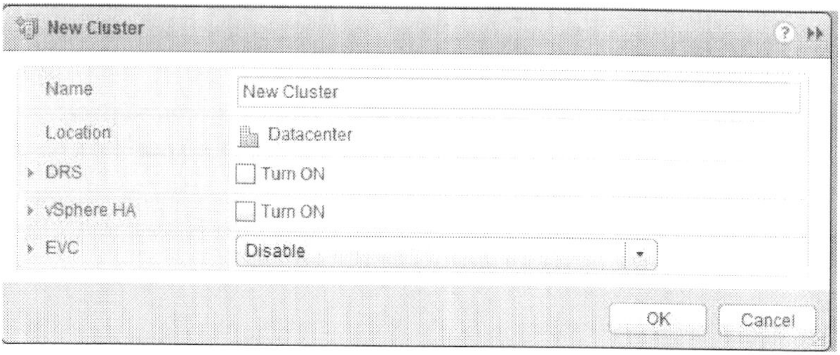

4. Give the new cluster an appropriate name. We recommend at a minimum including the location of the cluster and a sequence number i.e. ams-hadrs-001.
5. Select a Location.
6. Select Turn ON DRS and click Next.

Figure 47: DRS options expanded

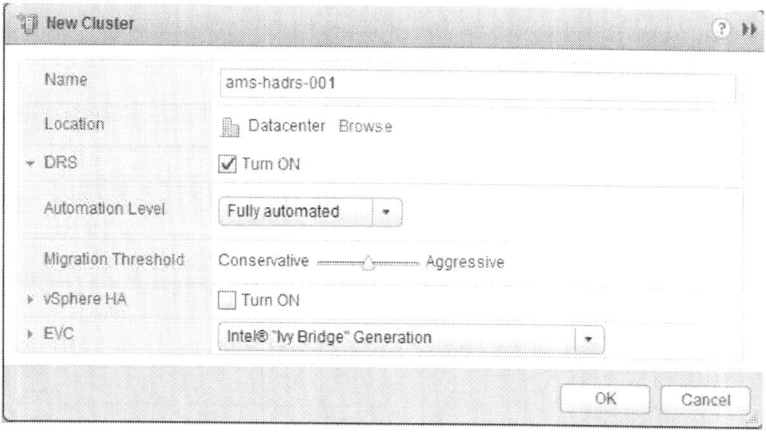

7. Verify the Automation Level is set to Fully automated.
8. Leave the migration threshold at the default and click OK.
9. Select the appropriate EVC mode.

Please note that an EVC mode cannot be selected before selecting a location for the cluster.

Automation Level

The automation level determines the level of autonomy of DRS, ranging from generating placement and load-balancing recommendations to automatically applying the generated recommendations. Three automation levels exist:

Manual: DRS generates initial placement recommendations for each virtual machine. If the cluster is unbalanced, DRS generates migration recommendations and presents these recommendations to the user via the DRS tab on the cluster object. The user must manually apply each recommendation.

Partially automated: When a virtual machine is powered on, DRS automatically places it on the most suitable host. If the cluster is unbalanced, DRS suggests migration recommendations via the DRS tab on the cluster object. The user must apply each recommendation manually.

Fully automated: When a virtual machine is powered on, DRS automatically places it on the most suitable host. If the cluster is unbalanced, DRS automatically migrates the virtual machine to a more suitable host.

Table 6: DRS automation level

Automation level	Initial VM Placement	Load Balancing
Manual	Recommended host(s) displayed	Migration recommendation is displayed
Partially automated	Automatic placement	Migration recommendation is displayed
Fully automated	Automatic placement	Automatic migration

Initial Placement

Initial placement occurs when a virtual machine is powered on or resumed. Due to the lack of historical performance data, DRS will assume that the virtual machine is 100% busy and will select an ESXi host that can host the virtual machine. During initial placement, DRS will take the current demand of the virtual machines and the capacity of each host into account.

For example, if a 4-vCPU virtual machine is powered on in a cluster comprising heterogeneous hosts. Assume this cluster consists of a host containing 4 physical cores and a host containing 8 physical cores. During initial placement, the 8 physical core ESXi host may look like a better candidate, depending on the virtual machine workload currently active on the host. However, DRS may place the virtual machine on the ESXi host configured with 4 cores as long as the sum of virtual machine resource demand is comparable to the load of the other ESXi host in the cluster.

If the cluster is configured with the Manual automation level, DRS will create a prioritized list of recommended hosts for virtual machine placement. This list is presented to the user to help select an appropriate host.

Impact of Automation Levels on Procedures

When a Manual or Partially automated automation level is selected, the user must manually apply the recommendations issued by DRS. DRS reviews the state of the cluster at an interval of five minutes and publishes recommendations to solve any calculated imbalance of the cluster. Consequently, administrators should check the recommendations after each DRS invocation to solve the cluster imbalance. Besides inefficiency, it is possible that DRS rules may be violated if the administrators apply the recommendations infrequently. DRS rules are explained in section "Rules" of chapter 15.

The automation level of the cluster can be changed without disrupting virtual machines. It is easy to change, so why not try Fully automated for a while to get comfortable with it?

Basic design principle

Set automation level to *Fully automated* to fully benefit from DRS capabilities.

vCenter sizing

The impact of the resource utilization by the DRS threads on vCenter must be taken into account when sizing the vCenter server and designing the cluster environment.

To ensure performance of vCenter, be sure to provide sufficient CPUs/cores and memory. The technical paper: "*VMware vCenter Server Performance and Best Practices*" lists the minimum hardware recommendations for three deployment sizes, ranging from 50 hosts and 500 virtual machines to 1.000 hosts and 10.000 powered-on virtual machines. It is recommended to follow these hardware recommendations when sizing the machine that will run vCenter.

Number of Clusters

A lower number of virtual machines inside a cluster will reduce the number of load-balancing calculations, therefore ensuring fast DRS performance. A lower number of virtual machines generally require a smaller number of hosts per cluster. However, the potential danger is creating too many small clusters. Having 200 x 3-host clusters instead of 100 x 6-host clusters could drive up CPU utilization of the vCenter as each cluster will invoke the periodic load-balancing process every 5 minutes. Whatever your decision, please size your vCenter accordingly.

DRS Cluster configuration

The configuration of cluster sizes, combination of workload types, virtual machine management and number of virtual machines all have an impact on the behavior and performance of the vCenter and therefore influence the performance of DRS threads. This, in turn, can impact the performance of the virtual machines due to slow or insufficient load-balancing migration recommendations and dynamic entitlement calculations.

Note

The DRS thread itself does not execute migrations, these are handled by vCenter. DRS can run while migrations are in flight.

DRS Threads Per Cluster

vCenter creates and runs a single DRS thread per cluster. The DRS thread communicates with the management agent (VPXA) on each ESXi host inside the cluster.

Figure 48: DRS-thread components

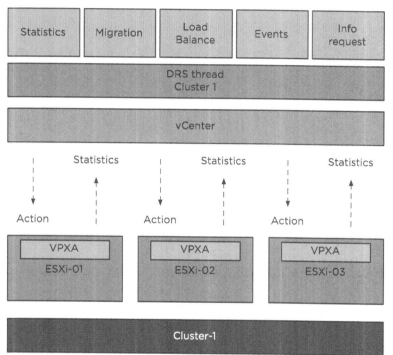

By default, a load balance calculation thread is invoked every five minutes. This thread calculates the imbalance of the cluster, applies resource settings and, if needed, generates migration recommendations. In practice, the thread may be invoked more frequently due to changes made inside the cluster. For example, DRS will be invoked if the cluster detects changes in its resource pool tree, operations and events such as changes in resource supply, or modification of resource settings.

Table 7: Events invoking DRS calculations

Change in resource supply	Change in resource demand	Resource setting changed
A host was added to the cluster	A virtual machine is transitioned from powered-on to powered-off	Resource settings of a virtual machine or a resource pool are changed
Host has maintenance mode status change.		A resource pool or a virtual machine is moved in or out the resource pool hierarchy

DRS Events and Statistics

The vCenter agent (VPXA) runs inside each ESXi host in the cluster and enables a two-way communication between the ESXi host and vCenter. VPXA keeps the status of both ESXi and virtual machines in sync with the status shown in vCenter.

The VPXA sends information when a virtual machine's power state changes or when a virtual machine is migrated with vMotion. Periodically, the VPXA sends additional notification and statistics to the vCenter server. DRS sends messages to the ESXi host, such as proposed migrations and information requests.

vCenter servers in Virtual Desktop Infrastructure (VDI) environments experience more load due to the larger number of virtual machines and higher frequency of virtual machine power state changes, leading to more frequent invocation of DRS threads.

Separate VDI Workloads From VSI Workloads

In large environments, we recommend separating VDI workloads and server workloads and assigning different clusters to each workload in order to reduce the number of DRS invocations. By isolating server workloads from VDI workloads, only the VDI clusters experience increased DRS invocations, reducing overall overhead, complexity and the number of calculations performed by DRS.

Basic design principle

Separate VDI workloads and server workloads and assign different clusters to each workload to reduce the DRS invocations.

Cluster Sizing

The general guideline is that the more hosts you have in the cluster, the more opportunities DRS has to place the virtual machines. The maximum number of hosts supported in vSphere 5.0 for a DRS cluster is 32. Although the maximum number of hosts has not increased over the vSphere 4 maximum, vSphere 5.0 is capable of running more virtual machines per cluster, supports more vCPUs per host, and can assign more memory per virtual machine. It is expected that DRS will not be the limiting factor when designing cluster configurations. However, the following can impact DRS cluster and virtual machine sizing:

Size of host versus the maximum amount of virtual machines in a cluster:
In vSphere 5.0, the maximum number of virtual machines inside a cluster is 4000. Current server hardware configurations are able to run more than 512 virtual machines per ESXi host. Please take the maximums into considerations when researching scale-up versus scale out cluster configurations.

Number of virtual machines versus number of LUNs required:
vSphere 5 allows up to 256 LUNs connected to an ESXi 5 host. DRS only considers hosts compatible for virtual machine migration if hosts are connected to the same VMFS datastore. Consistent VMFS datastore connectivity across all hosts in the DRS cluster is considered a best practice. If more than 256 VMFS datastores need to be connected, consider using multiple DRS clusters and size them accordingly.

Hardware configuration – Heterogeneous or Homogeneous:
Heterogeneous host configurations can impact the effectiveness of DRS. DRS will not migrate virtual machines if the physical configuration cannot host the virtual machines. By leveraging EVC, multiple hardware configurations can exists within a DRS cluster and allow older hardware configurations to be mixed with new hardware configurations. Although we recommend enabling EVC, we advise you to refrain from mixing hardware configurations that are too different.

For example, vSphere 5.0 and up allows up to 32 vCPUs and 1TB of memory to be assigned to a virtual machine and we expect to see an increase in the number of larger virtual machines within the virtual infrastructure. Larger virtual machines such as 12 or 16 vCPU virtual machines cannot be hosted on a system containing two Quad Core CPUs.

DRS is a simple clustering solution that will allow you to reach higher consolidation ratios while providing optimal utilization of available resources. Understanding the architecture of DRS will enable you to design vCenter and DRS clusters that are able to provide the best performance while operating as efficiently as possible. The following chapters will discuss the fundamental concepts of resource management. We will also discuss all decision-making moments to ensure you configure DRS in such a way that it meets the requirements of your or your customer's environment.

Chapter 11

vMotion and EVC

vMotion

vMotion is probably the best example of an industry-changing feature. When virtualization was first introduced, it was all about flexibility and portability of virtual machines. However, portability and flexibility was somewhat limited based on the power state of the virtual machine. VMware changed the world of IT when they introduced vMotion. vMotion was literally developed on top of existing components, basically leveraging the "suspend and resume" functionality that already existed. Please don't misread the last sentence, as vMotion truly is a brilliant piece of technology.

As hopefully all of you know, vMotion is a feature that enables you to migrate powered-on virtual machines from one host to another without any downtime. The question still remains how it works. It is a fairly complex process that has been optimized over the years to the point where it allows you to do 8 concurrent vMotions on a single host with 10GbE capabilities. At the time of this writing, the limit is 4 concurrent vMotions for hosts with 1GbE.

What does the workflow of a vMotion process look like?

1. Validate destination host is compatible.
2. Create a shadow virtual machine on the destination host.
3. Copy each memory page from the source to the destination via the vMotion network. This process is known as pre-copy.
4. Perform another pass over the virtual machine's memory, copying any pages that changed during the last pre-copy iteration.
5. Continue this iterative memory copying until no changed pages (outstanding to be-copied pages) remain.
6. Stun the virtual machine on the source and resume it on the destination.

That sounds simple, doesn't it, in only 6 steps? However, there are some corner cases where the amount of memory that changes exceeds the throughput capabilities of the vMotion network. Don't we all want to know what would happen in a scenario like that? We are bound to run into it at some point, for instance, with large memory-active database servers.

In vSphere 4.1, VMware introduced a feature as part of vMotion called Quick Resume. Quick Resume enabled the source virtual machine to be stunned while starting the destination virtual machine, before all pages were copied. However, as the virtual machine would already be running at the destination, it could possibly attempt to touch (read or write) a page which had not yet been copied. In that case, Quick Resume would request the page from the source and allow the guest to complete the requested action. Meanwhile, continuing to copy the remaining memory pages until all pages were migrated. So, what would happen if the vMotion network failed at this point? Wouldn't you end up with a destination virtual machine that could not access certain memory pages because they were "living" remotely? To address this scenario in vSphere 4.1, a failsafe mechanism was implemented using storage. A special file, on the order of a couple MBs would be created when Quick Resume was used. This file was basically used as a backup buffer. In the case of a network failure, this file would allow the migration to complete and provided bi-directional communication between the two hosts involved. Is that cool, or what?

The typical question that would arise immediately is whether this would impact performance. It is good to realize that, without Quick Resume, vMotioning large memory-active virtual machines would be difficult. The switchover time could potentially be too large and lead to temporary loss of connection with the virtual machine. Although Quick Resume would impact performance when pages were accessed but not yet copied, the benefits of being able to vMotion very large virtual machines with minimal impact by far outweighed this temporary increase in memory access time. In vSphere 5.0, new features were introduced which make Quick Resume obsolete. Let's look at what has changed.

Changes to vMotion?

There are some fundamental changes made to vMotion in vSphere 5.0 when it comes to scalability and performance:

- Multi-NIC vMotion support
- Stun During Page Send (SDPS)
- Higher Latency Link Support
- Improved error reporting

Multi-NIC vMotion Support

One of the most substantial and visible changes that we want to discuss is multi-NIC vMotion capabilities. vMotion is now capable of using multiple NICs concurrently to decrease the amount of time required for a vMotion operation. That means that even a single vMotion can leverage all of the configured vMotion NICs. Prior to vSphere 5.0, only a single NIC was used for a vMotion-enabled VMkernel interface. Enabling multiple NICs for your vMotion-enabled VMkernel interfaces will remove some of the bandwidth and throughput constraints that are commonly associated with large and memory-active virtual machines. The following list shows the currently supported maximum number of NICs for multi-NIC vMotion:

- 1GbE – 16 NICs supported
- 10GbE – 4 NICs supported

It is important to realize that in the case of 10GbE interfaces, it is only possible to use the full bandwidth when the server is equipped with the latest PCI Express busses. Ensure that your server hardware is capable of taking full advantage of these capabilities when this is a requirement.

Basic design principles

When sizing your environment, take virtual machine sizes into account when designing the network infrastructure. Having sufficient bandwidth for vMotion will result in faster migration times, and therefore host evacuation.

When designing your server platform, take peak network bandwidth requirements into account - not only for the NICs, but also for the PCI bus.

Stun During Page Send

This brand new feature replaces Quick Resume. The "stun" in Stun During Page Send (SDPS) refers to the vCPU of the virtual machine that is being vMotioned. vMotion will track the rate at which the guest pages are changed, or as the engineers prefer to call it, "dirtied." The rate at which this occurs is compared to the vMotion transmission rate. If the rate at which the pages are dirtied exceeds the transmission rate, the source vCPUs will be placed into a sleep state to decrease the rate at which pages are dirtied and to allow the vMotion process to complete. It is good to know that the vCPUs will only be put to sleep for a few milliseconds at a time at most. SDPS injects frequent, tiny sleeps, disrupting the virtual machine's workload just enough to guarantee that vMotion can keep up with the memory page change rate and allow for a successful, non-disruptive completion of the process. You could say that, thanks to SDPS, you can vMotion any type of workload, regardless of how aggressive it is.

It is important to realize that SDPS only slows down a virtual machine in the cases where the memory page change rate would have previously caused a vMotion to fail. If, for whatever reason, it is desired to have the vMotion to fail instead of slowing down the workload, it is possible to tune this behavior on a per-virtual machine basis through an advanced virtual machine setting.

To disable SDPS for all virtual machines on a particular host:
In the vSphere client, select the host and then click the **Configuration** tab.

- Under Software, click Advanced Settings.
- Click Migrate in the left side and the scroll down to Migrate.SdpsEnabled on the right side.
- Change the value of Migrate.SdpsEnabled to 0.
- Click OK.

Please note that we strongly discourage disabling SDPS. SDPS kicks in when the rate at which pages are dirtied exceeds the rate at which the pages can be transferred to the other host. In other words, if your virtual machines are not extremely memory active then chances of SDSP ever kicking in is small, very very small. If it does kick in, it kicks in to prevent the vMotion process from failing for this particular virtual machine. Now note that by default SDPS is not doing anything, normally your virtual machines will not be throttled by vMotion and it will only be throttled when there is a requirement to do so.

Note

vMotion of highly active virtual machines may fail when SDPS is disabled. There is also a higher probability that metro vMotion (vMotion over a link with up to 10ms of latency) might fail as the virtual machine's memory is dirtied faster than it can be copied over the slower link.

Higher Latency Link Support – Metro vMotion

When discussing long distance vMotion, the biggest constraint is usually latency. Pre-vSphere 5.0, the maximum supported latency for vMotion was 5ms. As you can imagine, this restricted many customers from enabling cross-site clusters. As of vSphere 5.0, the maximum supported latency has been doubled to 10ms for environments using Enterprise Plus licensing. This should allow more customers to enable DRS between sites when all the required infrastructure components are available like, for instance, shared storage.

Enhanced vMotion Capability

Enhanced vMotion Compatibility

VMware Enhanced vMotion Compatibility (EVC) facilitates vMotion between different CPU generations through use of Intel Flex Migration and AMD-V Extended Migration technologies. When enabled, EVC ensures that all CPUs within the cluster are vMotion compatible.

Interaction of EVC and hardware virtualization support

VMware's hypervisor is unique in that it supports a variety of execution modes depending on the capabilities of the underlying hardware. The VMkernel automatically selects the hypervisor execution mode that will deliver the best virtual machine performance given the capabilities of the hardware and type of guest OS. Virtualization acceleration features such as VT-x/AMD-V and RVI/EPT are available for use by the hypervisor independent of EVC or the EVC baseline and the VMkernel switches on the fly to whichever mode is the best performing one for the Guest OS as the virtual machine is migrated around the cluster.

What is The Benefit Of EVC?

Because EVC allows you to migrate virtual machines between different generations of CPUs, older and newer server generations can be mixed in the same cluster and still allow vMotion migration between these hosts. This makes adding new hardware into your existing infrastructure easier and helps extend the value of your existing hosts.

How Does EVC Work?

EVC leverages a defined baseline that allows all the hosts in the cluster to advertise the same CPU feature set. The EVC baseline does not disable the features within a CPU, but indicates to a virtual machine that specific features are not available.

It is crucial to understand that EVC only focuses on CPU features specific to CPU generations, such as SIMD (SSE) or AMD-now instructions. EVC hides these CPU features from software running inside virtual machines by not advertising these features. This means that the features are still available and active, but they are not "publically broadcasted."

When enabling EVC, a CPU baseline must be selected. This baseline represents a feature set of the selected CPU generation and exposes specific CPU generation features. When a virtual machine powers-on within an EVC cluster, this cluster's baseline will be attached to the virtual machine until it powers-off.

Note

The EVC baseline is attached to the virtual machine until it powers off even if it is migrated to another EVC cluster.

If an ESXi host with a newer generation CPU is joined to the cluster, the baseline will automatically "hide" the CPU features that are new and unique to that CPU generation.

For example: A cluster contains ESXi hosts configured with Intel® Xeon® Core™ i7 CPUs, commonly known as Intel Nehalem. The baseline selected – *Intel® "Nehalem" Generation* – presents the cumulative features of the *Intel® "Merom" Generation*, *Intel® "Penryn" Generation* and the *Intel® "Nehalem" Generation* to the virtual machine. This has the net effect of providing the standard *Intel® "Merom" Generation* features plus SSE4.1, SSE4.2, Popcount and RDTSCP features available to all the virtual machines

Figure 49: Intel EVC baselines

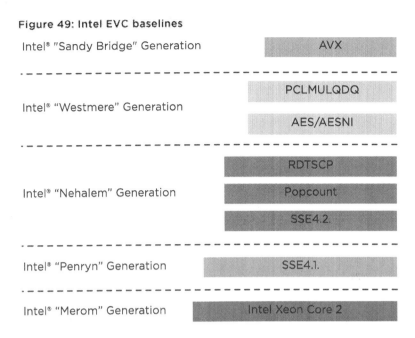

When an ESXi host with a Westmere (32nm) CPU joins the cluster, the additional CPU instruction sets like AES/AESNI and PCLMULQDQ will be suppressed automatically.

Will EVC Impact Application Performance?

It is possible, but highly unlikely, that an application running in a virtual machine would benefit from the instruction set hidden by EVC. However, keep in mind that enabling EVC may impact the performance of applications specifically written to benefit from these special instructions.

In general, it should be expected that your applications will incur no noticeable performance loss from using EVC. Although EVC hides CPU features from the virtual machine Guest OS and applications, these features do not influence performance for most software commonly found inside a virtual infrastructure. For example, EVC does not affect the number of instructions per second, number of cores, hardware acceleration, caching or other CPU features that most software uses.

After new CPU generations are released, software vendors might update or release new versions of their software to take advantage of the new instructions introduced by the latest CPU generations. Software development cycles always trail hardware development, resulting in a delayed implementation and utilization of new instruction sets.

Furthermore, new instruction sets often have specialized use cases, meaning that most new instructions are typically irrelevant to the business applications active in the virtual infrastructure.

One exception is encryption and decryption acceleration using the AES-NI instruction set. Many popular applications that perform encryption, including SSL libraries, now utilize this instruction set in their latest releases. Depending on workload, using these AES instructions can provide over 500% performance improvement.

Communication between virtual machines utilizing mutual SSL for authentication and transport level security leverages this AES instruction set.

Building Block Approach

A very popular design methodology is the use of a building block strategy. Building blocks extend the concept of a framework and outline a pre-defined set of items or modules that allow for scalability while maintaining standardization. Cluster configuration is usually treated as a building block. While some companies buy one cluster at a time, others use a modular approach and buy a fixed subset of physical hosts, planning to expand their clusters gradually. EVC allows mixing different generations of CPUs, allowing for future expansion of clusters and aligning with building block architectures.

One potential caveat of mixing hardware from different major generations in the same cluster can be fluctuating performance. Newer generation CPUs can offer a substantial performance increase over older generation CPUs, resulting in different progress of the virtual machine and its application. For example, 500MHz on Intel Xeon Nehalem EX from 2010 can result in quicker computations than 500 MHz on an Intel Xeon Core 2 "Merom" from 2006. Configurations like this can increase the complexity of performance troubleshooting. This is an extreme example, as most customers mix different but adjacent generations of processor hardware rather than combining radically different hardware into a single cluster.

EVC's impact on DRS Automation of Fault Tolerance Virtual Machines

As of vSphere 4.1, EVC allows DRS to generate initial placement for Fault Tolerance (FT) enabled virtual machines and allows DRS to move them around during load balancing operations. Without EVC enabled, FT primary virtual machines are powered on by DRS on their registered host and pinned there. DRS will automatically place the secondary virtual machine, but will never move primary and secondary virtual machines during load balancing operations.

Basic design principle
By enabling EVC, DRS-FT integration will be supported

Allowing DRS to control initial placement of FT-enabled virtual machines can lead to better virtual machine performance as DRS is able to select the most suitable host. Permitting DRS to incorporate FT-enabled virtual machines in load-balancing calculations helps DRS to reach steady state sooner. Fixed virtual machines impact load-balancing calculations and can constrain DRS's ability to achieve a proper load-balanced state. By allowing DRS to move the FT-enabled virtual machines, DRS has fewer restrictions to deal with and more virtual machine candidates to move around to find a better distribution. Furthermore, FT-DRS integration allows for hosts to be placed into maintenance mode because DRS will be able to evacuate FT-enabled virtual machines. DPM becomes more effective because DRS is able to migrate FT-enabled virtual machines off the hosts that are not required to provide resources to virtual machines.

FT-Enabled Virtual Machine Initial Placement

When calculating initial placement recommendations, DRS selects a host for the primary virtual machine and a host for the secondary virtual machine. DRS defines a compatible host set that contains ESXi hosts which are capable of vMotioning the FT-enabled machines. EVC assists with defining the host compatibility set. By applying an EVC baseline, each ESXi host in the cluster presents an identical instruction set, resulting in a general host compatibility set. For example, with EVC enabled, if virtual machine VM1 powers up on host ESXi-02, its host compatibility set contains ESXi-01 and ESXi-03 as it can vMotion to these hosts. It is also true that VM1 can be hosted by ESXi-03 and vMotion to ESXi-01 and ESXi-02. Likewise, if powered-on at ESXi-01, it is able to vMotion to hosts ESXi-02 and ESXi-03.

Figure 50: Host compatibility set

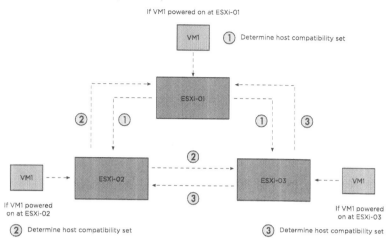

Without EVC, DRS needs to determine the host compatibility set by computing a separate host-to-host compatibility for each host. For example, with 32 hosts in the cluster, the calculation is N*(N-1), where N= number of hosts * (number of hosts - the host itself) = 32 *(32-1) = 992 compatibility checks. Besides the increased overhead, the power-on operation of the FT-enabled virtual machine would take an enormously long time if DRS is required to execute this number of compatibility checks.

During initial placement, DRS also ensures that the secondary virtual machine will not run on the same host as the primary virtual machine.

FT-Enabled Virtual Machine Load Balancing

As mentioned previously, both primary and secondary virtual machines can be migrated by DRS if EVC is enabled. However, DRS is still restricted when generating particular migration recommendations for FT-enabled virtual machines: due to an internal anti-affinity rule, DRS is prevented from swapping places of the primary and secondary FT virtual machines and FT-enabled virtual machines are never allowed to run on the same host at any time, so DRS will not move a primary virtual machine to the host where its secondary is running and vice versa within one recommendation. In addition, DRS is not allowed to place more than four FT-enabled virtual machines on a single host and will take this into account during load-balancing calculations.

FT-Enabled Virtual Machine DRS Automation Settings

The DRS automation settings can be configured for an FT-enabled virtual machine. The secondary virtual machine inherits the primary virtual machine's DRS automation settings, resulting in an identical configuration of both virtual machines. It is not possible to configure the automation setting of the primary and secondary virtual machines independently. If the automation setting is set to Disabled, vCenter powers on the primary and secondary virtual machines on their currently registered hosts and will not move them.

Enabling And Disabling EVC

EVC can be enabled even when virtual machines are active. Powered-on virtual machines will not block configuration of EVC for a cluster as long as the virtual machine itself is compatible with the desired EVC mode.

If EVC is disabled, the virtual machines continue to operate at the same EVC mode and are not forced to restart. If complete removal of the EVC mode is required, the virtual machine must go through a complete power-cycle; a reboot is not sufficient.

If EVC is disabled on a cluster containing FT-enabled virtual machines, their DRS automation settings are changed to Disabled and DRS will be unable to migrate the primary and secondary during load-balancing and maintenance mode operations. If EVC is enabled again, these virtual machines will once again receive the default cluster DRS automation level.

Power Off Virtual Machine Instead Of Reboot

It is important to remember that EVC baselines are applied only during power-on operations. If the EVC cluster mode is changed, active virtual machines are required to complete a full power-cycle to receive the new baseline. A virtual machine continues to run if the EVC mode is increased, for example from Intel® "Merom" Generation to Intel® "Nehalem" Generation, but will operate with the knowledge of the instruction set of the original Intel® "Merom" Generation baseline until it is power-cycled, at which point the new (Intel® "Nehalem" Generation) baseline will be propagated to the virtual machine.

EVC Requirements

To enable EVC on a cluster, the cluster must meet the following requirements:

- All hosts in the cluster must have CPUs from a single vendor, either AMD or Intel.
- All hosts in the cluster must have advanced CPU features, such as hardware virtualization support (AMD-V or Intel VT) and AMD No eXecute (NX) or Intel eXecute Disable (XD) and must be enabled in the BIOS.
- All hosts in the cluster should be configured for vMotion. See the section, Host Configuration Requirements for vMotion.
- All hosts in the cluster must be connected to the same vCenter Server system.

In addition, all hosts in the cluster must have CPUs that support the EVC mode you want to enable. To check EVC support for a specific processor or server model, see the VMware Compatibility Guide at:

http://www.vmware.com/resources/compatibility/search.php

Chapter 12

DRS Dynamic Entitlement

In this section we will explain DRS dynamic entitlement and the concepts of resource management. Understanding elements such as dynamic entitlement, resource pools and resource allocation settings will allow you to troubleshoot DRS behavior more easily and gain optimal performance for your virtual machines.

Before diving into DRS and local host resource management, it is essential that we step back and grasp the fundamentals of dynamic (resource) entitlements.

Dynamic entitlement: *Dynamic entitlement defines a target that represents the ideal amount of resources eligible for use. Both DRS and the host-local schedulers compute this target and it is up to the virtual machine or resource pool to use the available resources or not. Entitlement is comprised of static elements and dynamic elements. The static elements are based on user-provided resource specifications, while dynamic elements are based on estimated demand and the level of contention in a system. A virtual machine will have a separate dynamic entitlement target for each resource type (i.e. CPU and memory).*

You, as an administrator, can influence the dynamic entitlement of a virtual machine by configuring the resource allocation settings: reservations, shares and limits. Resource allocation settings not only affect the performance of the virtual machine, but also impact performance of other virtual machines. Therefore, it is important to understand how dynamic entitlement is calculated and how to configure the virtual machine without introducing a denial-of-service for the virtual machine or the rest of the environment.

Both the dynamic and static elements are explained in detail later in this chapter. For now, let's start with the architecture of the scheduler responsible for calculating dynamic entitlements.

Resource Scheduler Architecture

The VMkernel of an ESXi host runs multiple host-local resource schedulers, including the CPU scheduler and memory scheduler. DRS introduces a global scheduler, effectively creating a two-layer scheduler which is responsible for dividing the cluster resources and allocating the local resources.

Figure 51: DRS and Host-local scheduler

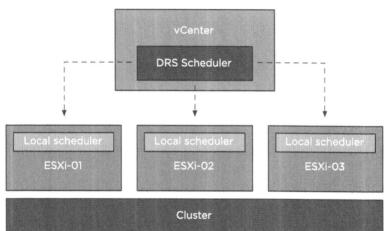

DRS Scheduler

The global scheduler is responsible for dividing the cluster resources. After receiving the active usage and demands of virtual machines, DRS determines the dynamic entitlement of each virtual machine.

The DRS scheduler computes the ideal CPU and memory entitlements that would have been reached if the cluster were a single large host but relies upon host-level scheduling to implement DRS resource pool and virtual machine-level resource settings. Resource pools are expanded upon in chapter 13.

The interesting case is when resource pools contain virtual machines that are running on different hosts. Host-local resource schedulers are responsible for allocating resources to virtual machines, requiring translation of cluster resource pool settings to host-level resource pool settings.

DRS solves this by mirroring the cluster resource pool tree to each host and mapping the appropriate resource settings to each resource pool node. The host-local scheduler places the resource pools in the /host/user hierarchy, resulting in a DRS resource pool tree rooted at /host/user on every host containing a resource pool hierarchy pushed by DRS.

Figure 52: Mapping Cluster RP tree to ESXi host-local RP tree

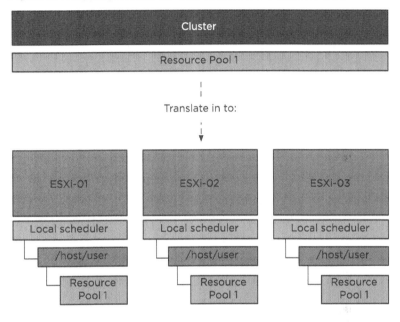

DRS sends resource pool settings to each host-local resource pool tree that are consistent with the dynamic entitlement of all virtual machines active on that host. DRS prunes the resource pool tree and sends the host only the allocations for the virtual machines running there. In Figure 53, none of the virtual machines within Resource Pool 1 are active on ESXi-02. Consequently, that specific resource pool tree will not exist on ESXi-02.

Figure 53: Dividing RP level resources across Host-Local RP trees

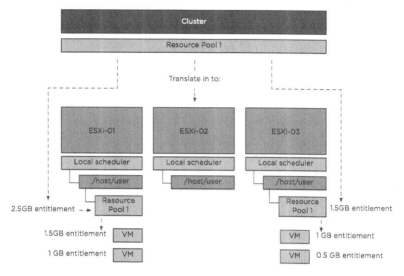

Local Scheduler

The local scheduler treats the host-local resource pool tree similar to if the user had set up the tree directly on the host. Following the resource allocation settings of the resource pool tree, the host-local scheduler computes the dynamic entitlement with regards to the tree and flows resources between virtual machines when that is appropriate. The host-local resource scheduler can allocate additional resources if necessary - if resources are available - and can quickly respond to changes in demand.

Dynamic Entitlement target

During normal operations in a non-overcommitted cluster, the dynamic entitlement of a virtual machine can fluctuate depending on its activity. In a non-overcommitted cluster, the virtual machine receives all the resources it requires. Artificially capping resource allocation requires extra calculations from the host-local schedulers. This unnecessary overhead is avoided by the host-local schedulers as much as possible, resulting in a less-restrictive resource allocation policy.

The dynamic entitlement target of a virtual machine will be increased as the demand of the virtual machine increases. In other words, the virtual machine is effectively capped on resource usage by its maximum configured size (i.e. number of vCPUs and configured memory size).

The dynamic entitlement target consists of demand and usage metrics. By integrating demand metrics in the calculation, both host-local schedulers and DRS understand how many resources the virtual machine wanted to use over how many resources it actually received.

The metrics used by DRS for dynamic entitlement calculations are CPU active and memory active. CPU active metrics exported by the host-local CPU scheduler include %Run + %Ready. The host-local scheduler includes some parts of the ready time in the active time, depending on the adjustments for specific CPU features such as Hyperthreading and power management.

Memory active is exported by the host-local memory scheduler and is the main memory metric used by DRS to determine the memory entitlement. The active memory represents the working set of the virtual machine, which signifies the number of active pages in RAM. By using the working-set estimation, the memory scheduler determines which of the allocated memory pages are actively used by the virtual machine and which allocated pages are idle. To accommodate a sudden rapid increase of the working set, 25% of idle consumed memory is allowed. The active memory part of the dynamic entitlement also includes the virtual machine's memory overhead.

Figure 54: Dynamic entitlement target

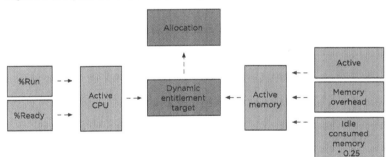

Let's use an 8 GB virtual machine as example on how DRS calculates the dynamic memory entitlement. The guest OS running in this virtual machine has touched 50% of its memory size since it was booted but only 20% of its memory size is active. This means that the virtual machine has consumed 4096 MB and 1638.4 MB is active. To calculate the idle consumed memory, the active memory 1638.4 MB is subtracted from the consumed memory, 4096 MB, resulting in a total 2457.6 MB idle consumed memory. By default DRS includes 25% of the idle consumed memory, i.e. 614.4 MB.

The virtual machine has a 90 MB memory overhead reservation. The memory demand, part of the dynamic entitlement target, DRS uses in it's load balancing calculation is as follows: 1638.4 MB + 614.4 MB + 90 MB = 2342.8 MB.

Figure 55: Dynamic memory entitlement

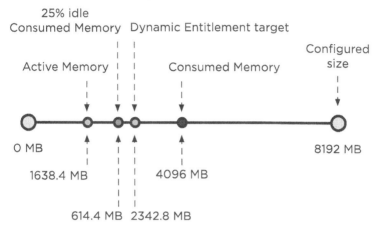

Contention

Contention will impact the dynamic entitlement. Contention, sometimes called overcommitment, can take all forms and shapes. If the virtual infrastructure is correctly sized, long-term contention will not occur. However, short-term contention can occur when resource usage rapidly increases to the point where demand temporarily exceeds availability.

Host failovers, boot storms, application scheduling, load correlation and load synchronicity can cause contention. Load correlation is the relationship between loads running in different machines. If an event initiates multiple loads, for example, a search query on front-end webserver, this may result in increased load on the supporting stack and backend. Load synchronicity is often caused by load correlation but can also exist due to user activity such as morning startup routines of users such as logon, checking mail and database connectivity. When contention occurs, both the reservation and share resource allocation settings affect entitlement.

DRS Dynamic Entitlement versus Host-Local Entitlement

Although both DRS and the host-local schedulers compute the dynamic entitlement of a virtual machine, they do not exchange these calculations. DRS calculates the average and peak demand for a target for the resource pool tree every invocation period (by default, 5 minutes) while the host-local schedulers compute the dynamic entitlement every schedule period for each different host-local scheduler.

Resource Allocation Settings

Resource allocation settings can be set for both virtual machines and resource pools. Chapter 13 explains resource pools and resource allocation policies. This section describes the function and impact of virtual machine allocation settings. Other policies at resource pool levels are described to further explain the topic.

Table 8: Resource allocation settings

Attribute	Specification
Reservation	Also referred to as "MIN". A reservation is the amount of physical resources (MHz or MB) guaranteed to be available for the virtual machine.
Shares	Shares specify the relative importance of the virtual machine. Shares are always measured against other powered-on sibling virtual machines and resource pools on the host.
Limit	Also referred as "MAX". A limit specifies an upper bound for resources that can be allocated to a virtual machine.

Figure 56: Resource allocation settings and dynamic entitlement

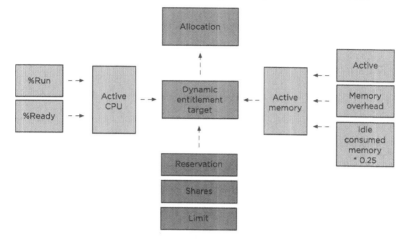

Reservation

A reservation is the amount of physical resources guaranteed available to a virtual machine. When contention occurs, the host-local schedulers need to determine how many resources need to be reclaimed. The scheduler cannot reclaim resources protected by reservation. In other words, a reservation creates a minimum dynamic entitlement target that is at least as large as the reservation.

For example, during memory contention the host-local memory scheduler compares the memory usage of the virtual machine to the dynamic entitlement. If the usage is above the dynamic entitlement, memory is ballooned, compressed or swapped until physical memory usage is at or below the entitlement. Reclamation of resources stops when the target set by a reservation is reached, as it is the minimum guaranteed dynamic entitlement.

Continuing with the previous memory example, depicted in Figure 57. The virtual machine has a dynamic entitlement of 2342.8 MB (1638.4 MB + 614.4 MB + 90 MB = 2342.8 MB). A 1024 MB reservation is set, resulting in a minimum entitlement target of 1024 MB. If contention occurs, the host-local memory scheduler will take the minimum entitlement into account when recalculating a new target and can reclaim memory from the virtual machine up to its minimum entitlement.

Figure 57: Minimum entitlement

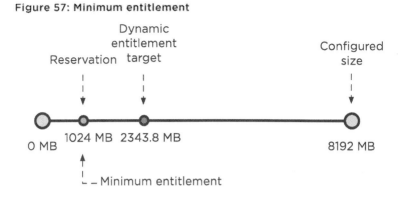

Resource Pool-Level Reservation Behavior

Reservations can exist at both the virtual machine and resource pool levels. Reservations set on a resource pool behave differently than a reservation set on a virtual machine. Reserved resources belonging to the resource pool are divided among the active virtual machines. No ownership of resources is transferred between the resource pool and the virtual machine, as the cluster-level resource pool reservation is divided between the host-local resource pool trees. The resources reserved by the host-local resource pool trees are available to each virtual machine and flow between them depending on their dynamic entitlements. In other words, reservations set at the resource pool-level act as dynamic targets, updated each time usage and demand changes inside the resource pool.

Virtual Machine-Level Reservation Behavior

Virtual machine-level reservations have a less dynamic nature than resource pool-level reservations. On top of this, a CPU reservation has a different effect than a memory reservation on the availability of resources for other virtual machines.

A reservation set at the virtual machine-level (statically) defines the minimum entitlement of that specific virtual machine. During contention, the host-local schedulers can reclaim resources up to the minimum entitlement of the virtual machine. Unlike resource pool-level reservations where resources are provided based on the usage and demand of a virtual machine, the reservations set at the virtual machine level are static. This means that the virtual machine is entitled to have these resources available at all times, whether it uses them or not. This impacts availability of that resource for other virtual machines.

A difference exists between reserving a resource and using the resource. As reservations are a part of the dynamic entitlement calculation, a virtual machine can use more or less that it has reserved. The static nature of the virtual machine-level entitlement impacts the sharing of resources. By not incorporating usage and demand, reserved resources are static and the host-local schedulers are not allowed to reclaim any idle resources beyond the dynamic entitlement of a virtual machine.

But when, exactly, will a virtual machine hit its full reservation? Popular belief is that the virtual machine will hit full reservation immediately when a virtual machine becomes active, but that is not entirely true. With a memory reservation on virtual machine-level, only the physical RAM that is used is protected by the reservation. And physical RAM only gets allocated to the virtual machine when the virtual RAM is accessed. However, in practice, it depends on the Guest OS running inside the virtual machine. During startup, Windows zeroes each page available during boot, hitting the full reservation during boot time. Linux, however, only accesses the memory pages it requires. For example, a 4GB Linux virtual machine configured with a 2GB memory reservation and accessing 1GB would have only 1GB of physical RAM allocated and protected by the reservation. Its minimum entitlement would be 1GB. A Windows machine with a similar configuration would have minimum entitlement of 2GB directly after Windows completed the boot-process.

Fortunately, it is not all bad. Sharing of reserved resources is determined by the agility of the workload: CPU instructions are transient and can quickly finish. For this reason, the CPU scheduler allows other virtual CPUs to use the physical CPU while the entitled virtual machine is not active. If the entitled virtual machine requests resources, the "squatter" can be de-scheduled quickly and placed in a queue. Physical RAM holds data and if memory space was loaned out to other virtual machines for temporary use, this data needs to be moved if the rightful owner wants to use this memory space. Clearing out this data takes significant time and may delay the entitled virtual machine unfairly. To avoid this, the memory scheduler does not loan out reserved physical memory for temporary use.

Admission Control and Dynamic Entitlement

Often mistaken as related, dynamic entitlement and admission control are independent mechanisms that are both affected by defined reservations.

The admission control mechanism is active prior to power-on and validates that enough system resources (total system resources - total reservations made by other virtual machines) are available to meet the reservation. The power- on succeeds only if the admission control is successful whereas dynamic entitlement is active during operation of the virtual machine and will not reclaim used resources protected by reservation.

In other words, admission control exists during the first lifecycle phase of the virtual machine (pre-power-on), while dynamic entitlement controls the virtual machine during the operational stage of its lifecycle.

Shares

Shares determine the relative priority of virtual machines and resource pools at the same hierarchical level and decide how resources (total system resources - total reservations) are divided.

Relative Priorities

Shares are pool-relative, which means that the number of shares is compared between the child-objects of the same parent. Since, they signify relative priorities; the absolute values do not matter, comparing 2:1 or 20.000 to 10.000 will have the same result. Chapter 13 zooms in on the use of shares in clusters.

Shares of CPU

After obeying the minimum entitlement of the virtual machines, shares of CPU are used to divide the available physical CPU resources. If a virtual machine is not using its reserved CPU time, the unused CPU time can be used by other virtual machines. The CPU scheduler calculates a MHzPerShare value for correct distribution of CPU time. This metric is used by the CPU scheduler to identify which virtual machines are "ahead" of their entitlement and which virtual machines are "behind" and do not fully utilize their entitlement.

When a virtual machine wants to run, the CPU scheduler identifies the progress of the virtual machine and places it in one of its queues. If the virtual machine is behind its entitlement, it will be placed it in the main scheduler queue. If it is ahead of its entitlement, it will be placed in the extra queue. Before scheduling, the CPU scheduler will compare the MHzPerShare values of the virtual machines in the main queue and will select the virtual machine with the lowest *MHzPerShare* value. If no virtual machines are in the *main* queue, the scheduler will select a virtual machine from the *extra* queue.

The *MHzPerShare* is calculated as follows:

MHzPerShare = MHzUsed / Shares

MHzUsed is the current utilization of the virtual machine measured in megahertz, while Shares indicates the currently configured number of shares of the virtual machine.

For example, consider Figure 58: VM1 is using 2500 MHz and has 2000 shares, resulting in a *MHzPerShare* value of 1.25. VM2 is consuming 2500MHz as well but has 1000 shares, resulting in a *MHzPerShare* value of 2.5. VM1 will be placed in front of the queue due to its lower *MHzPerShare* value.

Figure 58: Order of Priority

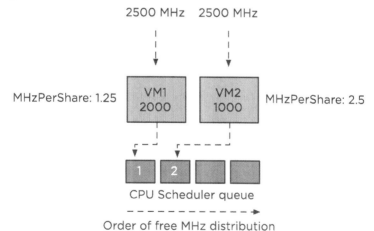

CPU Scheduler queue

Order of free MHz distribution

If the virtual machine with the lowest *MHzPerShare* value decides not to utilize the cycles, the cycles can be allocated to the virtual machine with the next lower *MHzPerShare* value.

Reservations override shares and guarantee the amount of physical resources regardless of the number of shares issued in the pool. This means that the virtual machine can always use the CPU cycles specified in its reservation, even if the virtual machine has a higher MHzPerShare value.

For example: three virtual machines are present in a resource pool possessing 8 GHz.

Table 9: Shares and Reservations overview

Virtual machine	Shares	Reservation
VM1	2000	None
VM2	1000	2500
VM3	2000	None

VM1 is running a memory-intensive application and does not require many CPU cycles. Both VM2 and VM3 host a CPU-intensive application. VM1 is running at 500 MHz, with 2000 shares, the *MHzPerShare* equals 0.25. 1000 shares are issued to VM2 plus a reservation is set at 2500MHz on VM2. VM3 owns 2000 shares, but is powered off. Because VM2 is in need of CPU cycles, the CPU scheduler allocates CPU cycles up to its reservation resulting in a MHzPerShare value of 2.5 (2500/1000). At this point 5000 MHz remains available in the resource pool.

Figure 59: VM2 claiming MHz up to its reservation

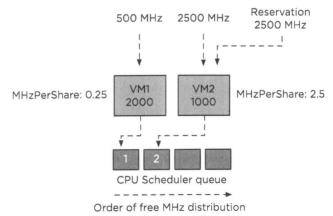

In the next scenario VM3 just powered up and is behind its entitlement; the CPU scheduler compares the *MHzPerShare* values of the virtual machines and selects the virtual machine with the lowest *MHzPerShare* value. Step 1 - VM3 has a *MHzPerShare* of 0 and can claim up to 0.25, the *MHzPerShare* value of VM1. Step 2 - VM1 does not need additional CPU cycles and forfeits it claim, VM3 can now claim CPU resources until it reaches a *MHzPerShare* value equal to 2.5 before the CPU scheduler will consider providing CPU cycles to VM2.

VM3 owns 2000 shares, meaning it can be allocated up to 4500 MHz to reach a MHzPerShare value of 2.5 (4500/2000). The CPU scheduler allocates 4500 MHz to equalize distribution before considering the share value of VM2 to allocate the remaining 500 MHz

This previous scenarios demonstrates that shares of CPU play a significant role in distributing CPU cycles.

Shares of Memory

The memory scheduler is invoked every 15 seconds to recompute the dynamic entitlement memory statistics in order to determine and update the virtual machine memory allocations.

This metric is pushed to DRS for its calculations to divide the resource pools across the ESXi hosts in a cluster. However, the host-local memory scheduler is responsible for allocating the resources. As mentioned before, every virtual machine is allowed to allocate additional resources if no contention exists.

The dynamic entitlement will still be calculated every 15 minutes, but a virtual machine is allowed to exceed its dynamic entitlement and allocate additional memory when required.

If contention occurs, the memory scheduler reclaims memory based on the dynamic entitlement of the virtual machine. ESXi determines the level of contention by calculating the free memory state (*MinFreePct*). Based on the level of contention and the free memory state, the memory scheduler determines which reclamation mechanism to use.

In vSphere 4.1, *MinFreePct* is defined as 6% and the other memory states are defined as a percentage of *MinFreePct*:

Table 10: Soft, Hard and Low states percentage of MinFreePct

Free memory state	Threshold	Reclamation mechanism
High	6%	None
Soft	64% of MinFreePct	Balloon, compress
Hard	32% of MinFreePct	Balloon, compress, swap
Low	16% of MinFreePct	Balloon, compress, **swap**

With today's server configurations, 6% might be a bit too much to trigger memory reclamation techniques. Servers with a memory configuration of 512GB become more and more common and with a 6% MinFreePct threshold, 30GB will be idling most of the time. To counteract wasting this amount of memory, vSphere 5 introduces a sliding scale.

Table 11: MinFreePct sliding scale

Free memory state threshold	Threshold
6%	0-4 GB
4%	4-12 GB
2%	12-28 GB
1%	Remaining memory

On a server configured with 96GB RAM, the *MinFreePct* threshold will be set at 1597.44 MB, opposed to 5898.24 MB if 6% was used for the complete range 96GB.

Table 12: Memory reclamation threshold of a 96GB server

Free memory state	Threshold	Range	Memory & reclamation technique	Memory threshold in MB
High	6%	0 - 4 GB	245.76MB	
	4%	4 - 12 GB	327.68MB	
	2%	12 - 28 GB	327.68MB	
	1%	Remaining	696.32MB	**1597.36**
Soft to High	64-100		Balloon	1022.31 − 1597.36
Low to Hard	16-64		Balloon, compress, swap	255.57 − 1022.31

To reduce the impact of memory reclamation, idle memory is selected for reclamation in order to provide the "liberated" physical memory to virtual machines that require more memory <u>and</u> have more priority.

To determine which physical memory can be redistributed, the memory scheduler computes the *Share-Per-Page* metric. Memory is reclaimed from the virtual machine or resource pool that owns the fewest shares per allocated physical memory page. *Shares-per-Page* is determined by dividing the number of shares by the allocation of pages, corrected with the number of active pages and the idle memory tax percentage. The idle memory tax is applied in a progressive fashion: the tax rate increases as the ratio of idle memory to active memory for the virtual machine. Adjusting the number of shares with active and idle pages helps to avoid a pure proportional-share state where idle virtual machines with disproportionate numbers of shares are able to hoard memory.

Contention Occurs, Now What?

If the free memory state transitions from high to another state such as soft, hard or low, the memory scheduler is invoked and a new target is recalculated for each virtual machine. The new target is adjusted by the idle memory tax, after statistical sampling of the virtual machine's working-set memory is classified as idle or active. Up to 75% of memory unprotected by the minimum entitlement can be reclaimed. The memory scheduler will hold a buffer of 25% to accommodate rapid increase of the working set.

Using the previous example and Figure 60, assume the virtual machine is running Windows. Due to the zero-out technique used by Windows at boot time, the virtual machine has allocated memory equal to the configured size. 20% of its configured size is active. If 1024 MB is protected by memory reservation, after estimating the active memory of the working set size and keeping 25% consumed idle memory as buffer to be able to respond rapidly to workload increase, the dynamic entitlement is determined at 3366.8 MB for this virtual machine. The calculation is as follows: 20% of 8192 MB = 1638.4 MB active consumed memory. As all memory is consumed, the calculation of idle consumed memory is: 8192 MB – 1638.4 MB = 6553.6 MB. 25% of idle consumed memory = 6553.6 * 0.25 = 1638.4 MB. The memory overhead reservation is 90 MB, making the total of 1638.4 MB + 16384.MB + 90 MB = 3366.8 MB dynamic entitlement.

Figure 60: Dynamic entitlement to determine reclamation

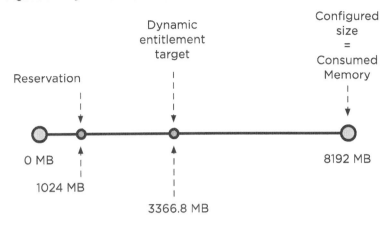

The memory scheduler will respect the reservation and cannot reallocate memory that is protected by the reservation. Depending on the level of contention, memory is reclaimed from each virtual machine. A low level of contention results in a small number of memory pages reclaimed from each virtual machine on the host. High levels of contention result in increased levels of reclamation. The memory scheduler tries to reclaim pages up to the dynamic entitlement of each virtual machine, but it can happen that the memory is reclaimed up to the reservation. This point is normally reached only if memory demand is excessive.

Figure 61: Reclamation and level of contention

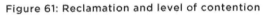

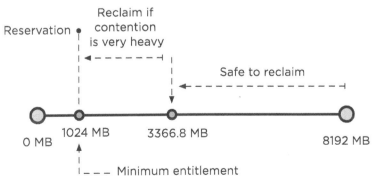

Worst Case Allocation

When memory is reclaimed up to the minimum entitlement, the virtual machine experiences its worst-case allocation. This value is presented in vCenter as the worst-case scenario column of the resource allocation tab. This value is meant as a theoretical value to help understand how bad resource allocation can become for the virtual machine.

Limits

Limits are a part of the resource allocation settings and define the allowed upper limit of physical resources. Both the CPU and memory scheduler allocate resources up to the limit. Even if there are enough free resources available, a limit will define the maximum entitlement and will be strictly enforced by the host-local resource schedulers. In Figure 62, the virtual machine has a configured size of 8192 MB and an additional limit is configured of 6144 MB. The resource scheduler may allocate physical memory up to 6144 MB. This means that the virtual machine maximum consumable memory is also 6144 MB, this results in a lower dynamic entitlement target as the total idle consumed memory is 4505.6 MB instead of 6553.6 MB.

Figure 62: Limits

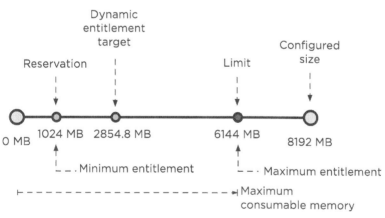

Limits can function to allocate a specific amount of resources to a resource pool, but we strongly recommend not applying limits on virtual machines as a day-to-day operational tool or management instrument.

Initially, limits were used as a troubleshooting tool by developers to induce a state of overcommitment at the virtual machine level without having to overcommit the entire ESXi host. A limit is a boundary for dynamic entitlement calculations which is not exposed to the guest OS inside the virtual machine. The Guest OS resource manager is only aware of the configured size of the virtual machine, i.e. configured memory and number of vCPUs.

CPU Limits

A limit specifies an upper boundary for CPU resources that can be allocated to a virtual machine. If the vCPU exceeds its CPU time, it is descheduled until it is allowed to run again. While the virtual machine is descheduled, available CPU cycles are wasted.

Memory Limits

The Guest Operating Systems will size and tune their caching algorithms and memory management accordingly and tend to use whatever memory they detect. Therefore, a limit set smaller than the configured memory size will hurt performance as the Guest OS or applications within a virtual machine try to use memory that is not stored in physical memory. The memory scheduler needs to acquire memory by ballooning, compressing or swapping, which generates overhead on the ESXi host and on the storage level if memory is swapped.

Setting limit equal to the memory size

We are aware that some administrators set a limit equal to the memory size of the virtual machine. This is not a proper use for limits and can be harmful in many ways:

The configured size is the explicit limit for the memory scheduler; the Guest OS cannot use more memory because it will not detect more memory. The VMkernel will reserve memory for each virtual machine for virtualization overhead, called the virtual machine memory overhead reservation. This amount of memory is not affected by the memory limit and is based on the configured size of the virtual machine. A limit is a static resource allocation setting and will not be affected by reconfiguration of the memory size of the virtual machine. This can result in unintentional compressing, ballooning and swapping of memory if the virtual machine requires more memory than the specified limit.

Tying It All Together

Looking at the true essence of resource allocation settings, reservations, shares and limits are just components used in calculating dynamic entitlement. When contention occurs, the virtual machine resource target is at least as large as the reservation. This minimum entitlement identifies the reclamation boundary for host-local schedulers; they cannot reclaim resources beyond this point. Limits define the maximum target for the host-local schedulers and will restrict the physical resource allocation. Shares, activity and contention define the remainder of the entitlement. If a virtual machine's resource usage is either above or below its entitlement, resource reclamation occurs until the virtual machine's usage is at or below the minimum entitlement.

At the deepest level in the world of host-local resource schedulers, reservation, ownership and shares do not exist. There is only a dynamic target that must be honored. In other words the host only tries to allocate resources according to the entitlement target.

Chapter 13

Resource Pools and Controls

Clusters aggregate ESXi host capacity into one large pool and provide an abstraction layer between the resource providers (ESXi hosts) and resource consumers (virtual machines). Resource pools create an additional abstraction layer to provide sharing resources within pools and isolate resources between pools.

Isolation and sharing of resources are accomplished by using the resource allocation controls: reservations, shares and limits. These resource allocation settings are similar to the virtual machine resource allocation settings explained in chapter 12. How do these settings work at the resource pool level and what impact do they have on virtual machine workloads?

Root Resource Pool

When enabling DRS, a root resource pool is created at the cluster level. Whenever an ESXi host is added to a DRS cluster, the host's resources are added to the root resource pool. Resources required to run the ESXi virtualization layer are not available to the cluster:

Total amount of host resources - virtualization overhead = available resources associated with the cluster.

If HA is enabled, resources required to satisfy HA failover are drawn from the root resource pool, because HA failover places virtual machines into the root resource pool. The resources required to run the virtualization layer are not visible when reviewing the capacity of the root resource pool, while the resources required to satisfy HA failover will be marked as reserved resources.

For example; the root resource pool contains 36GB of total memory resources if a cluster consists of 3 hosts, each providing 12GB of available memory resources.

Figure 63: Root resource pool

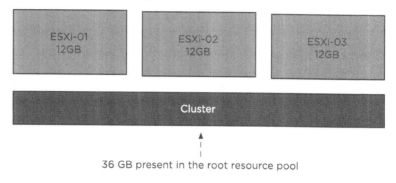

36 GB present in the root resource pool

Resource Pools

As a cluster distributes resources from hosts to virtual machines, the hosts play the role of resource providers, while virtual machines are resource consumers. Resource pools play both roles as they consume resources from the cluster and provide resources to the virtual machines.

Figure 64: Resource providers and consumers

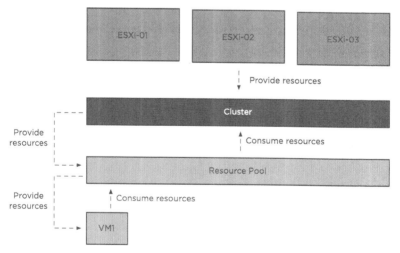

It is important to realize that resource pools can be both consumers and providers of resources as this might impact the way you design your resource pools from a shares perspective.

Inflating or Deflating Resource Pools

Resource pools span the entire cluster. When adding host to the cluster, its resources are immediately available to the resource pool. The opposite is true when removing hosts from the cluster: resources provided by the ESXi host are subtracted from the cluster and will not be available for use by the resource pool and its child-objects.

Please note that removing hosts can place a cluster in an overcommitted state. An overcommitted state occurs when the available cluster resources cannot satisfy the reservations of all resource pools. Resource allocations for the active virtual machines are reduced during an overcommitted state.

Host-Local Resource Pools

Using resource pools, you can hierarchically partition CPU and memory resources from the cluster. Resources can be shared with other child-objects within the pool while providing isolation between resource pools. A resource pool can have two types of child-objects: virtual machines or resource pools. How, exactly, are these resources shared and isolated?

Virtual machine workloads are executed by the host-local CPU and memory schedulers, requiring resource pool settings to be translated from the cluster level to the ESXi host level. As described in the previous chapter, DRS maps and mirrors the cluster resource pool tree to each host. DRS distributes the resources across the host-local resource pool tree, dividing the available resources across the hosts based on the active virtual machines and their dynamic entitlements. Once the resource pool allocations are propagated to the host-local resource pool tree, the host-local CPU and memory scheduler takes care of the actual resource allocation.

Note

As of vSphere 5.0, vCenter manages resource pool structures exclusively. Up to vSphere 4.1, changes made to the host-local resource pool structure would override the vCenter managed resource pool structure. Mismatches between vCenter's view of the host and the real resource structure on the host are undesirable and can have unexpected effects.

In order to prevent users from modifying resource settings by connecting directly to a host when it is already managed by DRS, no resource changing operations are permitted on the host. In this situation, all resource settings are read-only and vCenter displays the following message:

Figure 65: Host management

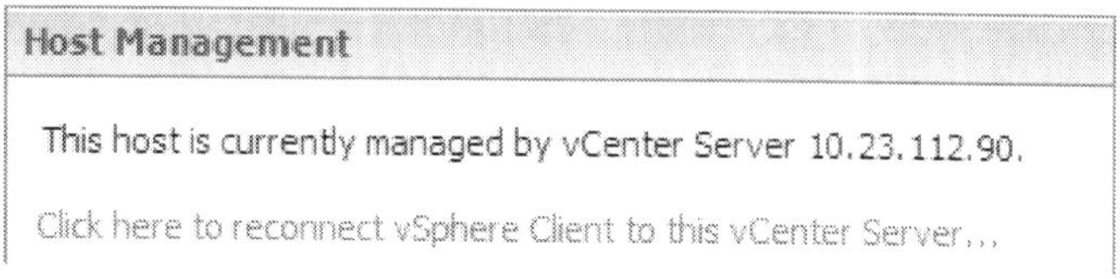

Host Management
This host is currently managed by vCenter Server 10.23.112.90.
Click here to reconnect vSphere Client to this vCenter Server…

Dividing Resources

DRS divides cluster resources with a coarser granularity than the host-local resource schedulers. DRS computes the dynamic entitlement target of all virtual machines during each invocation period (default *PollPeriodSec* = 300 seconds), versus the timescale of the host local schedulers of milliseconds for CPU scheduling and minutes for memory. During every DRS invocation, each host conceptually receives a target of resources based upon the dynamic entitlement of its active virtual machines.

For example, between the DRS invocations, the host-local memory scheduler is responsible for the distribution of available memory. The host-local memory scheduler makes a bottom-up pass over the resource pool tree to compute the demand at each resource pool node. If the resource demand is less than or equal to the amount of resources provided, the entitlement of each virtual machine is equal to the demand. If the demand exceeds the amount of memory provided, the dynamic entitlement is adjusted. After the entitlement is calculated, the memory scheduler makes a top-down pass to compute the new targets for all resource pools and their member virtual machines. The host-local memory scheduler then allows the resource pools to allocate memory to their targets.

Resource Pools Are Not Folders

Understanding how resources are divided across the resource pool tree makes it obvious that resource pools should not be used as a folder structure. Often, we come across environments that use resource pools as a folder structure in the "Hosts and Clusters" view of vCenter, because it helps the administrator identify relationships between the virtual machines. Using resource pools for this purpose generates unnecessary load on both vCenter and the ESXi hosts that can affect virtual machine performance.

Basic design principle

Do not use resource pools as a folder structure in Host and Cluster view, but use the appropriate folder view.

Resource Pool Tree Structure

Officially there is no cluster-wide limit on the number of resource pools inside a cluster; however, each host has a limit on number of resource pools it can support. That limit is a complicated formula depending on number of virtual machines the host can support, which can depend on the configuration of the virtual machines or the overall maximum limit. DRS will not instantiate all resource pools on a single host, but our recommendation is not to exceed 2048 resource pools per cluster.

For a host, the maximum resource pool tree depth for user created pools is 8; 4 levels are taken internally on each ESXi host. These internal resource pools are independent of the DRS resource pools. To avoid complicated proportional share calculations and complex DRS dynamic entitlement calculations, we advise not to exceed a resource pool depth of 2. The flatter the resource pool tree, the easier it is to manage and reduces overhead during dynamic entitlement calculations.

Basic design principle

Attempt to keep the resource pool tree depth to a minimum.

Resource Pool Resource Allocation Settings

Resource allocation settings are applied to resource pools. Although similar to virtual machines, their behavior can differ somewhat.

Table 13: Resource pool resource allocation settings

Attribute	Specification
Shares	Shares specify the relative importance of the virtual machine or resource pool. Shares are always measured against other powered-up virtual machines or resource pools at the same hierarchical level. Shares have two properties: level and amounts. The value of level can be low, normal, high and custom.
Reservation	The minimum available resources also referred to as "MIN". Reservation is the amount of physical resources guaranteed to be available for the virtual machine or resource pool. Reserved resources are not wasted if they are not used. If the utilization is less than the reservation, the resources can be utilized by other running virtual machines. Units are MB for memory, MHz for CPU.
Limit	The maximum allowed physical resource usage Also referred as "MAX". Limit specifies an upper bound for resources that can be allocated to a virtual machine or resource pool. The utilization of a resource pool will not exceed this limit, even if there are available resources. Units are MB for memory, MHz for CPU.
Expandable reservation	[DEFAULT] Expandable reservation determines whether or not the reservation on a resource pool can grow beyond the specified value, if the parent resource pool has unreserved resources. A non-expandable reservation is called a fixed reservation.

Shares

Shares determine the priority of a resource pool or virtual machine compared to their siblings. Siblings can be resource pools or virtual machines that exist at the same hierarchical level, i.e. share the same parent.

Priority is determined by comparing the number of shares to the total amount of shares issued by the object's parent. For example, a resource pool is created with 4000 CPU shares. If it is the only object, its parent (the cluster) has issued only 4000 CPU shares. Because the resource pool owns all issued shares, it is entitled to all the CPU resources available in the cluster.

In Figure 66, Resource Pool 2 is added to the cluster and is configured with 8000 shares. The cluster issues 8000 more shares, increasing the total shares to 12,000 and diluting the share ratio of Resource Pool 1 from 100% to 33%. In a worst-case scenario, Resource Pool 1 is entitled to 33% of the cluster resources. Worst-case scenario describes the state where all virtual machines request 100% of the resources within the boundaries of their configured size.

Shares are a part of the dynamic entitlement calculation. During computation of dynamic entitlement, reservation and limits take precedence over shares, but this does not imply that shares are unimportant!

Note

Shares are not simply a weighting system for resources. In the following chapters we explain the working of shares during a **worst-case scenario** situation: every virtual machine claims 100% of their configured resources, the system is overcommitted and contention occurs. In real life, this situation (hopefully) does not occur very often. During normal operations, not every virtual machine is active and not every active virtual machine is 100% utilized.

Activity and amount of contention are two elements determining dynamic entitlement of active virtual machines. For ease of presentation, we tried to avoid as many variable elements as possible and used a worst-case scenario situation in each example.

Figure 66: Resource Pool 1 and 2 share ratio

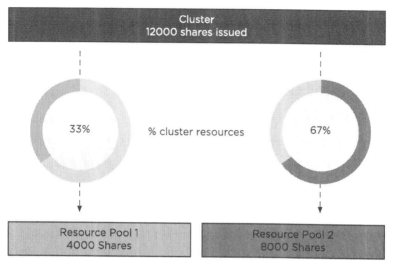

Resource Pool Shares

Because resource pool shares are relative to other resource pools or virtual machines with the same parent resource pool, it is important to understand how vCenter sizes resource pools internally.

The values of CPU and memory shares applied to resource pools are similar to virtual machines. By default, a resource pool is sized like a virtual machine with 4 vCPUs and 16GB of RAM. Depending on the selected share level, a predefined amount of shares are issued. Similar to virtual machines, four share levels can be selected. There are three predefined settings: *High*, *Normal* or *Low*, which specify share values with a 4:2:1 ratio, and the *Custom* setting, which can be used to specify a different relative relationship.

Table 14: Share level overview

Share Level	Shares of CPU	Shares of Memory
Low	2000	81,920
Normal	4000	163,840
High	8000	327,680

Caution must be taken when placing virtual machines at the same hierarchical level as resource pools, as virtual machines can end up with a higher priority than intended. For example, in vSphere 5, the largest virtual machine can be equipped with 32 vCPUs and 1TB of memory. If a virtual machine is configured with a High share level, it can own up to 64,000 CPU shares and 20,80,000 memory shares. Figure 67 depicts the share ratio between a resource pool and the virtual machine both configured with a *Normal* share level.

Figure 67: Shares ratio of RP and a 32 vCPU, 1TB virtual machine

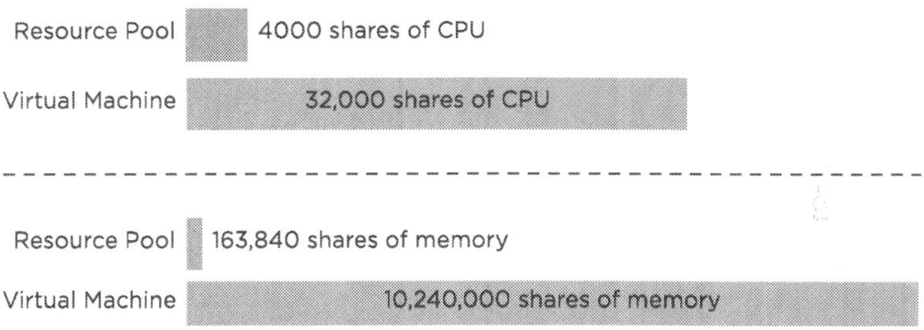

Resource Pool   4000 shares of CPU

Virtual Machine   32,000 shares of CPU

Resource Pool   163,840 shares of memory

Virtual Machine   10,240,000 shares of memory

Basic design principle

It is not recommended deploying virtual machines at the same hierarchical level as resource pools.

Sibling Rivalry

As shares determine the priority of the resource pool or virtual machine relative to its siblings, it is important to determine which objects compete for priority.

Figure 68: Sibling level

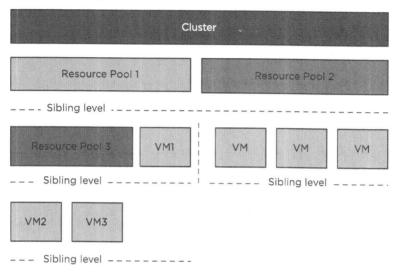

In the scenario depicted in Figure 68, multiple sibling levels are present. Resource Pool 1 and Resource Pool 2 are child objects of the Cluster and therefore are on the same sibling level. Resource Pool 3 and VM1 are child objects of Resource Pool 1 and are active on the same sibling level. The VMs of Resource Pool 2 are active on their respective sibling level. VM2 and VM3 are siblings and both compete for resources provided by Resource Pool 3. Their share values can be compared to each other. The share values of VM1 and VM3 cannot be compared with each other because they each have different parent resource pools and don't have sibling rivalry.

Shares indicate the priority at that particular hierarchical level, but the relative priority of the parent at its level will determine the availability of the total amount of resources.

In the example depicted in Figure 69, the cluster resources are divided between Resource Pool 1 and Resource Pool 2. Resource Pool 1 receives 33% of the cluster resources based on its share value. Resource Pool 1 divides its resources between Resource Pool 3 and VM1. Both child-objects own an equal amount of shares and therefore receive each 50% of the resources of Resource Pool 1. This 50% of Resource Pool 1 resources equals to 16.5% of the cluster resources. 16.5% resources is the result of 50% of pool of resources that is equal to 33% of the total amount of cluster resources. Resource Pool 3 divides its resources between VM2 and VM3. These child-objects of Resource Pool 3 compete with each other with an unequal amount of shares. In a worst-case scenario situation, VM2 ends up with 67% of Resource Pool 3's resources that in turn equals 11% of the cluster resources.

Figure 69: Cluster resource distribution

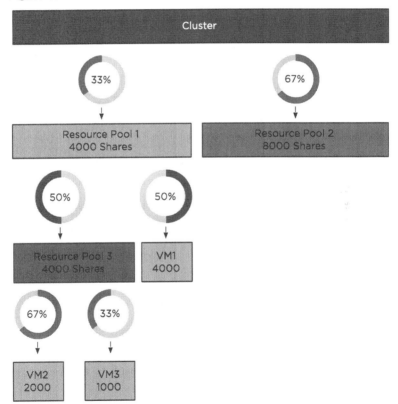

Virtual Machines and Resource Pools as Siblings

Having virtual machines as siblings to resource pools can affect the resource allocation of the subsequent layers. This section illustrates why placing virtual machines as siblings to resource pools is considered to be a misconfiguration. Depicted in Figure 70, VM1 competes for resources with Resource Pool 3. Based on their share values, each can receive up to 50% of the parent resource pool. The resources Resource Pool 3 obtains need to be divided among its child-objects, contrary to VM1 that can use its allocated resources for its own sake.

In the previous example, two virtual machines are active inside Resource Pool 3 and the resources are divided between those two virtual machines. When adding more virtual machines to the resource pool, each share value of the virtual machine gets diluted, while the share value of VM1 remains the same.

Figure 70: Share value dilution

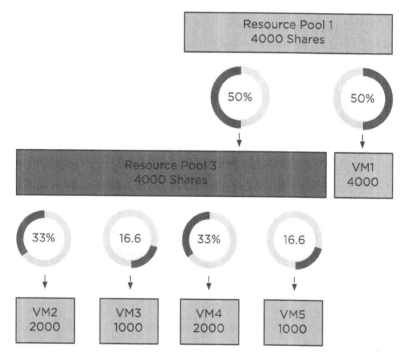

Mixing virtual machines and resource pools at the same hierarchical level may create an unintended imbalance in the proportional share values at that hierarchical level and affects the resource allocation of subsequent layers.

Share Levels are not Resource Classes

Share levels set at a parent are not inherited by child-objects. When a virtual machine is associated with a resource pool, it will retain its share level. If a virtual machine with a *Custom* share level is moved to a resource pool, an error is generated if the virtual machine is configured with a share amount that is too high or low:

The CPU resource shares for VM <name> are much lower than the virtual machines in the resource pool. With its current share setting, the virtual machine will be entitled to 0% of the CPU resources in the pool. Are you sure you want to do this?

When creating a virtual machine or a resource pool, vCenter assigns the Normal share level by default, independent of the share level of its parent. In Figure 71, VM1 has 4000 shares, caused by a High share level, whereas Resource Pool 3 is configured with a *Normal* share level. Although their share levels are different, both Resource Pool 3 and VM1 own 4000 shares each. Both compete with each other based on share **amounts**, not based on share level values. The number of shares and 'share level' are related but different, the number of shares is important while the 'share level' is simply a convenience for generating the values.

Figure 71: Share levels

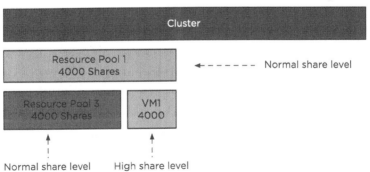

To summarize: all shares are the same and none are more important than the others: 4000 shares = 4000 shares.

The Resource Pool Priority-Pie Paradox

When resource pools are used to hierarchically partition cluster resources, cluster dynamic entitlements cascade down the resource pool hierarchy. On every level, the siblings compete for resources and dilute the remaining resources available at every subsequent level. However, the amount of resources available to each sibling depends on the number of rivals and their configurations inside the resource pool. This means that a few virtual machines inside a resource pool configured with a Low share level can end up with a higher dynamic entitlement than many virtual machines in a resource pool that is configured with a High share level. Virtual machines depicted in Figure 72 are all configured identically and their size is scaled proportionally to their dynamic entitlement within the cluster.

Figure 72: VM dynamic entitlement based on RP share value

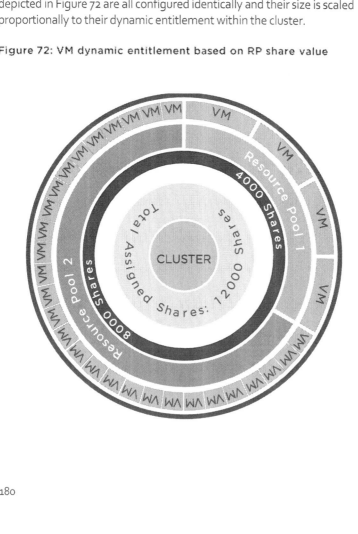

From Resource Pool Setting to Host-Local Resource Allocation

How do resource pool shares affect virtual machine workloads? As mentioned before, DRS mirrors the resource pool hierarchy to each host and divides the entitled resources of the resource pool across the host-local RP tree based on the number of active virtual machines, their share amounts and their current utilization. Once the resource allocation settings are propagated to the host local RP tree, the local host CPU and memory scheduler takes care of the actual resource allocation.

For example, a resource pool in a 2-host cluster is configured with a *Normal* CPU share level. Here, Resource Pool 1 holds 4000 shares of CPU. Four virtual machines running inside the resource pool can be configured as follows:

Figure 73: Single resource pool configuration

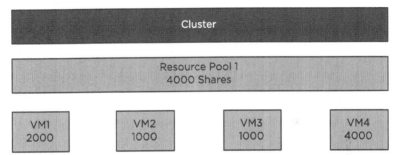

Table 15: Share configuration Resource Pool 1 virtual machines

Virtual machine	Share level	Number of vCPUs	Shares	Share ratio	Host
VM1	Normal	2	2000	2/8	ESXi-01
VM2	Low	2	1000	1/8	ESXi-01
VM3	Low	2	1000	1/8	ESXi-01
VM4	High	2	4000	4/8	ESXi-02

Assume that all of the virtual machines are running equal and stable workloads. DRS will balance the virtual machines across both hosts and creates the following resource pool mapping:

Figure 74: Host-local resource pool mapping

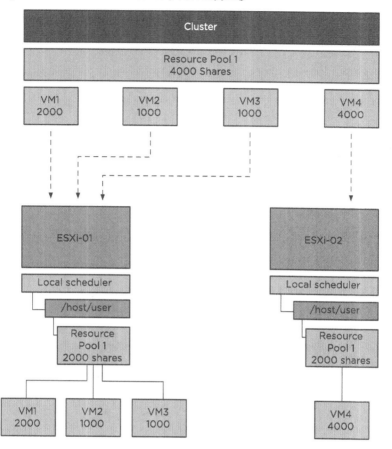

The number of shares specified on virtual machines VM1, VM2 and VM3 add up to 4000, which equals half of the amount of total configured shares inside the resource pool.

In this example, DRS places VM1, VM2 and VM3 on ESXi-01 and for that reason assigns 2000 of the total 4000 shares to Resource Pool 1 of the host local RP tree. VM4 runs on ESXi host ESXi-02 and receives the other half of the resource pool shares.

At this point we create Resource Pool 2. Resource Pool 2 is configured with a High share level and receives 8000 CPU shares. The virtual machine members of Resource Pool 2 are configured identically to the virtual machines in Resource Pool 1.

Table 16: Share configuration Resource Pool 2 virtual machines

Virtual machine	Share level	Number of vCPUs	Shares	Share ratio	Host
VM5	Normal	2	2000	2/8	ESXi-01
VM6	Low	2	1000	1/8	ESXi-01
VM7	Low	2	1000	1/8	ESXi-01
VM8	High	2	4000	4/8	ESXi-02

Figure 75: Share ratio result

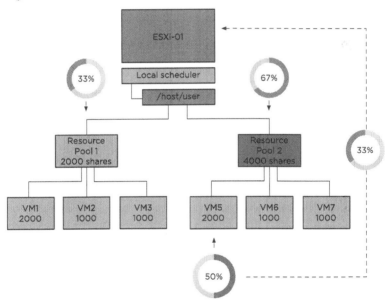

The host-local resource pool tree of ESXi-01 is updated with Resource Pool 2; Resource Pool 2 is configured with twice the number of shares as Resource Pool 1. Introducing 4000 more shares increases the total number of shares to 6000. Since Resource Pool 2 owns 4000 of the total of 6000, it gets 66.6 percent of the ESXi host's resources.

Due to the 67%- 33% ratio at resource pool level, the local resource scheduler will allocate more resources to Resource Pool 2 when contention occurs. The resources allocated to Resource Pool 2 are distributed across the virtual machines based on their hierarchical level (sibling rivalry). This means that virtual machine VM5 is entitled to 50% of Resource Pool 2's resources during contention; this translates to 33% of the ESXi host's resources.

The Resource Allocation tab of clusters or resource pools contains the %shares column. This column displays the percentage of resources assigned to the object. This value is related to the total shares issued by the parent and therefore applies only to that particular hierarchical level.

To emphasize, the example used virtual machines with equal and stable workloads. During normal conditions, some virtual machines have a higher utilization than others. As the active resource utilization is part of the dynamic entitlement calculation, active workload is taken into consideration when dividing the resource pool shares and resources across hosts and local resource pool trees.

Furthermore, virtual machine utilization often changes and usually affects the resource distribution after each DRS invocation.

Resource Pool-Level Reservation

Setting reservation guarantees permanent availability of physical resources to the resource pool. Because reservations are applied before shares, resources protected by a reservation are not reclaimed during contention. Setting a reservation at resource pool-level ensures that the reserved resources are available for its child-objects.

Reservations associated with a resource pool apply to all the virtual machines within the resource pool collectively. Resource pool-level reservations do not implicitly define a reservation at the child-object layer, but rather "lends out" a portion of the protected resource. Because a resource pool reservation does not become a static setting on the child-object, the amount of resources protected by the reservation can fluctuate for each child object from time to time.

The resource pool reservations are divided amongst its children based on the dynamic entitlement of each child-object. Described in chapter 12, dynamic entitlement is based on the configured size, resource allocation settings, demand and the level of contention.

Because it is based on dynamic entitlement, the activity and level of contention play a big part in the acquisition of protected resources. By using the virtual machine's dynamic entitlement, resource pool reservations have a dynamic nature and are more in line with the concept of consolidation and fairness. Reserved resources are divided among the virtual machines that require them; unused resources will flow back to the resource pool, ready to be used by other virtual machines.

Let's take a closer look at this behavior. A memory reservation is set at 12GB on Resource Pool 1. Resource Pool 1 contains 4 virtual machines, each configured with 4GB of memory and no virtual machine reservation. VM2 and VM3 are configured with a Low share level, VM1 has a Normal share level, while VM4 is configured with a High share level. Figure 76 shows the distribution of protected memory from the resource pool to each single virtual machine at 08:00. VM1 and VM3 are rather busy, while VM2 and VM4 are each running a very light workload.

Figure 76: Distribution of resource pool reservation at 08:00

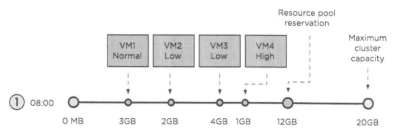

Although VM3 is configured with a Low share level, the availability of resources and the lack of contention allow VM3 to receive 4GB of protected memory. In other words, all of its memory pages are stored in physical memory.

Figure 77 shows the same environment at 11:00. At that particular time, VM1, VM3 and VM4 are highly utilized. The reserved memory owned by the resource pool is divided based on share level and utilization of each virtual machine. This means that the resource pool distributes the most memory to VM4 due to its High share level, VM1 gets 3GB according to its resource demand, the rest of the reserved memory is divided between VM2 and VM3. As VM3 is highly utilized, its dynamic entitlement is higher than that of VM2 and therefore VM3 can allocate 3GB of reserved resources.

Figure 77: Distribution of resource pool reservation at 11:00

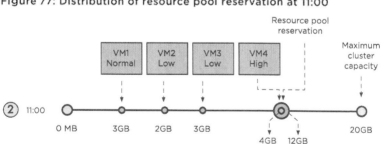

At 19:00 (Figure 78), all systems are idle, except VM2, which is running a backup operation. All memory required is distributed to VM2 while the resource pool has enough reserved memory available satisfy the dynamic entitlement of the other virtual machines.

Figure 78: Distribution of resource pool reservation at 19:00

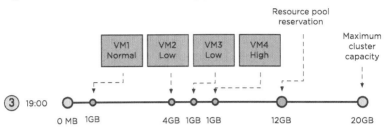

The dynamic nature of resource pool reservation might not be suitable for certain virtual machines: virtual machine-level reservations are more suitable if guaranteed availability of physical resources is required.

Child-Object-Level Reservation Inside a Resource Pool

If a child-object inside a resource pool is configured with a reservation, that reservation is left untouched by DRS. DRS relies upon host-level scheduling and host-level resource pools to implement DRS-level resource pools and to enforce resource pool and virtual machine-level resource settings. DRS passes virtual machine-level reservations straight through to the host, where the host-level CPU and memory schedulers enforce the reservation.

Any virtual machine-level reservation is withdrawn from the resource pool-level reservation amount and reduces the amount of reserved resources available to its siblings. Physical resources allocated by the virtual machine reservation are available only for that virtual machine and will not be shared with siblings or virtual machines and resource pools external to the parent resource pool.

Figure 79: Virtual Machine reservation

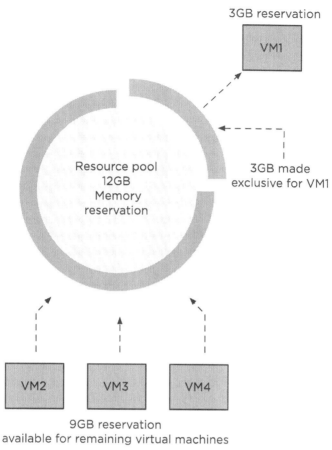

Basic design principle

Set per-virtual machine reservations only if a virtual machine absolutely requires guaranteed resources.

Activation of Reservation

Virtual machine reservations only take effect when a virtual machine is powered on. A resource pool-level reservation applies from the moment it is set, regardless of child virtual machines' activity. Because of this instant activation, the reservation immediately reduces the amount of unreserved resources in the pool.

Neither DRS nor the VMkernel will power on a virtual machine if its reservation cannot be honored. In addition to virtual machine-level reservations, the VMkernel requires unreserved memory to host the memory overhead of each virtual machine. Configuring resource pool-level reservations can impact the consolidation ratio of virtual machines in the cluster.

Basic design principle

We recommend to right-size resource pool-level reservations to avoid unnecessary reduction of the pool of unreserved resources. Adjust resource pool-level reservations according to the requirements of the current virtual machines.

Memory Overhead Reservation

For each running virtual machine, ESXi reserves physical memory for its virtualization overhead. ESXi requires this extra space for the internal VMkernel data structures like virtual machine frame buffer and mapping table for memory translation (mapping physical virtual machine memory to machine memory). Two kinds of virtual machine overheads exist:

Static Overhead

Static overhead is the minimum overhead that is required for the virtual machine to startup. DRS and the host-local memory scheduler use this metric for Admission Control and vMotion calculations. The destination ESXi host must be able to accommodate the sum of the virtual machine reservation and the static overhead otherwise the vMotion will fail.

Dynamic Overhead

Once a virtual machine has started up, the virtual machine monitor (VMM) can request additional memory space. The VMM will request the space, but the VMkernel is not required to supply it. If the VMM does not obtain the extra memory space, the virtual machine will continue to function but this could lead to performance degradation. The VMkernel treats overhead reservation the same as virtual machine-level memory reservation and it will not reclaim this memory once it has been used.

To power-up virtual machines in the resource pool, a pool of reserved resources needs to be available. If no resource pool-level reservation is set, the resource pool is required to allocate unreserved resources from its parent. To allow resource pools to retrieve unreserved resources, enable the Expandable Reservation setting on the resource pool.

Memory Overhead Reservation Impact

The total amount of unreserved resources required to power-up a virtual machine consist of virtual machine-level reservation (if set) plus the *memory overhead reservation*. Admission control will prevent power-up of a virtual machine if the required amounts of unreserved resources are not available.

Basic design principle

Memory overhead reservations need to be taken into account while designing the cluster and resource pool structure.

The *vSphere Resource Management* guide lists the overhead memory of virtual machines. The table listed below is an excerpt from the Resource Management guide and lists the most common ones.

Table 17: Virtual machine memory overhead

Memory (MB)	1 vCPU	2 vCPU	4 vCPU	8 vCPU
256	20.29	24.28	32.23	48.16
1024	25.90	29.91	37.86	53.82
4096	48.64	52.72	60.67	76.78
16384	139.62	143.98	151.93	168.60

The improvement in reducing memory overhead from version 4.1 to 5.x is enormous, for example an 8 vCPU virtual machine with 4096MB vRAM would consume on average a memory overhead of 561.52MB. In vSphere 5 the overhead is down to 76.78MB.

Please be aware of the fact that memory overheads may vary with each new release of ESXi, so keep this in mind when upgrading to a new version. Verify the documentation of the virtual machine memory overhead and check the specified memory reservation on the resource pool.

Memory Overhead Reservation Appears as Resource Pool Reservation

When a virtual machine is powered on, the memory overhead reservation is added to the total amount of resource pool reservation. If a resource pool is configured without a reservation, the total amount of memory overhead reservation is displayed in the resource pool summary.

Size by Numbers

Although the VMkernel requires a small amount of memory to satisfy the memory overhead reservation of a virtual machine, a large amount of memory can be required when running many virtual machines. Right sizing virtual machines can save a lot of reserved and non-shareable memory.

Expandable Reservation

The *Expandable Reservation* option allows a resource pool to acquire unreserved resources from its parents to satisfy virtual machine-level and memory overhead reservations.

If the *Expandable Reservation* setting is enabled, Admission Control considers the capacity in the parent resource pool tree available for satisfying VM-level reservations. If the *Expandable Reservation* setting is not enabled, Admission Control considers only the available resources of the resource pool to satisfy the reservation.

Figure 80: Expandable reservation workflow

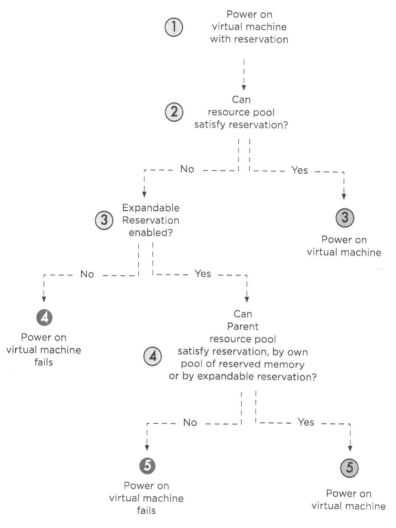

To verify whether the resource pool can satisfy the reservations, add the virtual machine-level reservations and static overhead reservations of every active virtual machine in the resource pool. The result of the calculation cannot exceed the resource-pool level reservation, unless Expandable is checked.

Traversing the Parent Tree

Admission Control only considers unreserved resources from parents, not siblings. The search for unreserved capacity halts at a resource pool configured with a limit or if Expandable Reservation is not enabled. If the requested capacity would allocate more resources than the limit of the parent resource pool specifies, the request is rejected, and the virtual machine will not be started.

Figure 81: Traversing the parent tree

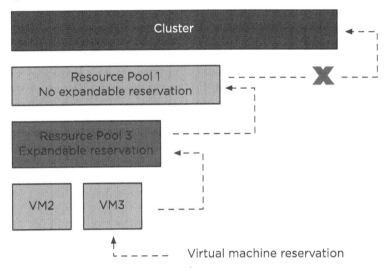

Basic design principle

In order to have available reserved memory to satisfy memory overhead reservations, enable *Expandable Reservation* if no reservations are set at the resource pool-level.

Reservations are not Limits.

A reservation at the resource pool-level defines the amount of protected physical resources; it does not define the maximum amount of available physical resources. Child-objects are able to allocate resources beyond the specified reservation, however allocating additional resources is based on share value and this will not guarantee that the required resources are available for use.

Figure 82: Reservation and shares

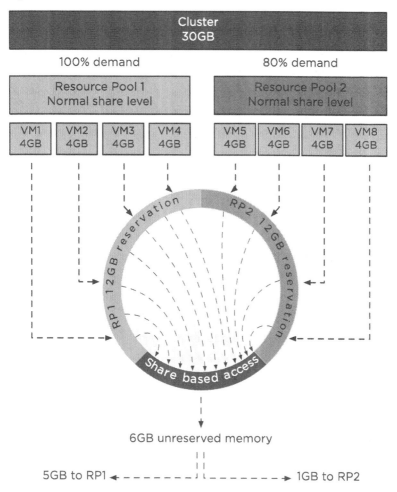

Reservations and Shares

In Figure 82, Resource Pool 1 has a 12GB memory reservation configured, but the total amount of configured memory of its virtual machines is greater than the reservation (Configured memory + memory overhead reservation = +/- 17 GB). The maximum amount of memory that Resource Pool 1 can allocate is a total of the combined configured memory of all virtual machines plus their memory overhead reservations.

Resource Pool 1 is configured with 12GB memory reservation, relying on the shares to obtain the remaining 5 GB to satisfy resource demand of the virtual machines inside the pool. Both resource pools have an equal amount of shares, providing them with equal chances of obtaining resources. Due to the difference in activity of virtual machines, Resource Pool 1 receives 5 GB, while Resource Pool 2 receives 1GB. Although it appears equal distribution based on shares is not the case in this scenario, both resource pools get the resources they require, as 80% demand of 16GB equals to 12.8GB.

Limits

A limit defines the maximum amount of available physical resources that can be allocated. Limits are an excellent way of specifying a boundary with regards to physical resource utilization of objects. The limit prohibits a resource pool from allocating more physical resources than the configured amount, even when they are available. Setting limits on resource pools or virtual machines can not only affect the performance of the virtual machines, but may also negatively affect the rest of the environment.

Limits associated with a resource pools apply to all the child-objects within the resource pool collectively. Resource pool-level limits do not implicitly define a limit at the child-object layer, but rather adjust the maximum amount of resources any child object can utilize. Because a resource pool limit does not become a static setting on the child-object, the availability of resources capped by the limit can fluctuate for each child object from time to time. Meaning that the dynamic entitlement of a virtual machine can fluctuated depending on the level of contention inside the resource pool.

The resource pool limits are divided amongst its children based on the dynamic entitlement of each child-object. Mentioned in chapter 12, dynamic entitlement is based on the configured size, resource allocation settings, demand and the level of contention. Because allocation is based on dynamic entitlement, actual activity and level of contention play a big part in the availability of resources.

Limits, Reservations and Memory Overhead Reservation

A limit must be equal to or exceed the configured reservation. If virtual machines are configured with a reservation, that reservation is directly subtracted from the resource pool unreserved memory pool. In order to power-on a virtual machine vCenter must be able to reserve the defined amount of reserved memory plus the memory overhead of the virtual machine.

Basic design principle

When calculating the limit on a resource pool, take both reservations and memory overhead reservations into account.

Expandable Reservation and Limits

As explained in the previous section, *Expandable Reservation* is used to allocate unreserved memory for virtual machine reservations and virtual machine memory overhead reservations on behalf of the virtual machines inside the resource pool. If the resource pool is unable to provide enough unreserved resources, it will traverse the ancestor tree to allocate sufficient unreserved resources.

However, when a limit is set at the resource pool level, the resource pool cannot allocate more physical resources than defined by its limit setting. Although the expandable reservation setting allows the resource pool to allocate additional unreserved resources, the limit parameter will prohibit the resource pool from allocating more physical resources than the configured limit.

Chapter 14

Calculating DRS Recommendations

DRS takes several metrics into account when calculating migration recommendations to load balance the cluster: the current resource demand of the virtual machines, host resource availability and high-level resource policies. The following section explores how DRS uses these metrics to create a new and better placement of virtual machines than the current location of the virtual machines, while still satisfying all the requirements and constraints.

When is DRS Invoked?

DRS is invoked every 300 seconds by default. When the invocation interval expires, DRS will compute and generate recommendations to migrate virtual machines. Each recommendation that is not applied is retired at the next invocation of DRS; DRS might generate the exact recommendation again if the imbalance is not solved.

The interval in which the DRS algorithm is invoked can be controlled through the vpxd configuration file (vpxd.cfg) with the following option:

vpxd config file

```
<config>
 <drm>
  <pollperiodsec>
  300
  </pollperiodsec>
 </drm>
</config>
```

The default frequency is 300 seconds, but can be set to anything in the range of 60 seconds to 3600 seconds. Changing this value from its default is strongly discouraged. A less frequent interval might reduce the number of vMotions and therefore overhead but would risk leaving the cluster imbalanced for a longer period of time. Shortening the interval will likely generate extra overhead, while providing little additional benefit.

The DRS imbalance calculation is also triggered if the cluster detects changes in its resource pool tree, operations and events such as changes in resource supply, or modification of resource settings.

Table 18: Events invoking DRS calculations

Change in resource supply	Change in resource demand	Resource setting changed
A host was added to the cluster	When a virtual machine is transitioned from powered-on to powered-off	Resource settings of a virtual machine or a resource pool are changed
Host has maintenance mode status change.		A resource pool or a virtual machine is moved into or out of the resource pool hierarchy

Recommendation Calculation

DRS performs multiple calculations and passes in order to generate migration recommendations. DRS determines the cluster imbalance and makes a selection of suitable virtual machines to migrate in order to solve the imbalance.

Constraints Correction

Prior to determining the current load imbalance, DRS checks for constraint violations. The constraint correction pass determines whether DRS needs to:

- Evacuate hosts that the user requested to enter Maintenance or Standby mode.
- Correct Mandatory VM-Host affinity/anti-affinity rule violations.
- Correct VM/VM anti-affinity rules violations.
- Correct VM/VM affinity rules violations.
- Correct host resource overcommitment
  (Rare, since DRS is controlling resources).

These constraints are respected during load balancing. Understand that constraints may cause an imbalance, which may not be fixable while respecting these constraints. The imbalance information on the cluster summary page informs the administrator if an unfixable imbalance was identified.

Imbalance Calculation

To establish cluster imbalance, DRS compares the Current Hosts Load
Standard Deviation (CHLSD) metric to the Target Host Load Standard
Deviation (THLSD). If the CHLSD exceeds the THLSD, the cluster is
considered imbalanced.

Current Host Load Standard Deviation

DRS determines the Current Host Load Standard Deviation (CHLSD) by
computing the average and standard deviation of the normalized
entitlement across all active hosts in the cluster.

Normalized entitlement is the measure of the utilization of available capacity.
DRS receives the usage and demand of each virtual machine to compute its
dynamic entitlement then sums the entitlements of all virtual machines on
the host and divides this by the capacity of the host. The available capacity of
the host is the amount of resources remaining after subtracting the
resources required for running the virtualization layer.

$$Normalized\ entitlement = \frac{VM\ entitlements}{Capacity\ of\ host}$$

Because the virtual machine entitlement contains demand metrics, such as
%ready time for CPU and %idle for memory, the standard deviation of the
normalized entitlement is very similar to the state of a cluster that does not
experience contention.

Target Host Load Standard Deviation

The *Target Host Load Standard Deviation* (THLSD) is derived from the DRS
migration threshold, which defines the cluster imbalance tolerance level.

DRS Migration Threshold

The migration threshold determines the maximum value under which the
load imbalance is to be kept. The DRS migration threshold offers five levels,
ranging from Conservative to Aggressive.

Figure 83: Migration Threshold

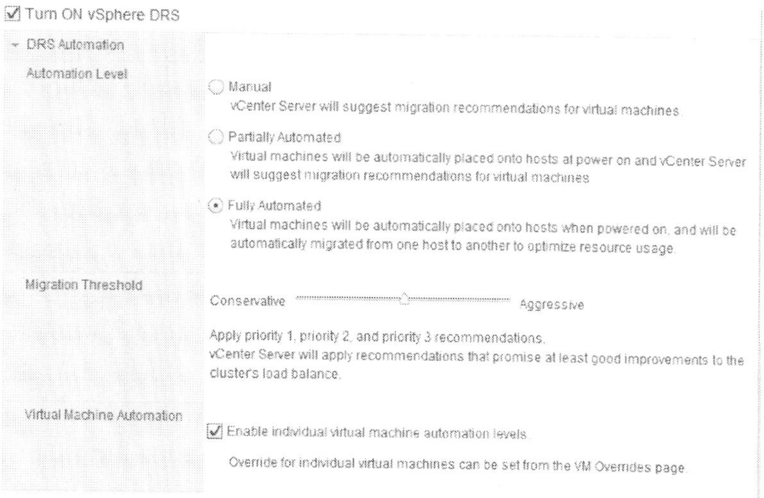

☑ Turn ON vSphere DRS

- DRS Automation

Automation Level

○ Manual
vCenter Server will suggest migration recommendations for virtual machines

○ Partially Automated
Virtual machines will be automatically placed onto hosts at power on and vCenter Server
will suggest migration recommendations for virtual machines

⊙ Fully Automated
Virtual machines will be automatically placed onto hosts when powered on, and will be
automatically migrated from one host to another to optimize resource usage

Migration Threshold

Conservative ———————————————— Aggressive

Apply priority 1, priority 2, and priority 3 recommendations.
vCenter Server will apply recommendations that promise at least good improvements to the
cluster's load balance.

Virtual Machine Automation

☑ Enable individual virtual machine automation levels

Override for individual virtual machines can be set from the VM Overrides page.

Each threshold level sets an imbalance tolerance margin. The Aggressive threshold sets a tight margin allowing for little imbalance, while the more conservative thresholds tolerate bigger imbalances. The most conservative threshold does not compute a THLSD and will only recommend mandatory moves to correct constraint violations. More information about thresholds can be found later in the chapter.
A higher frequency of migrations can be expected when selecting a more aggressive migration threshold as DRS is required to keep the CHLSD lower than the THLSD.

The metric *Current Host Load Standard deviation* is presented in vCenter, while CHLSD is often referred as the Load Imbalance Metric inside DRS. In the next section, Load Imbalance Metric is interchangeable with CHLSD.

Figure 84: DRS migration recommendation workflow

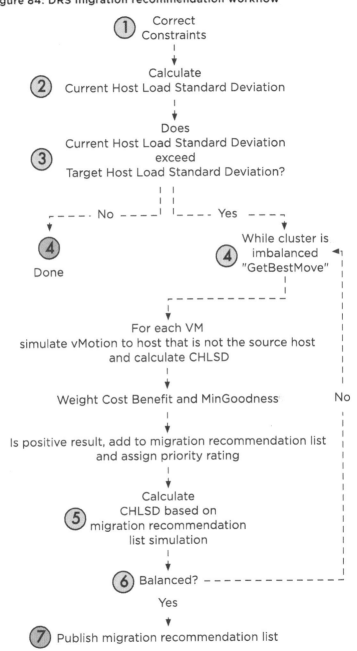

① Correct Constraints

② Calculate Current Host Load Standard Deviation

③ Does Current Host Load Standard Deviation exceed Target Host Load Standard Deviation?

No — ④ Done

Yes — ④ While cluster is imbalanced "GetBestMove"

For each VM simulate vMotion to host that is not the source host and calculate CHLSD

Weight Cost Benefit and MinGoodness

Is positive result, add to migration recommendation list and assign priority rating

⑤ Calculate CHLSD based on migration recommendation list simulation

⑥ Balanced?

No

Yes

⑦ Publish migration recommendation list

If the Current Hosts Load Standard Deviation exceeds the Target Hosts Load Standard Deviation, DRS will initiate the *GetBestMove*.

DRS procedure

```
while (load imbalance metric > threshold) {
move = getbestmove();
if no good migration is found:
stop;
else:
add move to the list of recommendations;
update representation of cluster to the state after the move is added; }
```

Contrary to popular belief, the algorithm adds all the recommendations to the list before allowing vCenter or the user to execute the recommendations list.

GetBestMove

The *GetBestMove* procedure aims to find the virtual machine that will give the best improvement in the cluster wide imbalance. The *GetBestMove* procedure consists of the following instructions:

GetBestMove

```
GetBestMove() {
for each virtual machine v:
 for each host h that is not source host:
  if h is lightly loaded compared to source host:
   if cost-benefit and risk analysis accepted
    simulate move v to h
    measure new cluster-wide load imbalance metric as g
    return move v that gives least cluster-wide imbalance g.
}
```

This procedure determines which migration offers the most improvement. DRS cycles through each DRS-enabled virtual machine and each host that is not the source host. The source host is the ESXi host currently running the virtual machine under consideration. DRS compares the normalized entitlement of the source host to each destination host. Hosts with a lower normalized entitlement are selected for further simulations.

After the *GetBestMove* is completed and the result is positive, DRS will select a host from the previous normalized entitlement selection and simulate a migration. DRS computes the possible CHLSD of both hosts after the simulated migration and, if they still exceed the DRS Migration threshold, DRS repeats the procedure but selects a different target host. This procedure is repeated for every VM-to-host combination. The migration recommendation lists the migrations that result in the biggest reduction in load imbalance.

Basic design principle

When sizing vCenter take into account the number of clusters and virtual machines. DRS migration calculations for large numbers of virtual machines can impact the performance of vCenter.

Cost-Benefit and Risk Analysis Criteria

The purpose of the cost-benefit and risk analysis is to filter out expensive and unstable migrations. The term "unstable migration" indicates the effect of the migration on the cluster load balance and examines the stability of the workload pattern of the virtual machine. Please note it does not imply the vMotion process itself is unstable.

DRS invokes a cost-benefit risk analysis to throttle migrations and avoid a constant stream of vMotions. Both the source and destination hosts incur costs when performing a vMotion and constantly initiating vMotions can nullify the benefit of migrating a virtual machine.

The cost benefit and risk analysis also prevents spiky workloads from affecting the recommendations. If a virtual machine's workload changes directly after the recommendation, the recommendation becomes useless and creates a situation where the virtual machine is selected over and over again, resulting in "Ping-Pong" migrations.

Cost

The vMotion process will reserve 30% of a CPU core if a 1Gb connection is used. If 10Gb is available to the vMotion Portgroup, it will reserve 100% of a CPU core. This reservation is set to a host-local resource pool and is created on both source and destination hosts. If multiple vMotions are running, this reservation is shared between the vMotion tasks. A shadow virtual machine is created on the destination host during the vMotion process; the memory consumption of this shadow virtual machine is also factored into the cost of the recommendation.

Benefit

By moving a virtual machine, resources on the source host are released and made available for other virtual machines. The migrated virtual machine benefits due to the lower *normalized entitlement* on its new host. The migration of workloads identified by DRS will result in a much more balanced cluster.

If any host is overcommitted on a particular resource, DRS will give a higher benefit weight to that resource for all migrations. For example, if contention occurs primarily on CPU, DRS will apply a higher benefit weight on CPU to resolve contention. DRS re-examines overcommitment on a particular resource during each invocation.

Risk

Risk accounts for the possibility of irregular loads. Irregular load indicates inconsistent and spiky demand workloads.

Combining the Cost Benefit Risk

DRS recommends migrations for rebalancing if their estimated cost is lower than their potential benefit with respect to current and recent VM demand and to the relative imbalance between hosts. DRS combines the cost benefits and risk to compute a new placement of virtual machines that satisfies all constraints and improves load balance.

The cost-benefit and risk analysis determines the *resource gain* of a migration, whether positive or negative. To determine if a migration will likely have a positive result, the workload characteristics of the virtual machine over the last 5 minutes are analyzed. This is called the "stable time" and indicates how long the virtual machine has used resources similar to the active workload metric. A conservative estimation is used for the remaining time within the invocation period (invocation period duration – stable time). DRS assumes the virtual machine runs at its worst possible load and uses the peak value from the last 60 minutes.

DRS includes the cost of migration and considers the resource gain of both the source and destination hosts. DRS will only recommend a migration if the cost-benefit and risk analysis produces a positive result.

You can imagine what kind of impact adjusting the invocation interval would have on this analysis because the net resource gain is calculated for each of the periods and weighted by the length of the period. We do not recommend changing this interval unless you understand the full impact of that change.

MinGoodness

Besides the Cost Benefit analysis, DRS calculates a Goodness value for each move. This value indicates the positive or negative effect of a move on the load balance of the cluster. For both the Cost Benefit and Goodness metrics, DRS uses the same rating system:

Table 19: Rating system

Rating	Description
-2	Strongly reject
-1	Accept only if the other metric is rated strongly accept.
0	Neutral, leave the decision to the other metric.
+1	Accept, if the other metric is neutral or above.
+2	Strongly accept, reject only if other metric rating is definitely reject.

Each move gets a Goodness rating that is related to current load balance and the minimum migration threshold. If a move will severely hurt the load balance, the move will receive a rating of -2. A move that slightly reduces the load balance gets a -1 rating. One that improves the load balance but does not improve it enough to reach the minimum threshold receives a neutral rating. A move that improves the load balance slightly (0.1) receives a +1 rating. Moves with a Goodness rating of +2 improve the load balance by a significant amount.

As mentioned before, DRS uses the same values to weight the Cost Benefit of a move. These ratings are applied as follows: A move that reduces resource availability by at least 10% receives a -2 rating. A move that could have a slight decrease in resource availability receives a value of -1. If a move has a neutral effect on resource availability, i.e., it doesn't hurt or help, will receive a 0 value. If a move improves resource availability, a +1 rating is awarded, while a move that improves resource availability by at least 10% receives a +2 rating.

Before presenting the recommendations, the Goodness ratings are compared to the Cost Benefit ratings. As the Cost-benefit algorithm is more conservative than the Goodness algorithm, it is highly unlikely to see DRS recommend moves with a neutral or less Goodness rating. Therefore, recommendations made by DRS are usually moves with positive Cost Benefit and Goodness ratings.

Filtering moves by Goodness (MinGoodnessFiltering) and Cost Benefit (CostBenefitFiltering) could prevent DRS from recommending moves when a cluster is severely imbalanced. A cluster is regarded as severely imbalanced when any host's load differs more than 0.2 from the target host load deviation.

If you notice that DRS is not recommending any load balancing moves in your environment, it could be that each move has a too little impact on the cluster imbalance. It is possible that no possible move significantly improve the cluster wide balance (controlled by the MinGoodnessFiltering), or that the moves which improve the cluster wide imbalance have costs that are too high (controlled by the CostBenefitFiltering).

To solve this situation, DRS in vSphere 5.1 is equipped with three additional steps in the load-balancing algorithm. These steps are RelaxMinGoodness, RelaxCostBenfitFiltering and DropCostBenefitFiltering. How does this work?

Table 20: DRS invocation Steps

		Cost Benefit Ratings				
		-2	-1	0	1	2
Goodness Ratings	-2	R	R	R	R	R
	-1	R	R	R	R	R
	0	DCB	RCB	RMG	A	A
	1	DCB	RCB	A	A	A
	2	DCB	A	A	A	A

During normal operations, moves with neutral or negative Goodness ratings will be rejected (R); however, they can be reconsidered and accepted (A) if the cluster remains severely imbalanced. If the cluster remains severely imbalanced after the DRS load balancing step, and if the load balancing operation was not limited by the migration limit (MaxMovesPerHost), load balancing is re-run with the RelaxMinGoodness (RMG) flag activated. This means that a DRS considers recommending moves with a neutral goodness and cost-benefit rating previously dropped by MinGoodNessFiltering.

If the analysis shows that the cluster remains severely imbalanced, even after considering moves that improve the cluster-wide balance in a small - but still positive way, DRS sets the RelaxCostBenefitFiltering (RCB) flag. In this situation, moves are considered that would improve load balance on a small to medium scale, even if they have a slightly negative Cost Benefit value. If these additional moves do not solve the severe imbalance, DRS sets the DropCostBenefit (DCB) flag and considers moves that would have been strongly rejected during normal load balancing runs.

This new feature may result in DRS generating more moves than it would have in pre-vSphere 5.1 environments, but please note that these additional moves will only appear if the cluster is in state of severe imbalance. In essence, this feature is an automated way of implementing the manual workaround of setting minGoodness=0 and costBenefit=0. However, DRS applies this mechanism only during states when it's absolutely necessary; enabling these settings manually could possibly hurt virtual machine performance.

Calculating the Migration Recommendation Priority Level

The migration threshold specifies the tolerance of imbalance of the Current Host Load Standard Deviation (CHLSD) relating to the Target Host Load Standard Deviation (THLSD). The migration threshold factor is configured via the DRS setting on cluster level. To make the migration threshold setting more understandable, priority levels were introduced to exemplify which level of tolerance is used to generate migration recommendations.

During its calculations, DRS assigns a priority level to each recommendation and this priority level is compared to the migration threshold. If the priority level is less than or equal to the migration threshold, the recommendation is displayed or applied, depending on the automation level of the cluster. If the priority level is above the migration threshold, the recommendations are either not displayed or discarded. You can think of the migration threshold as a filter for recommendations generated by DRS.

Level 1 (conservative)

When selecting the conservative migration threshold level, only mandatory moves, priority-one recommendations, are executed. This means that the DRS cluster will not invoke any load-balancing migrations. Mandatory moves are issued when:

- The ESXi host enters maintenance mode
- The ESXi host enters standby mode
- An (anti-) affinity rule is violated
- The sum of the reservations of the virtual machines exceeds the capacity of the host.

It is possible that a mandatory move will cause a violation on another host. If this happens, DRS will move virtual machines to fix the new violation at the next DRS invocation. This scenario is possible when multiple rules exist on the cluster. It is not uncommon to see several migrations required to satisfy the configured DRS rules.

Level 2 (moderately conservative)

The level 2-migration threshold only applies priority-one and priority-two recommendations, priority two recommendations promise a very good improvement in the cluster's load balance.

Level 3 (moderate)

The level 3-migration threshold is the default migration threshold when creating DRS clusters. The moderate migration threshold applies priority-one, -two and priority-three recommendations, promising a good improvement in the cluster's load balance.

Level 4 (moderately aggressive)

The level 4-migration threshold applies all recommendations up to priority level four. Priority-four recommendations promise a moderate improvement in the cluster's load balance.

Level 5 (aggressive)

The level 5 migration threshold is the right-most setting on the migration threshold slider and applies all five priority level recommendations; every recommendation which promises even a slight improvement in the cluster's load balance is applied.

Guidance

A level 1 recommendation should always be applied, but a list of several priority level 5 recommendations could also collectively improve the cluster if those recommendations are applied.

Unnecessary migrations can occur while using an aggressive migration threshold in a cluster that hosts virtual machines running inconstant workloads.

A moderate migration threshold is more suitable in such a scenario. Aggressive thresholds, level 4 and 5 are considered suitable for clusters with equal-sized hosts running relatively constant workload demands.

Basic design principle

The default moderate migration threshold provides a higher tolerance for migrations, while offering sufficient balance. The algorithm considers the configured threshold and creates only recommendations that are worthwhile according to the tolerance. The default setting is typically aggressive enough to maintain workload balance across hosts without creating unnecessary overhead caused by too-frequent migrations.

Chapter 15

Guiding DRS Recommendations

Some DRS settings and features can influence the DRS migration recommendations. This chapter takes a closer look at the various settings and the impacts they can have on the DRS calculations and load balancing process.

Virtual Machine Size and Initial Placement

When a virtual machine is powered on, DRS selects a target host where the virtual machine should be initially placed. DRS prefers the registered host as long as the placement of the virtual machine on this host will not cause a cluster imbalance. During initial placement, DRS applies a worst-case scenario because it does not have historical data of the resource utilization of the virtual machine. DRS assumes that both the memory demand and CPU demand is equal to its configured size.

Virtual machines that are oversized can introduce a temporary cluster imbalance and cause pointless migrations of active virtual machine. If none of the cluster members is able to provide the full 100% of the resources requested DRS will defragment the cluster's resources, migrating virtual machines to make room.

If the actual utilization of a virtual machine is comparable to its configured size, the additional migrations are expected behavior as they will help the cluster reach a balanced state as quickly as possible. However, if a virtual machine is oversized (its active utilization does not compare to DRS's initial expectation), a number of migrations throughout several DRS rounds may be required to rebalance the cluster.

We are aware that many organizations still size their virtual machines based on assumed peak loads happing in the (late) life cycle of that service or application. This is similar to the policy historically used for sizing physical machines. One of the benefits of using virtual machines is the flexibility it offers with regards to resizing a machine during its lifecycle. We recommend leveraging these mechanisms and incorporating this into your service catalog and daily operations. In order to most effectively utilize your resources, size a virtual machine according to its current or near-future workload.

Basic design principle
Size a virtual machine according to its current or near-future workload.

MaxMovesPerHost

DRS evaluates the cluster and recommends migrations based on demand and cluster balance state. This process is repeated each invocation period. To minimize CPU and memory overhead, DRS limits the number of migration recommendations per DRS invocation period. Ultimately, there is no advantage recommending more migrations than can be completed within a single invocation period. On top of that, the demand could change after an invocation period which would render the previous recommendations obsolete.

vCenter calculates the limit per host based on the average time per migration, the number of simultaneous vMotions and the length of the DRS invocation period (*PollPeriodSec*).

PollPeriodSec: By default, *PollPeriodSec* – the length of a DRS invocation period – is 300 seconds, but can be set to any value between 60 and 3600 seconds. Shortening the interval will likely increase the overhead on vCenter due to additional cluster balance computations. This also reduces the number of allowed vMotions due to a smaller time window, resulting in longer periods of cluster imbalance. Increasing the *PollPeriodSec* value decreases the frequency of cluster balance computations on vCenter and allows more vMotion operations per cycle. Unfortunately, this may also leave the cluster in a longer state of cluster imbalance due to the prolonged evaluation cycle.

Simultaneous vMotions: Mentioned in the supporting deepdive about vMotion, vSphere 5.1 allows you to perform 8 concurrent vMotions on a single host with 10GbE capabilities. For 1GbE, the limit is 4 concurrent vMotions. However, vSphere 5.1 contains multi-NIC vMotion support: assigning multiple active NICs to the vMotion portgroup allows vMotion to leverage the available bandwidth for vMotion operations. Even a single vMotion can utilize all available NICs to decrease the amount of time required for a vMotion.

Estimated total migration time: DRS considers the average migration time observed from previous migrations. The average migration time depends on many variables, such as source and destination host load, active memory in the virtual machine, link speed, available bandwidth and latency of the physical network used by the vMotion process.

Basic design principle

When designing a DRS cluster, take the requirements of vMotion into account. By providing enough bandwidth, the cluster can reach a balanced state more quickly, resulting in better resource allocation (performance) for the virtual machines.

Rules

To control virtual machine placement, vSphere 5.1 offers both *Virtual Machine to Virtual Machine* (VM-VM) rules and *Virtual Machine to Host* (VM-Host) rules.

- VM-VM affinity rules specify whether virtual machines should stay together and run on the same hosts (affinity rules) or that they are not allowed to run on the same host (anti-affinity).

- A VM-Host affinity rule specifies whether the members of a *VM DRS group* can or should run on the members of a *Host DRS group*.

VM-VM Affinity Rules

A VM-VM affinity rule specifies which virtual machines should run on the same ESXi host.

Figure 85: Affinity rule

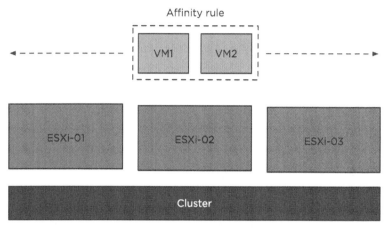

Affinity rules are useful to retain network traffic inside the virtual switch, reducing traffic on the physical network. For example, by keeping both the front-end and back-end servers of an application on the same host, internal application network traffic remains inside the virtual switch, reducing latency and decreasing load on physical network links and components.

Affinity rules are often recommended to realize greater benefit from memory consolidation: by containing multiple identical servers on the same ESXi host, transparent page sharing may reduce the overall amount of physical memory used. However, due to modern CPU architecture and onboard memory controller subsystems, memory savings might not be as great as anticipated. Today, almost any CPU architecture includes a *Non-Uniform Memory Architecture* (NUMA). NUMA provides separate memory for each processor, possibly resulting in different memory access times based on the relative locations of the memory and the processor being used. In order to avoid additional latency caused by cross-CPU memory access, ESXi will not share pages between two processors (NUMA nodes).

To expand further on memory management; if the ESXi hosts are equipped with recent AMD or Intel processor types, these processors offer hardware support for virtualization, such as Intel *Extended Page Tables* (EPT) and AMD *Rapid Virtualization Indexing* (RVI). These hardware extensions assist in memory management unit (MMU) virtualization, allowing the VMkernel to rely on hardware to keep track of the memory mappings inside the Guest OS. To optimize performance of synchronization between memory mappings inside the guest and the VMkernel; large pages are used to reduce the number of pages in these tables. A large page (2MB) is not shared by transparent page sharing (TPS) until the large page is broken down into small pages (4KB), and that only happens when the ESXi host has surpassed the free memory threshold. The free memory threshold is explained in chapter 13. Large Pages, NUMA and hardware virtualization assistance may reduce the effectiveness of TPS when applying VM-VM affinity rules for the purpose of optimizing memory consolidation.

VM-VM Anti-Affinity Rules

A VM-VM anti-affinity rule achieves the opposite of an affinity rule: it specifies which virtual machines are not allowed to run on the same host.

Figure 86: Anti-affinity rule

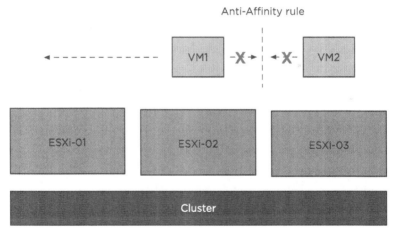

Anti-affinity rules can be used to offer host failure resiliency to services provided by multiple virtual machines; examples of such services are Active Directory domain controllers, DNS servers and web server farms. By running these virtual machines on separate hosts, it is possible to maintain service availability during an ESXi host failure.

Another example is separating virtual machines with network-intensive workloads. If they were to be placed on one host, they might saturate the host's networking capacity. Because DRS is unaware of network usage – it monitors CPU and memory demand – an anti-affinity rule resolves this problem by preventing DRS from placing them on the same host.

VM-VM Affinity Rules – impact on HA
Note that VMware HA is unaware of VM-VM affinity and anti-affinity rules. Following a host failure, VMware HA may restart the virtual machines on the same host, but DRS will correct this violation during the next invocation.

VM-VM Affinity Rules – impact on DRS
VM-VM affinity rules limit migration choices and place more constraints on virtual machine mobility. DRS will first obey affinity rules and correct constraint violations before determining optimal virtual machine placement to achieve cluster balance. In small clusters or large clusters with a large number of rules, this behavior can lead to sub-optimal cluster balance and resource allocation. Although DRS may temporarily violate VM-VM affinity rules if necessary for placement, it will correct the violation during the next invocation period if possible, probably affecting resource allocation again.

VM-Host Affinity Rules
A VM-Host affinity rule specifies whether virtual machines belonging to a virtual machine DRS group must (not) or should (not) run on the ESXi hosts in a host DRS group.

VM-Host affinity and anti-affinity can be configured as either mandatory rules, presented in the vSphere client as "*Must (not) run on*" or preferential rules, presented as "*Should (not) run on*".

Figure 87: VM-Host affinity rule

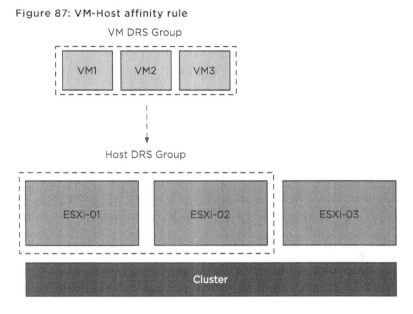

VM-Host affinity rules establish an association between a group of virtual machines and a group of ESXi hosts. Please note that virtual machines listed in the VM DRS group can independently run on the ESXi host listed in the Host DRS Group, they are not required to run all on the same host within the Host DRS Group – unless the host group contains only one host, of course.

Affinity VM-Host rules can be used to isolate virtual machines inside cluster-subsets of hosts to comply with ISV license regulations. A VM-Host Anti-affinity rule may be used to separate virtual machines across different failure domains for increased availability. An example of a failure domain could be a server blade chassis or hosts or sets of racks connected to the same power supplies. A VM-Host affinity rule consists of three components:

- Virtual machine DRS group
- Host DRS group
- Designation (i.e. Must/Should run on)

Note

VM-Host affinity rules apply to a specific cluster. Therefore they can only contain virtual machines and ESXi hosts belonging to that specific cluster.

Virtual machine DRS Group: The virtual machine DRS group contains the virtual machines to which the rule applies. Please note that if a virtual machine is removed from the cluster, it is automatically removed from the virtual machine DRS Group. However, the virtual machine is not automatically returned to the group if it is returned to the cluster.

Host DRS Group: The host DRS Group contains the ESXi hosts to which the rule applies. Similar to virtual machine behavior, if an ESXi host is removed from the cluster, it is automatically removed from the Host DRS Group. However, it is not automatically returned to the group if the host is returned to the cluster.

Designations: Two different types of VM-Host rules are available, a VM-Host affinity rule can either be a "*must*" rule or a "*should*" rule.

- **Should (not) run on:** The "should" rule is a **preferential** rule for DRS and DPM. DRS and DPM use best effort trying to satisfy these rules, but DRS and DPM can violate should rules if necessary.

- **Must (not) run on:** The "must"-rule is a **mandatory** rule for HA, DRS and DPM. It forces the specified virtual machines to run on or not run on the ESXi hosts specified in the ESXi host DRS Group.

Preferential Rules

Preferential rules are designed to influence DRS migration recommendations. DRS executes preferential rules if it does not over utilize the CPU or memory demand of the host. During load-balancing calculations, DRS runs the preferential rules. If they violate any other requirement, DRS drops the rule list and reinitializes a load-balance calculation without the preferential rules.

DRS does not provide any information regarding preferential rules to HA. Since HA is unaware of these "should" rules, it may unknowingly violate these rules during placement after a host failure. During the next DRS invocation cycle, DRS identifies the constraint and issues a (4 stars - priority 2) migration recommendation to correct this violation, if possible. Depending on the automation level of DRS, it will either display the recommendation or correct the situation itself.

Mandatory Rules

A mandatory rule applies to DRS, DPM, HA, and user-initiated operations. DRS takes the mandatory rules into account when generating or executing operations and will never produce any recommendations that violate the mandatory rule set. For example, DRS rejects the request for Maintenance Mode if it would violate a mandatory rule.

If a reservation is set on a virtual machine, DRS takes both the reservation and the mandatory rules into account. Both requirements must be satisfied during placement or power on. If DRS is unable to honor either one of the requirements, the virtual machine is not powered on or migrated to the proposed destination host.

When a mandatory rule is created and the current virtual machine placement is in violation of a rule, DRS corrects this violation or will report an error if the violation cannot be corrected.

It is important to realize that HA will not violate mandatory rules during virtual machine restart following a host failure; HA will failover virtual machines, if possible. If vCenter is available, HA will send an action list (which virtual machines needs to be failed over) to vCenter and will check periodically whether vCenter has freed up enough resources so that HA can handle the failover operations. If HA cannot restart the virtual machines after a configurable number of retries, it will generate an error.

A user operation, such as a vMotion of a virtual machine to a host external to the Host DRS Group, violates the mandatory rule and will fail with an error indicating host incompatibility.

Compliance with mandatory rules is deemed crucial and they are not removed when DRS is disabled. That bears repeating: **even after disabling DRS, mandatory rules will still be in effect for HA and user operations** and the cluster continues to track, report and alert if these mandatory rules are violated. For example if a vMotion operation would violate a mandatory rule, the cluster will reject the migration operation, citing *host incompatibility* as the reason. Mandatory rules can only be disabled if the administrator explicitly does so. If the administrator intends to disable DRS, he should remove mandatory rules before disabling DRS. Please note that once DRS is disabled, vCenter no longer displays the DRS options, prohibiting the user from viewing or managing the rules. When DRS is enabled once again, the rules will be displayed; disabling DRS does not permanently orphan the rules.

DPM does not place an ESXi host into standby mode if the result would violate a mandatory rule. Moreover, DPM will power-on ESXi hosts if these are needed to meet the requirements of the mandatory rules.

Mandatory rules place more constraints on virtual machine mobility, restricting the number of hosts a virtual machine can run on. In addition, HA and DPM operations are constrained as well. For example mandatory rules will:

- Limit DRS in selecting hosts to load-balance the cluster.
- Limit HA in selecting hosts to power up the virtual machines.
- Limit DPM in selecting hosts to power down.

Mandatory VM-Host affinity rules reduce the placement options for DRS when defragmenting the cluster. When HA "*Percentage based*" admission control is used, resource fragmentation can occur. During a failover, defragmentation of cluster resources can be requested by HA. To fulfill this request, DRS migrates virtual machines in order to free up enough resources to power-on all of the failed virtual machines. During defragmentation, DRS is allowed to use multi-hop migrations, which creates a chain of dependent migrations. For example, VM-A migrates to host 2 and VM-B migrates from host 2 to host 3. Mandatory rules reduce the options by allowing virtual machines to only move around within their associated DRS host groups.

A virtual machine that is a member of multiple mandatory rule sets is constrained to run only on the host(s) listed in both DRS host groups. For example rule 1 allows the VM2 to run on 4 hosts ESXi-01, -02, -03 and ESXi-04. Rule 2 allows the virtual machine to run on host ESXi-03, -04, -05 and ESXi-06. The net result is that the virtual machine is only allowed to run on the compatibility subset that contains ESXi-03 and ESXi-04.

Figure 88: Compatibility subset

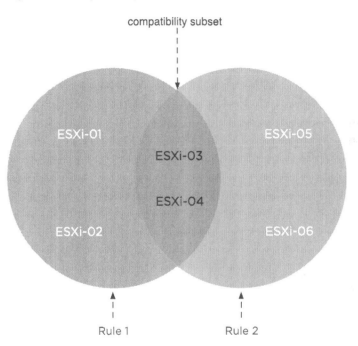

Rule Behavior

Mandatory rules must be obeyed and preferential rules are executed if they do not overcommit the host or cause constraint violations. This behavior can limit DRS in its goal to achieving a load-balanced cluster. As you can imagine, mandatory affinity rules can complicate troubleshooting in certain scenarios. For example, trying to determine why a virtual machine is not migrated from a highly utilized host to an alternative lightly utilized host in the cluster.

If a rule is created that conflicts with another active rule, the older rule overrides the newer rule and DRS will disable the new rule. When creating a new rule, a message indicating the conflicting rule will be displayed and the new rule will be visibly disabled.

Due to their limiting behavior, mandatory rules should be used sparingly and only for specific cases, such as licensing requirements. Preferential rules can be used to meet availability requirements such as separating virtual machines between blade enclosures or other failure domains.

Basic design principles

Use VM-Host and VM-VM affinity rules sparingly, as rules can have an impact on the effectiveness of the load balancing calculation; the DRS algorithm has less choice when rules are configured.

Mandatory affinity rules apply to DRS, HA and manual operations, even when DRS is disabled; use mandatory rules with caution.

Impact of Rules on Organization

Many users create rules but forget to create a backup or to document them. Anti-affinity rules can play an important role in meeting certain SLA or BC/DR requirements and creating a backup or documenting them seems appropriate. Using PowerCLI, the rules can easily be extracted from the vCenter database.

Virtual Machine Automation Level

Automation levels for individual virtual machines can be customized to override the DRS cluster automation level. There are five automation level modes:

- Fully Automated
- Partially Automated
- Manual
- Default (cluster automation level)
- Disabled

Each automation level behaves differently:

Table 21: Automation level DRS behavior

Automation level	Initial placement	Load Balancing
Fully Automated	Automatic Placement	Automatic execution of migration recommendation
Partially Automated	Automatic Placement	Migration recommendation is displayed
Manual	Recommended host is displayed	Migration recommendation is displayed
Disabled	VM powered-on on registered host	No migration recommendation generated

The default automation level is not listed in the table above as it aligns with the cluster automation level. When the automation level of the cluster is modified, the individual automation level is modified as well.

Disabled automation level
If the automation level of a virtual machine is set to disabled, then DRS operations are disabled for that specific virtual machine. DRS does not generate a migration recommendation or generate an initial placement recommendation. The virtual machine will be powered-on on its registered host. A powered-on virtual machine with its automation level set to disabled will still impact the DRS load balancing calculation as its consumes cluster resources. During the recommendation calculation, DRS ignores the virtual machines set to disabled automation level and selects other virtual machines on that host. If DRS must choose between virtual machines set to the automatic automation levels and the manual automation level, DRS chooses the virtual machines set to automatic as it prefers them over virtual machines set to manual.

Manual automation level
When a virtual machine is configured with the manual automation level, DRS generate both initial placement and load balancing migration recommendations, however the user needs to manual approve these recommendations.

Partially automation level
DRS automatically places a virtual machine with a partially automation level, however it will generate a migration recommendation which requires manual approval.

The impact of manual and partially automation level on cluster load balance

When selecting any other automation level than disabled, DRS assumes that the user will manual apply the migration recommendation it recommends. This means that DRS will continue to include the virtual machines in the analysis of cluster balance and resource utilization. During the analysis DRS simulates virtual machine moves inside the cluster, every virtual machine that is not disabled will be included in the selection process of migration recommendations. If a particular move of a virtual machine offers the highest benefit and the least amount of cost and lowest risk, DRS generates a migration recommendation for this move. Because DRS is limited to a specific number of migrations, it might drop a recommendation of a virtual machine that provide almost similar goodness. Now the problem with this scenario is, that the recommended migration might be a virtual machine configured with a manual automation level, while the virtual machine with near-level goodness is configured with the default automation level. This should not matter if the user monitors each and every DRS invocation and reviews the migration recommendations when issued. This is unrealistic to expect as DRS runs each 5 minutes.

We have seen a scenario where a group of the virtual machines where configured with manual mode. It resulted in a host becoming a "trap" for the virtual machines during an overcommitted state. The user did not monitor the DRS tab in vCenter and was missing the migration recommendations. This resulted in resource starvation for the virtual machines itself but even worse, it impacted multiple virtual machines inside the cluster. Because DRS generated migration recommendations, it dropped other suitable moves and could not achieve an optimal balance.

Disabled versus partially and manual automatic levels

Disabling DRS on a virtual machines have some negative impact on other operation processes or resource availability, such as placing a host into maintenance mode or powering up a virtual machine after maintenance itself. As it selects the registered host, it might be possible that the virtual machine is powered on a host with ample available resources while more suitable hosts are available. However disabled automation level avoids the scenario described in the previous paragraph.

Partially automatic level automatically places the virtual machine on the most suitable host, while manual mode recommends placing the host on the most suitable host available. Partially automated offers the least operational overhead during placement, but can together with manual automation level introduce lots of overhead during normal operations.

Risk versus reward
Selecting an automation level is almost a risk versus reward game. Setting the automation level to disabled might impact some operation procedures, but allows DRS to neglect the virtual machines when generating migration recommendations and come up with alternative solutions that provide cluster balance as well. Setting the automation level to partially or manual will offer you better initial placement recommendations and a more simplified maintenance mode process, but will create the risk of unbalance or resource starvation when the DRS tab in vCenter is left unmonitored.

Thoughts on Virtualized vCenter
Most admins like to keep track of the virtualized vCenter server in case a disaster happens. After a disaster occurs, for example a datacenter-wide power-outage, you only need to power-up the ESXi host on which the vCenter virtual machine is registered and then manually power-up the vCenter virtual machine.

An alternative to this method is keeping track of the datastore vCenter is placed on and then registering and powering on the virtual machine on a (random) ESXi host after the disaster. This is slightly more work than disabling DRS for the vCenter Server virtual machine, but it may offer better performance of vCenter during normal operations.

Due to expanding virtual infrastructures and additional features, vCenter is becoming more and more important for day-to-day operational management. Assuring good performance outweighs any additional effort necessary after a (hopefully) rare occasion, but both methods have merits.

Overall, you should select the automation level in accordance with your environment and level of comfort. Try to have virtual machines in DRS Fully Automated mode as much as possible, as DRS considers these virtual machines for cluster load balance migrations before the virtual machines not in Fully Automated mode.

Impact of VM Automation Level on DRS Load Balancing Calculation

Contrary to popular belief, a virtual machine set to Disabled automation level still impacts the calculation of the *Current Host Load Standard Deviation* as the sum of the active workload is divided through the capacity of the host. DRS does not need to be aware of virtual machine automation levels at that stage. During the recommendation calculation, DRS ignores virtual machines set to Disabled automation level and selects other virtual machines on that host. If DRS must choose between virtual machines set to the automatic automation levels and the Manual automation level, it chooses the virtual machines set to automatic as it prefers them over virtual machines set to Manual.

Chapter 16

Introduction to DPM

With VI 3.5, VMware introduced Distributed Power Management (DPM). DPM provides power savings by dynamically sizing the cluster capacity to match the virtual machine resource demand. DPM dynamically consolidates virtual machines onto fewer ESXi hosts and powers down excess ESXi hosts during periods of low resource utilization. If the resource demand increases, ESXi hosts are powered back on and the virtual machines are redistributed among all available ESXi hosts in the cluster.

Enable DPM

DPM is disabled by default and can be enabled by selecting the power management modes Manual or Automatic. DRS must be enabled first because of DPM's dependency on DRS for moving virtual machines around the cluster.

Figure 89: DPM settings

Power Management Automation Levels

DPM can be set to *Manual* or *Automatic* mode. All hosts inside the cluster will inherit the default cluster setting, but DPM settings can be configured on at the host-level as well. Host-level settings override the cluster default setting.

A reason for overriding DPM cluster default is virtual machine template placement. While DPM leverages DRS to migrate all active virtual machines on a host before powering it down, the registered templates are not moved. This means that templates registered on the ESXi host placed in standby mode will not be accessible as long as the host is in standby mode.

Basic design principle
Register templates on a single host and disable DPM on this host.

Each power management mode operates differently:

Disabled: No power recommendation will be issued.

Manual: A power recommendation will be generated; the user must manually confirm the recommendation.

Automatic: A power recommendation will be generated and will be executed automatically; no user intervention required.

DRS and DPM management modes are distinct and can differ from each other: DRS can be set to Automatic while DPM is set to Manual, or vice versa. Both DRS and DPM generate recommendations and each combination of management modes results in different behavior regarding initial placement and migration recommendations or operations. Keep in mind that certain combinations, while valid, do not make much sense to implement.

Table 22: Combining DPM and DRS

DPM level	DRS level	Effect
Manual	Manual	Recommendations generated for placement of virtual machines and power-on/off hosts; manual action required to apply all recommendations.
Manual	Automatic	Recommendations generated for power-on/off hosts; automatic placement of virtual machines.
Automatic	Manual	Recommendations generated for power-on/off hosts, but user must confirm virtual machine migrations before DPM will place ESXi host into standby mode. DPM will automatically power-up host if resources are needed.
Automatic	Automatic	Fully automatic placement of virtual machines and automatic power-on/off of ESXi hosts.

The goal of DPM is to keep the cluster utilization within a specific target range, but at the same time take various cluster settings, virtual machine settings and requirements into account when generating DPM recommendations. After DPM has determined the maximum number of hosts needed to handle the resource demand and HA requirements of the virtual machines, it leverages DRS to distribute the virtual machines across that number of hosts before placing the target ESXi hosts into standby mode.

Chapter 17

Calculating DPM Recommendations

DPM attempts to keep the resource utilization of each ESXi host in the cluster within a specified *Target Resource Utilization Range*, offering an optimum mix of resource availability and power savings. If the resource utilization of an ESXi host in the cluster is below the target resource utilization range, DPM will evaluate and provide power-off recommendations if deemed necessary. Conversely, if resource utilization is above the resource utilization target range, DPM provides power-on recommendation after evaluation

Evaluating Resource Utilization

DPM evaluates each ESXi host and calculates whether the CPU and memory resource utilization of the ESXi host is within the specified *target utilization range*. DPM computes the *target utilization range* as follows:

> Target Resource Utilization Range = DemandCapacityRatioTarget ± DemandCapacityRatioToleranceHost

Resource utilization: DPM calculates the resource utilization of an ESXi host based on the virtual machine demand and the available ESXi host capacity. The available capacity of a host is the amount of resources remaining after subtracting the resources required for running the virtualization layer. DPM calculates the resource demand as the sum of each active virtual machine over an historical period of interest plus two standard deviations. DPM uses different historical periods for recommending power-on recommendations than for calculating power-off recommendations. We will expand upon historical periods in a later section.

Similar to DRS, the calculation of demand is a combination of active usage plus unsatisfied demand during periods of contention. By using historical data over a longer period of time instead of using simply the current demand of active virtual machines, DPM ensures that an evaluated virtual machine demand is representative of the virtual machines' normal workload behavior. Using shorter periods of time may lead to unnecessary power state change recommendations. Not only does this impact the power-saving efficiency, it impacts DRS as it will try to load-balance the active virtual machines across a constantly changing landscape of available hosts.

DemandCapacityRatioTarget is the utilization target of the ESXi host. By default this is set at 63%.

DemandCapacityRatioToleranceHost specifies the tolerance around the utilization target for each host, by default this is set at 18%.

This means that DPM attempts to keep the ESXi host resource utilization centered at the 63% sweet spot, plus or minus 18 percent. This results in a range between 45 and 81 percent. The sweet spot of 63 percent is based on in-house testing and feedback from customers. If the ESXi hosts' resource utilization of each resource is below 45%, DPM evaluates power-off operations. If the resource utilization exceeds the 81% of either CPU or memory resources, DPM evaluates power-on operations of standby ESXi hosts.

Advanced options
At DRS advanced options, the user can specify a different *DemandCapacityRatioTarget* and *DemandCapacityRatioToleranceHost* value.

DemandCapacityRatioTarget and can be set from 40% to 90%, while *DemandCapacityRatioToleranceHost* and can be set from 10% and 40%.

Note
It is recommended to use the default values and to only modify the values when you fully understand the impact.

The advanced options interface, can be found at the DRS cluster settings. Right-click the cluster and select Edit Settings. Select vSphere DRS and then click *Advanced Options* at the lower right corner.

Figure 90: Power operations regarding to host utilization levels

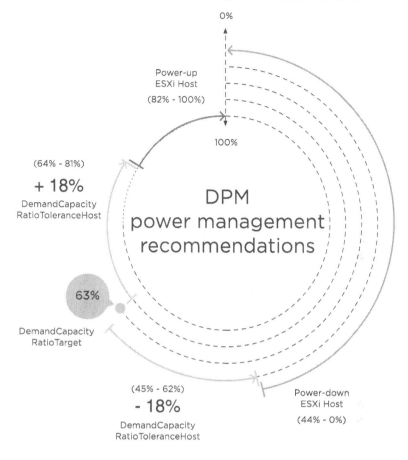

Finding a proper balance between supply and demand can be quite difficult as underestimating resource demand can result in lower performance while overestimating resource demand can lead to less optimal power savings.

Historical Period of Interest

As mentioned before, DPM determines the virtual machine average demand by calculating the demand over an historical period of interest. DPM uses two periods of interest when calculating the average demand:

DPM uses a shorter period of time for evaluating power-on recommendations, allowing itself to respond to demand increases relatively quickly.

Power-on recommendations: The period of interest of evaluating virtual machine demand for power-on operations is 300 seconds (5 minutes).

The longer period used to evaluate power-off operations ensures that DPM responds more slowly to a decrease in workload demand.

Power-off recommendations: DPM uses a longer period of evaluating resource demand for power-off operations; DPM evaluates the virtual machine workload of the past 2400 seconds (40 minutes).

DPM must be absolutely sure that it will not negatively impact virtual machine performance. Providing adequate resources for workload demand is considered more important by DPM than rapid response to decreasing workloads, so performance receives a higher priority by DPM than saving power. This becomes visible when reviewing the rules of power-on and power off operation recommendations; a power off recommendation is only applied when the ESXi host is below the specified target utilization range AND there are no power-on recommendations active.

Evaluating Power-On and Power-Off Recommendations

If the resource utilization evaluation indicates low or high resource utilization, DPM generates power-state recommendations that reduce the distance between the current resource utilization and the target resource utilization range. In other words, optimizing and aligning the power demand to the workload demand.

Both DRS and DPM evaluate every ESXi host in the cluster for power-state recommendations. To optimize the evaluation and selection process, hosts are placed in a particular order for evaluation. Candidate host can be rejected if they violate any DRS constraint, such as affinity rules or any resource reservation.

Power-Off recommendations

Host Selection for Power-Off Recommendations
Before selecting ESXi hosts for power off operations, DPM reviews the active hosts inside the cluster and sorts them in a specific order for its power off evaluation process. If the cluster contains hosts in both DPM automatic mode and manual mode, they are placed into separate groups. Hosts inside the automatic mode group are considered before the hosts inside the manual mode group.

If the cluster contains homogeneous-sized hosts, DPM considers hosts in order of lower virtual machine evacuation costs: hosts inside the automatic mode group with a lower number of virtual machines or smaller virtual machines are considered before heavily-loaded hosts in the same group.

If the cluster contains heterogeneous-sized hosts, DPM considers hosts in order of critical resource capacity. For power-off recommendations, smaller capacity hosts are favored over larger capacity hosts.

Host Power-Off Recommendations
DPM will evaluate the candidate hosts and uses DRS to run simulations in which the candidate hosts are powered off in the cluster.

These simulations are used by DPM to determine the impact of the power-off operations. DPM examines the positive gain of reducing the number of lightly loaded hosts and reducing the distance of the current utilization to the target resource utilization while minimizing the increase of utilization on the remaining hosts

To measure the amount of resource utilization under the target resource utilization range, DPM calculates a value for CPU and memory resources called *cpuLowScore* and *memLowScore*. To measure the amount of resource utilization above the target resource utilization range, DPM computes the resource HighScores called *cpuHighScore* and *memHighScore*.

The formula used for each resource is similar and calculates the weighted distance below or above the target utilization. For example, the memLowScore is calculated as follows:

> MemLowScore = Sum across all hosts below target utilization (target utilization – host utilization)

DPM compares the LowScore value of the cluster with all the candidate hosts' active workloads to the LowScore value of the simulations. DPM includes the critical resource state in this evaluation. If the hosts are overcommitted on memory, DPM determines that memory is the critical resource and will prioritize memory over CPU recommendations. If a simulation offers improvement of the LowScore and if the HighScore value does not increase, DPM generates a power-off recommendation. This power-off recommendation also contains virtual machine migration recommendations for the virtual machines running on this particular host.

Rejection of Host Power-Off Recommendations

DPM will not power down a host if it violates the minimum powered-on capacity specified by the settings *MinPoweredOnCpuCapacity* and *MinPoweredOnMemCapacity*.

Table 23: Advanced options

Option	Description
MinPoweredOnCpuCapacity	Minimum amount of powered-on CPU capacity maintained by VMware DPM.
MinPoweredOnMemCapacity	Minimum amount of powered-on memory capacity maintained by VMware DPM.

By default, both settings have a value of 1 MHz and 1MB respectively, which ensures that at least one host is kept powered-on. If these settings are altered, it might happen that DPM and DRS do not require all of the powered-on physical resources to run the virtual machines at a proper level. An ESXi host may be idle, leading to less efficient power utilization.

The CPU capacity kept powered on might not match the required CPU characteristics. If this setting is used in a cluster with heterogeneous CPU configurations, enable EVC to guarantee that the available CPU resources are compatible with all virtual machines.

Basic design principle

Enable EVC when adjusting *MinPoweredOnCapacity* settings with heterogeneous CPU/Memory configurations inside a cluster.

Another reason for DPM to not select a specific candidate host can be based on DRS constraints or objectives. For example, a host might be rejected for power off if the virtual machines that need to be migrated can only be moved to hosts that become too heavily utilized. This situation can occur when multiple DRS (anti) affinity rules are active in the cluster.

A third factor is that DPM does not select a candidate host to power down based on the negative or non-existing benefit indicated by the power-off cost/benefit analysis run by DPM. DPM continues to run simulations as long as the cluster contains ESXi hosts below the target utilization range.

DPM Power-Off Cost/Benefit Analysis

Before DPM generates a power-off recommendation, it calculates the costs associated with powering down a host. The following costs are taken into account:

- Migrating virtual machines off the candidate host
- Power consumed during the power-down period
- Unavailable resources of candidate host during power-down
- Loss of performance if candidate host resources are required to meet workload demand while candidate host is powered off
- Unavailability of candidate host resources during power-up period
- The power consumed during the power-up period
- Cost of migrating virtual machines to the candidate host

DPM runs the power-off cost/benefit analysis that compares the costs and risks associated with a power-off operation to the benefit of powering off the host. DPM will only accept a host power-off recommendation if the benefits meet or exceed the performance impact multiplied by the *PowerPerformanceRatio* setting.

The default value of *PowerPerformanceRatio* is 40 but can be modified to a value in the range between 0 and 500. A user specified *PowerPerformanceRatio* is set at the DRS advanced options interface.

As always, do not change these settings unless you understand the true impact of modifying them. Both cost and benefit calculations include CPU and Memory resources.

Power-Off Cost and Benefit Analysis Calculation

The power-off benefit analysis calculates the *StableOffTime* value, which indicates the amount of time the candidate host is expected to be powered-off until the cluster needs its resources because of an anticipated increase in virtual machine workload.

StableOffTime = ClusterStableTime – (HostEvacuationTime + HostPowerOffTime)

The time that the virtual machine workload is stable and no power-up operations are required is called the *ClusterStableTime*. DPM will use the virtual machine stable time, calculated by the DRS cost-benefit-risk analysis, as input for the *ClusterStableTime* calculation.

The time it takes from applying the power-off recommendation to the power-off state is taken into account as well. The analysis breaks this time down into two sections and calculates this as the sum of the time it takes to migrate all active virtual machines off the host (*HostEvacuationTime*) and the time it takes to power off the host (*HostPowerOffTime*).

The power-off cost is calculated as the summation of the following estimated resource costs:

- Migration of the active virtual machines running on the candidate host to other ESXi hosts
- Unsatisfied virtual machine resource demand during power-on candidate host at the end of the ClusterStableTime
- Migration of virtual machines back onto the candidate host

The last two bullet points can only be estimated by DPM; DPM calculates the number of hosts required to be available at the end of the *ClusterStableTime*. This calculation is, to some extent, a worst-case scenario as DPM expects all the virtual machines to generate heavy workloads at the end of the *ClusterStableTime*, hereby generating a conservative value.

As previously mentioned, DPM will only recommend a power-off operation if there is a significant gain in resource utilization efficiency. It might be possible that the *ClusterStableTime* is low, and this can result in a *StableOffTime* equal to or even less than zero. During this scenario, DPM will stop evaluating the candidate host for a power-off operation recommendation because it will not offer any benefit.

Power-On recommendations

Host Selection for Power-On Recommendations

Similar to power-off recommendations, ESXi hosts in automatic mode are evaluated before ESXi hosts in manual mode for power-on recommendations. In a cluster containing heterogeneous-sized hosts, the ESXi hosts with a larger capacity with regards to the critical resources are favored.

If the sort process discovers equal hosts with respect to the capacity or evacuation cost, DPM will randomize the order of hosts, done for a wear-leveling effect. Be aware that sorting of the hosts for power-on or power-off recommendations does not determine the actual order for the selection process to power-on or power-off hosts.

Host Power-On Recommendations

If the resource utilization evaluation indicates a host with high utilization inside the cluster, DPM considers generating host power-on recommendations.

Before selecting an ESXi host for power on, DPM reviews the standby hosts inside the cluster and sorts them in a specific order for DPM power on evaluation process.

DPM continues by evaluating each standby host and invokes DRS to run simulations. The simulations distribute current virtual machines across all hosts regardless if they are active or standby. By using the *HighScore* calculation, DPM determines the impact of a power-up operation on the current utilization ratio. It needs to determine how much improvement each power-up operation has on the distance of the resource utilization from the target utilization or the possible reduction of the number of highly utilized hosts. DPM compares the *HighScore* value of the cluster in its current state (standby host still down) to the *HighScore* value of the simulations. If a simulation offers an improved *HighScore* value when a standby host is powered-on, DPM will generate a power-on recommendation for that specific host.

In addition, DPM does not strictly adhere to its host sort order if doing so would lead to choosing a host with capacity far greater than needed, if a smaller capacity host that can adequately handle the demand is also available. Sometimes a host will not be selected if DPM expects that the candidate cannot offer the simulated load-reduction.

For example, if it is not possible to migrate specific virtual machines to the candidate due to vMotion incompatibility, the simulated reduction may not be achievable.

DPM continues to run simulations as long as there are hosts in the cluster exceeding the target utilization range. DPM is very efficient in homogeneous-sized clusters as DPM will skip every host that is identical regarding physical resources or vMotion compatibility to any host who is already rejected for power-on operation during the simulation.

Basic design principle
Use homogeneous clusters, as DPM will operate more efficiently.

Impact of Advanced Settings on Host Power-On Recommendations

Advanced options can be set to specify a particular minimum amount of CPU or Memory capacity be kept powered on regardless of DPM recommendations.

If the user sets a custom value in the advanced settings, *MinPoweredOnCpuCapacity* and *MinPoweredOnMemCapacity*, DPM needs to adjust its power-on operation recommendations to fulfill the requirements defined in these settings.

Contrary to a power-off recommendation, redistribution of virtual machines among the powered-on hosts is not included in a power-on recommendation. To satisfy that need, DPM relies on future invocation rounds of DRS.

Recommendation Classifications

DPM threshold

The DPM threshold slider works similarly to the DRS slider. Like DRS, threshold options range from conservative to aggressive. DPM recommendation priority levels can be compared to the DRS priority levels.

The aggressive level of DPM corresponds with the aggressive level of DRS in that it generates DPM recommendations up to priority 5. Similarly, the conservative level of DPM corresponds with the conservative level of DRS: selecting the conservative level threshold causes DPM to generate priority level 1 recommendations only. The following warning is displayed below the threshold slider when the conservative DPM level is selected:

Warning

"Apply only priority 1 recommendations. vCenter will apply power-on recommendations produced to meet HA requirements or user-specified capacity requirements" DPM will only automatically apply the power-on recommendations."

In this scenario, DPM will not generate power-off recommendations; this effectively means that the automatic DPM power saving mode is disabled. The user is able to place the server in the standby mode manually, but DPM will only power-on ESXi hosts when the cluster fails to meet certain HA or custom capacity requirements or constraints.

Priority Levels

The power-off and power-on Recommendations are assigned priorities ranging from priority one-recommendations to priority-five recommendations.

Priority level ratings are based on the resource utilization of the cluster and the improvement that is expected from the suggested host power state recommendation. It may be interesting to note that different ranges are applied to power-on recommendations than power-off recommendations: power-off recommendations can range from priority 2 to priority 5 while power-on recommendations range from priority 1 to priority 3.

Table 24: Priority levels range of power state recommendations

Priority level	Power-off recommendation	Power-on recommendation
1		X
2	X	X
3	X	X
4	X	
5	X	

Power-off recommendations

Recommendations with higher priority levels will result in more power-savings if the recommendations are applied. The highest power-off priority level 2 results in the largest reduction of excess capacity headroom, while applying a priority level 5 power-off recommendation results in a modest reduction in excess capacity headroom. Priority level 1 recommendations are not generated for power-off recommendations as providing adequate resources for workload demand is considered more important by DPM than rapid response to decreasing workloads.

Power-on recommendations

A priority level 1 is generated when conforming to VMware High Availability requirements or powered-on capacity requirements set by the user. Power-on priority level 2 indicates a more urgent recommendation to solve higher host utilization saturation levels than priority level 3.

Be aware that the generated migration recommendations are not mandatory. If DRS is set to the conservative migration threshold, these migration recommendations are ignored and will effectively disable DPM.

Basic design principle

Do not set DRS to the conservative migration threshold if DPM is required

Chapter 18

Guiding DPM Recommendations

DPM Standby Mode

The term "Standby mode" used by DPM specifies a powered down ESXi host. The term is used to indicate that the ESXi host is available to be powered on should the cluster require its resources. DPM requires the Host to be able to awake from an ACPI S5 state via Wake-On-LAN (WOL) packets or one of the two supported out-of-band methods: Intelligent Platform Management Interface (IPMI) version 1.5 or HP Integrated Lights-Out (iLO) technology. Both IPMI and iLO require the availability of a Baseboard Management Controller (BMC) providing access to hardware control functions and allowing the server hardware to be accessed from the vCenter server using a LAN connection. To use WOL, the ESXi host must contain a Network Interface Card that supports the WOL protocol. If the host does not offer the hardware support and configurations of any of these protocols, it cannot be placed into standby mode by DPM.

DPM WOL Magic Packet

If the ESXi host is not an HP server supporting iLO, does not support IPMI version 1.5, or if the appropriate credentials for using iLO or IPMI have not been configured and set up in vCenter, DPM uses Wake-On-LAN Packets to bring the ESXi host out of standby mode. The "magic packet," the network packet used to bring the server back to life, is sent over the vMotion network by another currently powered on ESXi server in the cluster. For this reason, DPM keeps at least one host powered on in the cluster at all times, managed by the DPM advanced controls, *MinPoweredOnCpuCapacity* and *MinPoweredOnMemCapacity*, both configured with the respective default values of 1 MHz and 1 MB.

Because the magic packet is sent across the vMotion network to a powered-off server, DPM impacts the configuration of the vMotion network as well. Because most NICs support WOL only if they can switch to 100 Mb/s, the switch port used by the vMotion NIC must be set to auto-negotiate link speed instead of setting the port to a fixed speed/duplex such as 1000 MB/s Full. Industry best practices advise setting both NIC and switch ports to identical settings, so ensure that vmknic speed is set to auto-negotiate as well.

Baseboard Management Controller

If both a BMC wake method (IPMI or iLO) and WOL are present and both are operational, DPM will attempt to use a BMC wake method as default. To ensure IPMI is operational, configure the *BMC over LAN channel* to always be available, some *BMC LAN channels* require the availability to send operator-privileged commands. A number of BMC boards require IPMI accounts set in the BIOS.

DPM uses MD5- or plaintext-based authentication with IPMI. If the BMC reports that it supports MD5 and has the operator role enabled, only then will vCenter use MD5 authentication. vCenter will switch to plaintext authentication if none or only one requirement is met. If neither MD5 nor plaintext is enabled or supported, vCenter will not use IPMI and attempts to use Wake-On-LAN.

Protocol Selection Order

If the server is configured for IPMI or iLO, DPM will try use the protocols in the order IPMI, iLO and then WOL: if vCenter is unable to successfully power on the ESXi host with the IPMI, it will try the second protocol, iLO, if this attempt fails, DPM will try to power on using the Wake-On-LAN and instructs a powered-on ESXi host to send the magic packet.
It is important to understand that placing the ESXi host into standby mode does not use any power management protocols; vCenter initiates a graceful shutdown of the ESXi host.

DPM Scheduled Tasks

DPM can be enabled and disabled via scheduled tasks. The DPM "Change cluster power settings" scheduled task allows the administrator to enable or disable DPM via an automated task. If the administrator selects the option "DPM off," vCenter will disable all DPM features on the selected cluster and all hosts in standby mode will be powered on automatically when the scheduled task runs.

This option removes one of the biggest obstacles to implementing DPM: the incurred (periodic) latency when DPM must bring hosts out of standby. If DPM places a host into standby mode, it can take up to five minutes before DPM decides to power up the host again, not counting the time it takes for the host to boot.

It is common for DPM to place ESXi hosts into standby mode during the night due to the decreased workloads. When the employees arrive in the morning and the workload increases, DPM must power on additional ESXi hosts to handle the increased (normal) demand. During this time, the environment may experience latency or suboptimal performance. The period between 7:30am and 10:00am is recognized as one of the busiest periods of the day and during that period the IT department wants their computing power lock, stock and ready to go.

This scheduled task option will give administrators the ability to disable DPM before the employees arrive so that the full capacity is available to meet the demand. Because the ESXi hosts remain powered-on until the administrator or a DPM scheduled task enables DPM again, another schedule can be created to enable DPM after the period of high workload demand ends.

For example, by scheduling a DPM disable task every weekday at 6:30am, the administrator is ensured that all ESXi hosts are powered on before the morning peak, rather than having to wait for DPM to react to the workload increase.

By scheduling the DPM disable task more than one hour in advance of the morning peak, DRS will have time to rebalance the virtual machines across all active hosts inside the cluster and the Transparent Page Sharing process can collapse the memory pages shared by the virtual machines on the ESXi hosts. By powering up all ESXi hosts early, the cluster will be ready to accommodate the expected increase in workload.

Chapter 19

Summarizing

Hopefully we have succeeded in giving you a better understanding of resource management; resource pools, DRS and DPM algorithms. We have tried to simplify some of the concepts to make it easier to understand, but we acknowledge that some concepts are difficult to grasp. We hope that after reading these sections of the book, everyone is confident enough to create and configure DRS clusters to achieve higher consolidation ratios at lower costs.

If there are any questions please do not hesitate to reach out to either of the authors.

Part III

vSphere Storage DRS

Chapter 20

Introduction to vSphere Storage DRS

vSphere 5.0 introduced Storage DRS to resolve some of the operational challenges associated with virtual machine provisioning, migration and cloning. Historically, monitoring datastore capacity and I/O load has proven to be very difficult. As a result, it is often neglected, leading to hot spots and over- or underutilized datastores. Storage I/O Control (SIOC) in vSphere 4.1 solved part of this problem by introducing a datastore-wide disk-scheduler that allows for proportional allocation of I/O resources to virtual machines based on their respective shares during times of contention.

Storage DRS brings this to a whole new level by providing smart virtual machine placement and load balancing mechanisms based on both space and I/O capacity. In other words, where SIOC reactively throttles hosts and virtual machines to ensure fairness, SDRS proactively makes recommendations to prevent imbalances from both space utilization and latency perspectives. More simply, Storage DRS does for storage what DRS does for compute resources.

There are five key features that Storage DRS offers:

- Resource aggregation.
- Initial Placement.
- Load Balancing.
- Datastore Maintenance Mode.
- Affinity Rules.

Resource Aggregation

Resource aggregation is the key component that all other Storage DRS features depend on. Resource aggregation enables grouping of multiple datastores into a single, flexible pool of storage called a *datastore cluster*. A datastore cluster is the new construct available in vSphere 5 and higher that provides access to Storage DRS functionality. The flexibility of this new abstraction, further separating the physical from the logical, greatly simplifies storage management by allowing datastores to be quickly, simply and dynamically added or removed from a datastore cluster to deal with maintenance, performance or out of space conditions. The Storage DRS load balancer will take care of initial VMDK placement as well as efficient and balanced use of datastores.

Initial Placement

The goal of Initial Placement is to place virtual machine disk files based on the existing load on the datastores, ensuring that neither the space nor the I/O capacity is exhausted prematurely. Initial placement provides a more simpler provisioning process by automating the selection of an individual datastore and leaving the user with the much smaller-scale decision of selecting a datastore cluster. Storage DRS selects a particular datastore within a datastore cluster based on actual space utilization and I/O capacity. In an environment with multiple seemingly identical datastores, initial placement can be a difficult and time-consuming task for the administrator. In many environments, the common practice is to find a datastore with the most free space and use that one. This is not always the best choice. Not only does a datastore with adequate available disk space need to be identified, but it is also crucial to ensure that the addition of this new virtual machine does not result in I/O bottlenecks. Storage DRS takes care of all of this and substantially reduces the amount of operational effort required to provision virtual machines; that is the true value of Storage DRS.

Load Balancing

Storage DRS can operate in two distinct load-balancing modes: *No Automation* (manual mode) or *Fully Automated*. Where Initial Placement reduces complexity in the provisioning process, Load Balancing addresses imbalances within a datastore cluster. Prior to Storage DRS, placement of virtual machines was often based on current space consumption or the number of virtual machines on each datastore. I/O capacity monitoring and space utilization trending was often regarded as too time consuming. Over the years, we have seen this lead to performance problems in many environments, and in some cases, even result in down time because a datastore ran out of space.

Storage DRS Load Balancing helps prevent these unfortunately common scenarios by generating placement recommendations based on both space utilization and I/O capacity. The load balance process in initiated periodically, by default every 8 hours. Placement recommendations are generated if the space utilization or I/O latency of a datastore exceeds the thresholds configured at the datastore cluster level. Depending on the selected automation level, these recommendations will be automatically applied by Storage DRS or will be presented to the administrator who then can decide to apply them manually.

Figure 91: Storage DRS Automation Level

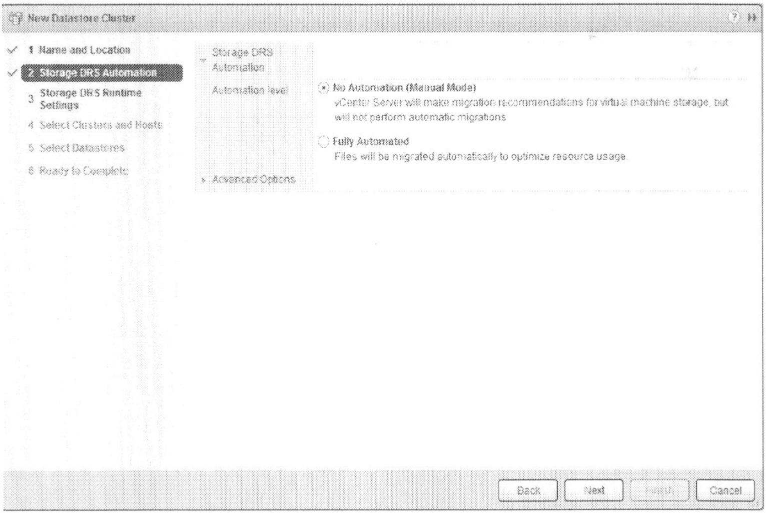

Although we see Load Balancing as a single feature of Storage DRS, it actually consists of two separately configurable options. When either of the configured thresholds for Utilized Space or I/O Latency is exceeded, Storage DRS will make recommendations to resolve the imbalance within the datastore cluster. In the case of I/O capacity load balancing, monitoring can be explicitly disabled (Figure 92).

Figure 92: Disable I/O load balancing

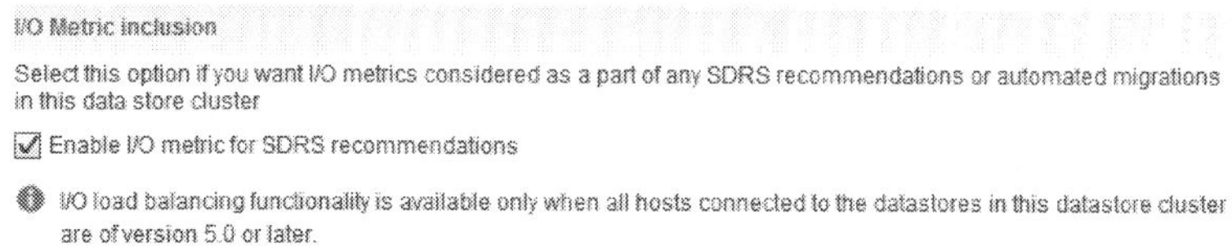

I/O Metric inclusion

Select this option if you want I/O metrics considered as a part of any SDRS recommendations or automated migrations in this data store cluster

☑ Enable I/O metric for SDRS recommendations

⊕ I/O load balancing functionality is available only when all hosts connected to the datastores in this datastore cluster are of version 5.0 or later.

Before anyone forgets, Storage DRS functionality can be enabled on fully populated datastores and environments without downtime. It is also possible to add fully populated datastores to existing datastore clusters. It is a great way to solve actual or potential bottlenecks in any environment with minimal required effort or risk.

Affinity Rules

Affinity Rules enable control over which virtual disks should or should not be placed on the same datastore within a datastore cluster in accordance with your best practices and/or availability requirements. By default, all of a virtual machine's virtual disks are kept together on the same datastore.

Datastore Maintenance Mode

Datastore Maintenance Mode can be compared to Host Maintenance Mode: when a datastore is placed in Maintenance Mode all registered virtual machines on that datastore are migrated to the other datastores in the datastore cluster. Typical use cases are data migration to a new storage array or maintenance on a LUN, such as migration to another RAID group.

Requirements

In order for Storage DRS to function correctly, the enviro
the following basic requirements:

- VMware vCenter Server 5.0 or later.
- VMware vSphere ESXi 5.0 or later.
- VMware vCenter Cluster (recommended).
- VMware vSphere Enterprise Plus license.
- Shared VMFS or NFS datastore volumes.
- Shared datastore volumes accessible by at least one l
  the cluster.*
- Datastores must be visible in only one datacenter.

* Full cluster connectivity is recommended, however this i

Chapter 21

Storage DRS Algorithms

Initial Placement

Storage DRS can automate initial placement of a virtual machine to avoid disk space imbalances and I/O hotspots on the datastores. By providing automatic datastore selection, Storage DRS initial placement minimizes the risk of over-provisioning a datastore, creating I/O bottlenecks or negatively impacting performance of the virtual machines.

User Interaction

In addition to smart placement, initial placement will speed up the process for the user by automating the datastore selection. Datastores used in a datastore cluster are by default not visible when selecting a datastore during the virtual machine creation process; only datastore clusters or "unclustered" datastores may be selected if a virtual machine must retain its automated mode.

Please note that one can drill down and pick a datastore from among one of the datastores in a cluster. If a datastore is picked, then the virtual machine placement sets the virtual machine automation mode to manual (as the user has selected a datastore) and Storage DRS does not consider automatic moves for that virtual machine so long its automation mode is manual.

Figure 93: Initial Placement

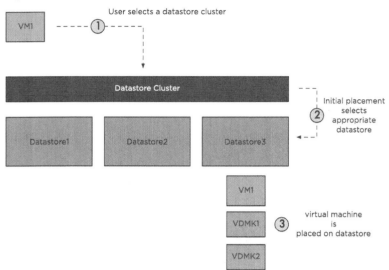

By default, Storage DRS place a virtual machine and its virtual machine disk (VMDK) files on datastore(s) within a datastore cluster according to the datastore cluster affinity rules. When creating a datastore cluster, Storage DRS preselects the VMDK affinity rule. In vSphere 5.1, the user interface allows changing the default affinity rule. Be aware that this only applies for newly created virtual machines. VMDK affinity rules are covered in a later chapter.

No partially automated mode available

Datastore clusters can be configured either with manual load balancing or automatic load balancing. Automated initial placement is excluded in both modes: Storage DRS generates an Initial placement recommendation that always requires a manual confirmation.

DRS and datastore connection

When connecting a datastore cluster to a DRS cluster, Storage DRS is in charge of virtual machine placement. It is responsible for virtual machine placement on compute and storage level. Storage DRS checks the datastore connectivity of all hosts to ensure that the virtual machines have the highest mobility on both host and datastore levels. Storage DRS will prefer datastores connected to all hosts of a DRS cluster – full connectivity – before considering partially-connected datastores – datastores connected to a subset of hosts within the DRS cluster. During initial placement, the selection of a partially connected datastore may impact the mobility of the virtual machine amongst the hosts, while selecting a partially connected host impacts the mobility of virtual machines amongst the datastores in the datastore cluster.

Space and I/O Load Consideration

When selecting a datastore, Initial Placement takes both DRS and Storage DRS threshold metrics into account. It will select the host with the least utilization and the highest connectivity to place the virtual machine. For datastores, Storage DRS weights the metrics according to the utilization of the datastores in the datastore cluster and combines space and IO metrics using a dynamic weighting. If space is running low, it will try to balance the space more than I/O (and vice versa). If neither resource is constrained the weight of both metrics is the same. For example, if the available datastores are close to the space utilization threshold, the weight of the space metric becomes higher and it is more likely that initial placement is based on space balancing.

Space utilization threshold

During initial placement, the total amount of free space is checked on datastore cluster level and datastore level. When initially placing virtual machines, Storage DRS avoids violating the space utilization threshold. (Space utilization threshold is covered extensively in the Space load-balancing chapter). It is important to understand that the space utilization threshold set on a datastore cluster applies to each datastore separately, not to the collective whole of the datastore cluster. This means that each datastore will have a buffer space which initial placement tries to avoid using. Figure 94, illustrates this concept.

Figure 94: Datastore space overview

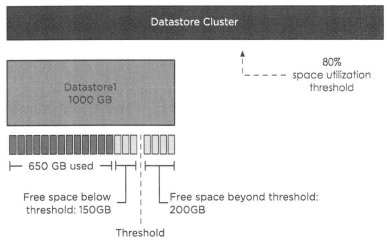

For example, setting the space utilization threshold to 80% on a datastore cluster containing a single 1000GB datastore will allow Storage DRS to place virtual machines that consume space up to 800 GB. In this scenario, 650GB of the datastore is used. This means that Storage DRS considers this datastore to have 350GB free but understands that a placement of a virtual machine bigger than 150GB will violate the threshold. If all the datastores are at or above the threshold, initial placement can still proceed if there is a datastore that can fit the incoming virtual machine. For example, if there is an incoming virtual machine of 200GB, and all the other datastores have also exceeded the space threshold, then this virtual machine can be placed at Datastore1.

Datastore cluster defragmentation

As mentioned previously, Storage DRS considers both free space at both datastore and datastore cluster levels. If enough free space is available in the datastore cluster but not enough space is available per datastore, the datastore cluster is considered fragmented. During this state, Storage DRS considers migrating existing virtual machines from one or more datastores to free up space if it cannot place the new virtual machine on any datastore.

Prerequisite migrations

Storage DRS starts by searching alternative locations for the existing virtual machines in the datastores and attempts to place the virtual machines on other datastores one by one. As a result, Storage DRS may generate sets of migration recommendations of existing virtual machines that allow placement of the new virtual machine. These migrations are called prerequisite migrations. The combination of prerequisite migration recommendations and the placement recommendation is called a recommendation set.

Depth of recursion

Storage DRS uses a recursive algorithm for searching alternative placement combinations. To keep Storage DRS from trying an extremely high number of combinations of virtual machine migrations, the "depth of recursion" is limited to 2 steps. What defines a step and what counts towards a step? A step can be best defined as a set of migrations out of a datastore in preparation for (or to make room for) another migration or placement into that same datastore. A step can contain migration of one VMDK, but can also contain migrations of multiple virtual machines with multiple virtual disks attached. In some cases, room must be created on that target datastore first by moving a virtual machine out to another datastore, which results in an extra step. The following diagram visualizes the process.

Figure 95: Depth of Recursion

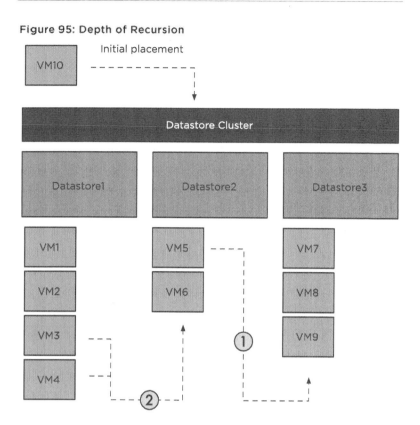

Storage DRS has calculated that a new virtual machine, VM10, can be placed on Datastore1 if VM3 and VM4 are migrated to Datastore2, however, placing these two virtual machines on Datastore2 will violate the space utilization, therefore room must be created. So, VM5 is moved out of Datastore2 as part of a step of creating space. This results in Step 1, moving VM5 out to Datastore3, followed by Step 2, moving VM3 and VM4 to Datastore2, and finally placing the new virtual machine on Datastore1.

Storage DRS stops its search if there are no 2-step moves to satisfy the storage requirement of an initial placement. An advanced setting can be set to change the number of steps used by the search. As always, changing the defaults is strongly discouraged since many hours of testing has been invested in researching the setting that offers good performance while minimizing the impact of the operation. If you have a strong case for changing the number of steps, set the Storage DRS advanced configuration option "MaxRecursionDepth". The default value is 1 the maximum value is 5. Because the algorithm starts counting at 0, default value of 1 allows 2 steps. Please note that this is a per-Datastore Cluster option.

Goodness value

Storage DRS will cycle through all the datastores in the datastore cluster and initiates a search for space on each datastore. A search generates a set of prerequisite migrations if it can provide space that allows the virtual machine placement within the depth of recursion. Storage DRS evaluates the generated sets and awards each set a goodness value. The set with the least amount of cost (i.e. migrations) is the preferred migration recommendation and is shown at the top of the list. Let's explore this a bit more.

Scenario

The datastore cluster contains 3 datastores; each datastore has a size of 1000GB and contains multiple virtual machines with various sizes. The space consumed on the datastores range from 550GB to 650GB, while the space utilization threshold is set to 80%. At this point, the administrator creates VM10 that requests 350GB of space. Although the datastore cluster itself contains 1225GB of free space, Storage DRS will avoid to place the virtual machine "as is" on any of the three datastores because placing the virtual machine without taking precautionary actions would violate the space utilization threshold of the datastores.

Figure 96 Space utilization datastore cluster prior to initial placement

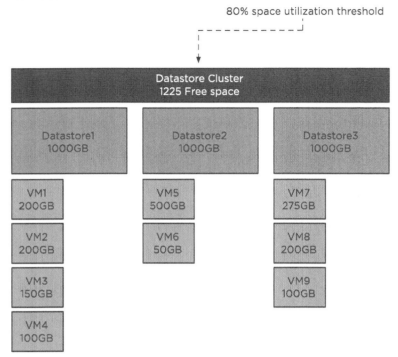

Search process

As each ESXi host provides information about the overall datastore utilization and the VMDK statistics, Storage DRS has a clear view of the most up to date situation and will use these statistics as input for its search. In the first step, it will simulate all the necessary migrations to fit VM10 in Datastore1. The prerequisite migration process with least number of migrations to fit the virtual machine on to Datastore1 looks as follows:

Figure 97: Prerequisite migrations - simulation 1

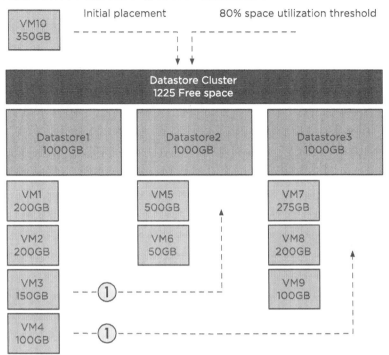

- Step 1: VM3 from Datastore1 to Datastore2.
- Step 1: VM4 from Datastore1 to Datastore3.
- Place new virtual machine on Datastore1.

Although VM3 and VM4 are each moved out to a different datastore, both migrations are counted as a one step prerequisite migration because both virtual machines are migrated out of a SINGLE datastore (Datastore1).

Next Storage DRS will evaluate Datastore2. Due to the size of VM5, Storage DRS is unable to migrate VM5 out of Datastore2 because it will immediately violate the utilization threshold of any selected destination datastore. One of the coolest parts of the algorithm is that it considers inbound migrations as valid moves. In this scenario, migrating virtual machines into Datastore2 would free up space on another datastore to provide enough free space to place VM5, which in turn frees up enough space on Datastore2 to allow Storage DRS to place VM10 onto Datastore2.

Figure 98: Prerequisite migration - simulation 2

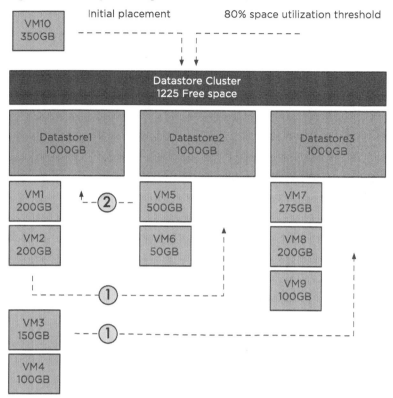

The prerequisite migration process with least number of migrations to fit the virtual machine on Datastore2 looks as follows:

- Step 1: VM2 from Datastore1 to Datastore2.
- Step 1: VM3 from Datastore1 to Datastore3.
- Step 2: VM5 from Datastore2 to Datastore1.
- Place new virtual machine on Datastore2.

The analysis of Datastore3 generates a single prerequisite migration. Migrating VM8 from Datastore3 to Datastore2 will free up enough space to allow placement of VM10. Selecting VM9 would not free up enough space and migrating VM7 generates more cost than migrating VM8. By default, Storage DRS attempts to migrate the virtual machine or virtual machine disk with a size that is closest to the required space.

Figure 99: Prerequisite migration - simulation 3

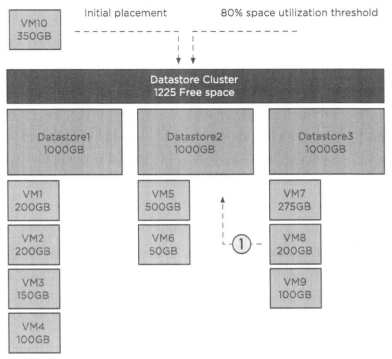

The prerequisite migration process with least number of migrations to fit the virtual machine on to Datastore3 looks as follows:

- Step 1: VM8 from Datastore3 to Datastore2.
- Place new virtual machine on Datastore3.

After analyzing the cost and benefit of the three search results, Storage DRS will assign the highest goodness factor to the migration set of Datastore3. Although each search result can provide enough free space after moves, the recommendation set of Datastore3 will result in the least number of moves and migrates the smallest amount of data. All three results will be shown; the most highly recommended set will be placed at the top.
A placement recommendation screen is displayed. Note that you can apply only the complete recommendation set and that applying the recommendation triggers the prerequisite migrations before the initial placement of the virtual machine occurs.

Load Balancing

Storage DRS takes both space and I/O load into consideration when recommending load-balancing recommendations: Storage DRS generates a unified load-balance recommendation.

Primary objective load balancing

Storage DRS generates migration recommendations when space utilization or I/O response time thresholds have exceeded and a significant space or I/O imbalance exists. However, if Storage DRS cannot correct the threshold violation, it will balance the load within the datastore cluster as much as possible.

Storage DRS Settings

The datastore cluster settings displays both space and I/O load balancing configuration options.

Figure 100: Storage DRS Thresholds

Storage DRS Thresholds

Runtime thresholds govern when Storage DRS performs or recommends migrations (based on the selected automation level). Utilized space dictates the minimum level of consumed space that is the threshold for action. I/O latency dictates the minimum I/O latency below which I/O load balancing moves are not considered.

Utilized Space:	50 % ———◇——— 100 %	80	▲▼	%
I/O Latency:	5 ms —◇———— 100 ms	15	▲▼	ms

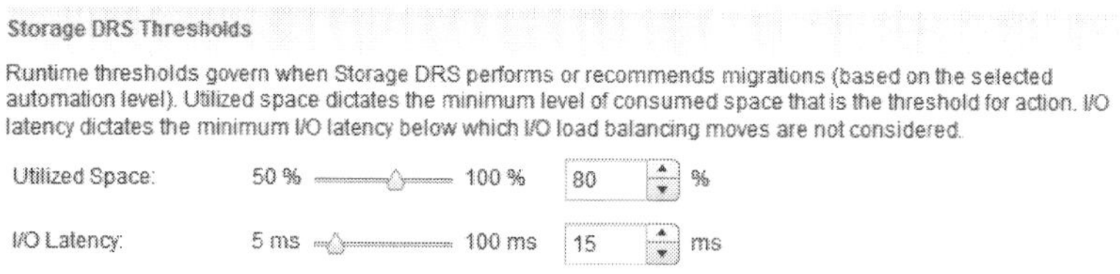

Figure 101: Advanced Options

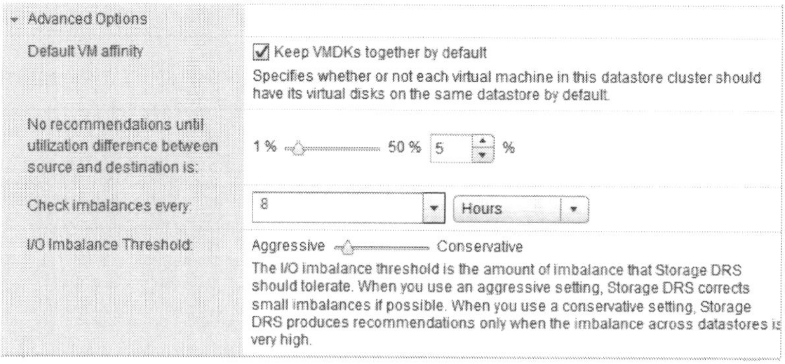

▾ Advanced Options

Default VM affinity	☑ Keep VMDKs together by default
	Specifies whether or not each virtual machine in this datastore cluster should have its virtual disks on the same datastore by default.
No recommendations until utilization difference between source and destination is:	1 % —◇———— 50 % 5 ▲▼ %
Check imbalances every:	8 ▾ Hours ▾
I/O Imbalance Threshold:	Aggressive —◇———— Conservative
	The I/O imbalance threshold is the amount of imbalance that Storage DRS should tolerate. When you use an aggressive setting, Storage DRS corrects small imbalances if possible. When you use a conservative setting, Storage DRS produces recommendations only when the imbalance across datastores is very high.

Storage DRS uses these settings to determine if migrations are required to balance load across datastores. Each of the load balancers generates recommendations independently. Storage DRS takes both recommendations into consideration before providing a unified recommendation. The following sections will examine each load balancer separately before expanding upon unified recommendations.

Space Load Balancing

Storage DRS distributes space utilization of the virtual machines across the datastores of the datastore cluster. The workflow is repeated for each space-overloaded datastore and more than one migration may be recommended to reduce load on a datastore. The space balance workflow looks as follows;

Figure 102: **Space balancing workflow**

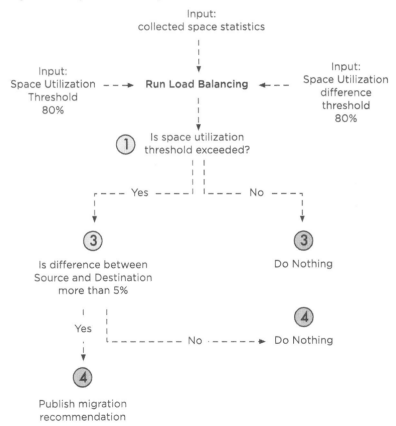

Collecting Statistics

Storage DRS retrieves virtual machine statistics from the vCenter database every two hours. The host on which the virtual machine is registered provides vCenter detailed information regarding the files associated with the virtual machine. Storage DRS collects this information from the vCenter database to understand the disk usage and file structure of each virtual machine.

Each ESXi host reports datastore utilization at a frequent interval and this is stored in the vCenter database. Storage DRS checks whether the datastore utilization is above the user-set threshold.

Figure 103: Space load balancing statistics input

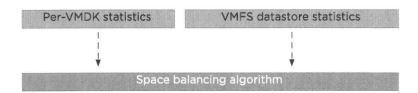

The user-set threshold – *space utilization ratio threshold* – defines the maximum acceptable space load of the VMFS datastore. The space load is the sum of the total consumed space on the datastore, divided by the capacity of the datastore.

$$space\ load = \frac{total\ consumed\ space\ on\ the\ datastore}{datastore\ capacity}$$

By default, the space utilization ratio is set to 80%, which indicates that the total consumed space on the datastore must not exceed 80% of the capacity of the datastore.

To avoid unnecessary migrations from one overloaded datastore to a datastore that is near the threshold, Storage DRS uses the *space utilization ratio difference threshold* to determine which datastores should be considered as destinations for virtual machine migrations.

Figure 104: Space utilization ratio difference threshold

The *space utilization ratio difference threshold* indicates the required difference of utilization ratio between the destination and source datastores. The difference threshold value is set by default to 5%.

Cost Benefit Risk Analysis

Similar to DRS, Storage DRS uses a cost-benefit metric to identify suitable migration candidates and to determine if the datastore cluster benefits from the move.

Benefit: The increase of free space after a virtual machine moves out of the datastore.

Cost: The size of the VMDK and activity of I/O workload impacts the cost calculation. The number of mirrored writes to the datastores and the expected duration of the migration are considered as the overhead of a migration.

Risk: Risk is involved when generating migration recommendations for virtual machines configured with thin-provisioned disks. Storage DRS considers the allocated disk space instead of the provisioned amount (configured size) when determining if load balancing is required. The data-growth rate is considered a risk when migrating thin disks. Storage DRS attempts to avoid migrating virtual machines with data-growth rates that will likely cause the destination datastore exceed the space utilization threshold in the near future.

The growth rate is estimated by means of historical usage samples; with recent samples weighing more than older samples. The "Near future" is a defined time window and defaults to 30 hours.

If the benefit outweighs the cost, Storage DRS considers the move for recommendation.

Migration candidate selection

When a datastore exceeds the space utilization threshold, Storage DRS will try to move the number of megabytes out of the datastore to correct the space utilization violation. In other words, Storage DRS attempts to select a virtual machine that is closest in size required to bring the space utilization of the datastore to the space utilization ratio threshold.

In order to minimize overhead, Storage DRS prefers moving powered-off virtual machines to powered-on virtual machines. The advantage of moving powered-off virtual machines is that Storage DRS does not have to track any block changes inside the VMDK during relocation and does not have to calculate the performance degradation on the virtual machine workload.

To reduce the overhead even more, if the virtual machine swap files are stored in a location explicitly specified by the user, such as Host Cache SSD Datastores, Storage DRS will not move these files. After evaluation of statistics, space utilization and utilization ratio thresholds, the Storage DRS space load-balancing algorithm will select a candidate virtual machine, which if moved, offers the highest benefit with the lowest overhead. These metrics will lead to one or more load balancing recommendations. However, Storage DRS does not apply or display the load balancing recommendation straight away; it considers the I/O load balancing recommendations before generating the actual recommendations.

On-Demand Space Load Balancing

Although Storage DRS load-balancing runs every 8 hours, a load balancing process is triggered by Storage DRS when the consumed space in a datastore exceeds the utilization ratio threshold. Storage DRS monitors utilization of the datastores and decides when the algorithm invocation needs to be scheduled. Depending on the fill-rate of the volume and the associated risk, Storage DRS decides if a load-balancing process needs to take place. It is possible that the threshold has been violated, but due to a slow fill-rate, space load balancing is not immediately necessary. This behavior was introduced to avoid generating unnecessary overhead.

I/O load balancing

The I/O load balancer's goal is to resolve the imbalance of performance delivered from datastores in a datastore cluster. To generate an I/O load balancer migration, Storage DRS runs the workflow outlined in Figure 105. Similar to the space-balancing algorithm, this algorithm is run for all overloaded datastores and the algorithm may recommend one or more migrations for each overloaded datastore.

Figure 105: I/O load-balancing workflow

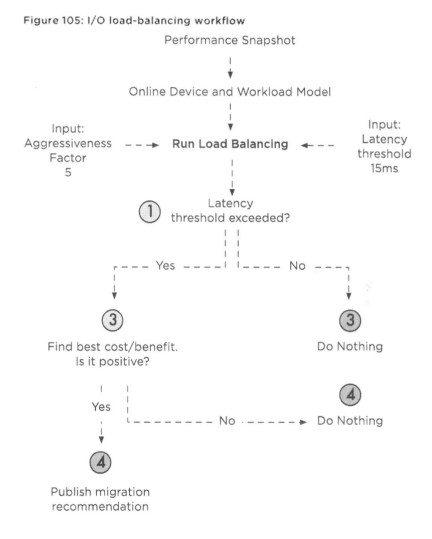

Stats Collection – Performance Snapshot

The main metric used by Storage DRS to represent performance is the average latency on each datastore. To solve the uneven distribution of average latency within the datastore cluster, Storage DRS requires input to recommend migrations. The required input is acquired by collecting a set of various statistics from vCenter. This set of statistics is commonly referred to as the "performance snapshot". Storage DRS uses the performance snapshot for its online device and workload modeling.

Online Device and Workload Modeling

To achieve better and more efficient utilization of storage resources in a datastore cluster, Storage DRS creates an online device and workload model. This model helps Storage DRS determine overall device performance capability and analyzes the impact of a specific set of workload data points on the latency of the datastore.

Device Modeling

Storage DRS captures device performance to create its performance models. Most storage devices hide RAID level and device characteristics from ESXi hosts and only present latency and the total capacity of a disk. It is important to understand that not every disk is the same and that device performance can vary due to a wide variety of configuration differences. For example, a 2TB disk spanning a disk group containing thirty-two 15K RPM Fibre-Channel disks usually offers better performance than a 2TB disk spanning eight 7.2K RPM SATA disks. To understand and learn the performance of each device, Storage DRS uses a workload injector and a reference workload to measure outstanding I/O's and latency. Paired together, they indicate the relative performance capability of a datastore.

Note

Please remember that Storage DRS does not require any support from the storage array to determine device characteristics. This means no additional third-party software is required to run Storage DRS.

Workload Modeling

The workload modeling process creates a workload metric of each virtual disk. Per virtual disk, 4 data points are collected:

- Number of Outstanding I/Os
- I/O size

- Read / Write ratio
- % Randomness

Storage DRS analyzes the impact of each data point on latency and returns an overall workload model metric.

Normalized Load

The device metric and workload metric are used to define the normalized load of a datastore. The normalized load allows Storage DRS to base its load balancing recommendation on both the intensity of the workload and the capabilities of the connected devices. The standard deviation of the normalized load of each datastore allows Storage DRS to determine the datastore cluster load imbalance.

Figure 106: I/O load balancing input

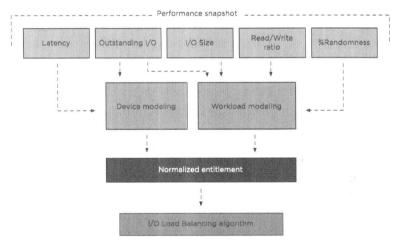

This performance snapshot contains read and write latency samples captured by the SIOC injector on the previous day. Although Storage DRS is invoked every 8 hours, the I/O load Storage DRS evaluates the same performance data from the previous day during each invocation. Effectively, I/O load balancing will recommend moves based on whole-day stats. This could lead to I/O load-balancer-related migrations once a day.

Data points

To avoid having its data polluted by peak load moments, Storage DRS does not use real-time statistics. Instead, it aggregates all the data points collected over a period of time. Storage DRS reviews the data points and if the 90th percentile I/O latency measured over a day for the datastore is greater than the threshold, Storage DRS considers the datastore as overloaded. By using the 90th percentile, Storage DRS uses the most busy 10% of the measurement period as a basis for its I/O load balancing decision. As workloads shift during the day, enough information needs to be collected to make an accurate assessment of the workloads. Therefore, Storage DRS must have at least 16 hours of data before recommendations are made. By using at least 16 hours of data, Storage DRS has enough data of the same timeslot so it can compare utilization of datastores. For example: Datastore1 to Datastore2 on Monday morning at 11:00. As 16 hours is 2/3 of the day, Storage DRS receives enough information to characterize the performance of datastores on that day. But how does this tie in with the 8-hour invocation period?

8-hour invocation period and 16 hours worth of data
Storage DRS uses 16 hours of data, however, this data must be captured in the current day otherwise the performance snapshot of the previous day is used. How is this combined with the 8-hour invocation periods?

Figure 107: Invocation period overview

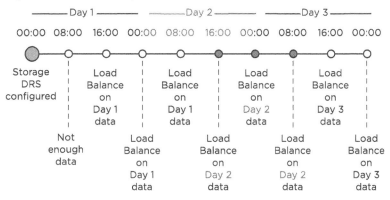

This means that the I/O load balancing is technically performed every 16 hours. Usually after midnight, after the day date, the stats are fixed and rolled up, this is is called the rollover event. The first invocation period (08:00) after the rollover event uses the 24 hours statistics of the previous day. After 16 hours of the current day have passed, Storage DRS uses the new performance snapshot and may evaluate moves based on the new stats.

Note: Storage DRS always uses past-day statistics regardless of the selected invocation period. For example if the invocation period is set to 72 hours, Storage DRS still reviews the data collected from the previous 16 hours.

Load Imbalance Recommendations

The I/O latency threshold defines the trigger point for considering load balancing to reduce latency. To do this, Storage DRS identifies the normalized load of each datastore. If a normalized load exceeds the user-set I/O latency threshold, Storage DRS reviews the load differences between the datastores in the datastore cluster and compares that to the value of tolerated imbalance set by the I/O imbalance threshold. If the load difference between the datastores matches or exceeds the tolerated imbalance, Storage DRS initiates the process to recommend migrations.

Figure 108: I/O imbalance threshold

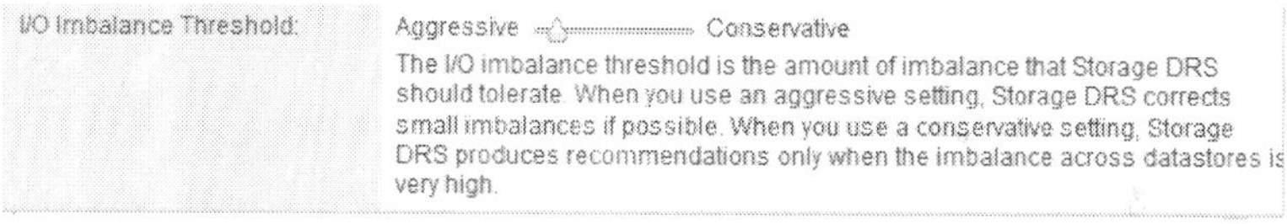

The I/O imbalance threshold can be set from Conservative to Aggressive by moving the slider to the appropriate side. A more conservative setting causes Storage DRS to generate recommendations only when the imbalance across the datastores is very high, while selecting a more aggressive setting would make Storage DRS generate recommendations to solve even small imbalances.

Cost-Benefit Analysis

The cost-benefit analysis is similar to the cost-benefit analysis of the space load balancer.

Cost: The cost is related to the duration of the Storage vMotion, which by itself is dependent on the size of the virtual machine disk files.

Benefit: The benefit is the estimated improvement of I/O latency that will be achieved on the source disk after the virtual machine has been migrated to the destination disk. If, after subtracting the cost from the benefit, the benefit remains greater than zero, Storage DRS will generate an I/O load balance recommendation. If the imbalance is very low between the source and destination datastores and the VMDK files are large, the value can be zero due to the fact that the estimated Storage vMotion time is so high that it does not make sense to recommend the move.

Ignoring Peak Moments

Storage DRS starts to generate I/O load-related recommendations once an imbalance persists for some period of time, usually at least 10% of a day (or approximately 2.4 hours). This prevents Storage DRS from being impacted by peak load moments. The duration of the imbalance period depends on the workload and the I/O imbalance threshold.

SIOC Latency and Storage DRS Latency

Although SIOC is leveraged by Storage DRS, its latency threshold setting is decoupled from Storage DRS. The configured latency threshold for Storage DRS is used by Storage DRS to classify a datastore as being overloaded and make recommendations to prevent bottlenecks and hotspots. The configured latency threshold for SIOC is used by SIOC to detect contention and throttle hosts based on this information to ensure each virtual machine receives the amount of resources it is entitled to.

To compute the latency metric, Storage DRS in vSphere 5.1 uses what is called vmObservedLatency while SIOC only uses device latency. vmObservedLatency is the time between the hypervisor receiving an I/O request from the virtual machine and getting I/O response back from the datastore. Storage DRS in vSphere 5.0 only measured the time between the I/O request leaving the ESXi host and the response coming back. By using vmObservedLatency, Storage DRS is also aware of any queuing delays (wait time) occurring inside the host.

To leverage vmObservedLatency, all hosts connected to the datastore cluster should be vSphere 5.1 or higher. This metric is included in the SIOC Performance Charts in the vSphere UI.

To avoid misaligned latency threshold settings, SIOC in vSphere 5.1 automatically determines the latency threshold for each device. The default latency threshold for datastores in a datastore cluster is based on the device model. This threshold corresponds to 90% of peak IOPS of the disks backing the datastore. SIOC will not set the threshold lower than the specified I/O latency threshold when the I/O metric is enabled.

Basic design principle

If you set the SIOC latency manually, set the SIOC latency higher than Storage DRS latency threshold, because Storage DRS latency is about correcting to reduce and avoid contention, whereas SIOC latency is about throttling workloads in a fair way when there is contention.

Datastore correlation detector

IO load balancing operations in vSphere 5.1 avoid recommending migration of virtual machines between two performance-correlated datastores. Performance-correlated datastores are datastores that share the same backend resource such as disk- or RAID-groups. When multiple datastores share the same disk- or RAID-group, their performance characteristics could be interrelated, i.e. if one datastore experiences high latency, the other datastores sharing the same disks might experience similarly high latency since the same disks service I/Os from both datastores.

In vSphere 5.0, Storage DRS depended on VASA to determine whether datastores are performance correlated. In vSphere 5.1, the SIOC injector has been extended to include datastore correlation detector capability.

How does it work? The datastore correlation detector measures performance during isolation and when concurrent IOs are pushed to multiple datastores. For example, Datastore1 and Datastore2 belong to the same datastore cluster. The SIOC injector uses a synthetic workload to measure to average IO latency of Datastore1 in isolation. Next, it measures the average IO latency of Datastore2 in isolation. The third step uses the same workload on both datastores simultaneously.

The first two steps are used to establish the baseline for each datastore. If the average latency of each datastore in step 3 has increased significantly, the datastores are marked as performance-correlated. If there is no performance correlation, concurrent IO to one datastores should have no effect on the other datastore. If two datastores are performance-correlated, the concurrent IO streams should amplify the average IO latency on both datastores.

When two datastores are marked as performance-correlated, Storage DRS does not generate IO load balancing recommendations between those two datastores. However Storage DRS can still generate recommendations to move virtual machines between two correlated datastores to address out of space situations or to correct rule violations.

Load balancing recommendations

Unified recommendations

Storage DRS generates both space and I/O load balancing recommendations separately. However, it will weigh and combine both recommendations to provide a unified recommendation.

A migration recommendation should not violate any user-set threshold. For example, migrating a virtual machine to resolve an I/O load imbalance should not create a situation that results in a space load balance violation on the destination datastore and require Storage DRS to generate another migration recommendation to resolve the space imbalance.

To avoid this scenario, Storage DRS calculates the space and I/O load imbalances for each candidate migration and selects the migration that improves the I/O load imbalance while not decreasing the space balance. To address any conflicting goals, each move is awarded a *goodness* metric that represents the weighted sum of the improvements to the I/O load and space load imbalances.

If the space load metric of each datastore is substantially below the space utilization threshold, the I/O load metric becomes the dominant factor in migration recommendations. However, if the space utilization of a datastore is above the threshold, the space metric receives more weight than the I/O load metric. Likewise, if I/O is overcommitted, the I/O load metric receives more weight than the space metric. Otherwise, both metrics receive equal weight.

If both thresholds are exceeded, Storage DRS can still decide not to generate migration recommendations if, for example, no valid moves exist. This can occur due to VM anti-affinity rules or because the cost of each move outweighs the benefit of that move. For example, the benefit value of a move can be zero if migrating virtual machines with large disks is the only way to solve a very low I/O imbalance. In this scenario, the cost of the Storage vMotion time would exceed the improvement on the I/O load balance in the datastore cluster.

Dependent Migration Recommendations

Dependent migration recommendations consist of multiple recommendations that must be executed in order, as a whole, to achieve a positive gain (load balanced). It is entirely possible that partial executions of this set may lead to a negative gain (worse imbalance). Storage DRS does not generate dependent migration recommendations during load balancing operations; however, Storage DRS may generate multiple independent moves which can lead to a positive gain of load balance. These independent moves can be executed in any order and still result in an improvement of load balance. Applying a subset of recommendations may also lead to an improvement, but with a smaller positive gain than applying the full set of recommendations.

Note that initial placement and migrations of virtual disks will be based on the space availability and that the Storage DRS algorithm can issue multiple Storage vMotion actions as part of its recommendation in order to accommodate a virtual disk within a datastore. See the cluster defragmentation section for more information.

Cultivation Time

Storage DRS migration recommendations will be delayed after Storage DRS is enabled for the first time. As mentioned in the data points section, Storage DRS requires at least 16 hours' worth of data before it can use the performance snapshot for migration recommendations. On top of this, Storage DRS will have a "warm-up" period in which it determines the capabilities of connected storage array(s) and the characteristics of the active workloads. This results in delays before the first set of migration recommendations is generated. In general, Storage DRS is being conservative about issuing load-balancing recommendations before it has collected enough information about the environment.

Invocation triggers

The I/O load balancing algorithm is automatically invoked every 8 hours. When the invocation interval expires, Storage DRS will compute and generate recommendations to migrate virtual machines. Each recommendation that is not applied is retired at the next invocation of Storage DRS; Storage DRS might generate the same recommendation again if the imbalance is not resolved.

The invocation period can be changed via the user interface and can range between 60 minutes and 43200 minutes (30 days). If the invocation period is set to 0, periodic load balancing is turned off.

Changing the default value is strongly discouraged. A less frequent interval might reduce the number of Storage vMotions and result in less overhead, but may lead to longer datastore cluster imbalance.
Shortening the interval will likely generate extra overhead while providing little additional benefit.

Besides periodic scheduling according to the configured invocation frequency, the Storage DRS imbalance calculation is also performed when it detects changes, such as:

- The datastore cluster configuration is updated.
- A datastore is entering maintenance mode.
- During initial placement. [No load balancing]
- A datastore is moved into a datastore cluster.
- A datastore exceeds its configured space threshold.
- When "Run Storage DRS" is invoked.

Cluster configuration change:
If the thresholds or invocation period is changed, Storage DRS triggers a new imbalance calculation.

Datastore maintenance mode:
When triggering maintenance mode, Storage DRS leverages vCenter APIs to retrieve a list of registered virtual machines on a given datastore. Storage DRS generates the migration recommendations and, depending on the automation level, it presents the list directly to vCenter for execution or presentation to the user.

Note

If there are any faults generated with respect to putting the datastore into maintenance mode, manual override kicks in. In this case, the user must cancel the request to enter maintenance mode or approve the recommendations and agree to manually address the faults.

Because Storage DRS retrieves information via vCenter APIs, and uses the vCenter APIs to move virtual machine files, it will only generate migration recommendations for virtual machines that are registered in vCenter. Orphaned virtual machines or other non-related files will not be migrated. When executing migration recommendations, vCenter only considers the remaining datastores of the datastore cluster as destinations. Datastores outside the cluster are not considered as suitable and compatible destinations.

Initial placement: Initial placement of a virtual machine or virtual disk will trigger the Storage DRS imbalance calculation when:

- A virtual machine is created.
- A virtual machine is cloned.
- A virtual disk is added to a virtual machine.
- A virtual machine or virtual disk is migrated into the datastore cluster.

Exceeding threshold: An invocation of Storage DRS will be scheduled to run when a host reports datastore usage above the user-set threshold or when a thin-provisioning out-of-space alarm is triggered.

Invocation Frozen Zone

Each ESXi host reports datastore space utilization statistics to vCenter on a regular basis. vCenter compares the utilization statistics to the imbalance threshold and schedules a Storage DRS invocation if the utilization exceeds the threshold.

Because ESXi hosts do not report on a synchronous basis, vCenter might keep on receiving utilization statistics while a virtual machine is being migrated to solve the space utilization violation. To counter possible Storage DRS schedule requests from vCenter due to space threshold issues, an invocation "frozen zone" is introduced. After each Storage DRS invocation, Storage DRS invocation cannot be scheduled for at least 10 minutes.

Future Storage DRS invocations take these recommendations into account; the best practice would be to apply such recommendations as soon as possible.

Recommendation Calculation

Storage DRS performs multiple calculations and passes in order to generate migration recommendations. Storage DRS determines the datastore cluster imbalance and selects suitable virtual machines to migrate to solve the imbalance. It monitors both space load and I/O performance in order to generate the migration recommendation. Before generating recommendations, Storage DRS checks for constraint violations.

Constraints Violation Corrections

The constraint correction pass determines whether Storage DRS needs to recommend mandatory Storage vMotions:

- To correct VMDK-VMDK anti-affinity rule violations
- To correct VMDK-VMDK affinity rule violations.
- To correct VM-VM anti-affinity rule violations.

If no acceptable move can be found to fix a violation, Storage DRS will display the reason why it cannot fix the violation in a fault message located in the Storage DRS view.

Chapter 22

Storage I/O Control

As Storage I/O Control is enabled by Storage DRS when a datastore cluster is created and "IO Metric" is enabled, we felt that a chapter on Storage I/O Control was appropriate. On top of that, Storage DRS leverages certain capabilities from Storage I/O Control to determine the capabilities of a datastore. Before we get to that, let's discuss the basics first.

Introduction

Storage I/O Control (SIOC) provides a method to fairly distribute storage I/O resources during times of contention. It enables administrators to run important workloads in a highly consolidated, virtualized storage environment without the risk of a self-inflicted denial of service attack. In addition, it helps prevent the noisy neighbor problem, where a single virtual machine could have a negative impact on the performance of other virtual machines on the same datastore. SIOC leverages virtual disk shares in order to fairly distribute storage resources. Shares for virtual disks were introduced long before SIOC was released, however, SIOC introduced datastore-wide scheduling. The main difference being that without SIOC scheduling is done on a per-host level. Although the algorithm used for SIOC is fairly complex, enabling and configuring SIOC is not (Figure 109). SIOC can be enabled in just a few steps and, when Storage DRS is used with the I/O metrics option, it will be automatically enabled. Before we show some examples, we want to make sure that everyone understands some of the basics around queuing and what the world looked like without SIOC.

Figure 109: Enabling Storage I/O Control

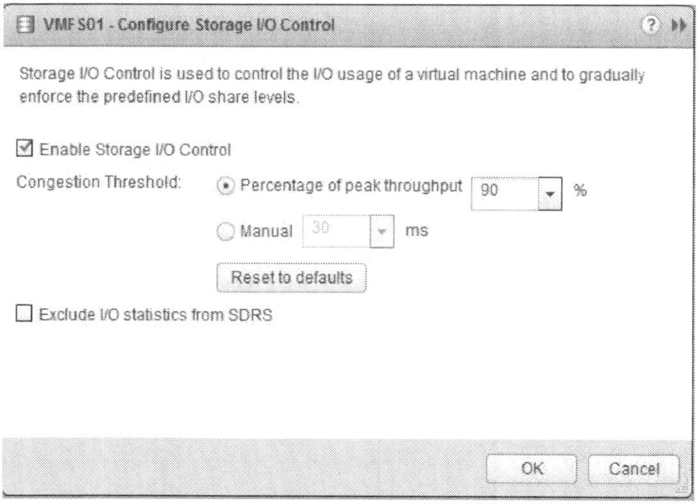

Queuing Internals

When discussing SIOC with many of our customers, we noticed there was a general misconception about how it actually ensures that resources are fairly distributed amongst all virtual machines and hosts. The examples include it, but the mechanism might not be obvious to everyone, so we will call it out specifically: Queue Throttling.

Before we will explain how the queue throttling works, we want to briefly explain the different queues that are part of the flow. When the guest OS initiates an I/O, this is the order of the flow and the queues encountered along the way:

- Guest device driver queue depth (LSI=32, PVSCSI=64).
- vHBA (Hard coded limit: LSI=128, PVSCSI=255).
- VMkernel Device Driver (FC=32, iSCSI=128, NFS=256, local disk=256).
- Multiple SAN/Array Queues (Includes port buffers, port queues, disk queues, etc.).

Those who are paying attention noticed that *Disk.SchedNumReqOutstanding* (DSNRO) is not mentioned. Normally it would be mentioned straight before the VMkernel Device Driver, however, when SIOC is enabled, DSNRO is no longer used since SIOC guarantees a certain level of fairness.

Although DSNRO does not come into play when SIOC is enabled, we do feel it is worth taking a sidestep to explain it:

When two or more virtual machines are issuing I/Os to the same datastore, *Disk.SchedNumReqOutstanding* will limit the number of I/Os that will be issued to the LUN. So, what does that mean?

Consider the situation in which you have set your queue depth for your HBA to 64 and a virtual machine is issuing I/Os to a datastore. If it is just a single virtual machine on the datastore, up to 64 I/Os will then end up in the device driver immediately. In most environments, however, LUNs are shared by many virtual machines and, in most cases, these virtual machines should be treated equally. When two or more virtual machines issue I/O to the same datastore, DSNRO kicks in. However, it will only throttle the queue when the VMkernel has detected that the threshold of a certain counter is reached. The name of this counter is *Disk.SchedQControlVMSwitches* and it is set to 6 by default. This means that the VMkernel will need to have detected 6 VM switches when handling I/O before it will throttle the queue down to the value of *Disk.SchedNumReqOutstanding*: by default, 32.

(VM Switches means that it will need to detect 6 times that the current I/O is not coming from the same VM as the previous I/O.)

The reason the throttling happens is because the VMkernel cannot control the order of the I/Os that have been issued to the driver. Just imagine you have VM-A issuing a lot of I/Os and another, VM-B, issuing just a few I/Os. VM-A would end up using most of the full queue depth all the time. Every time VM-B issues an I/O, it will be picked up quickly by the VMkernel scheduler (which is a different topic) and sent to the driver as soon as another one completes from there, but it will need to get in line behind the 64 I/Os from VM-A that are already in the queue. This will add significantly to the I/O latency experienced by VM-B, which is not desirable. By limiting the number of outstanding requests, we allow the VMkernel to schedule VM-B's I/O sooner into the I/O stream from VM-A, thus reducing the latency penalty for VM-B.

Now, that brings us to the second part of all statements out there: should we really set *Disk.SchedNumReqOutstanding* to the same value as your queue depth? Well, in the case where you want your I/Os processed as quickly as possible, without any fairness, you probably should. But, if you have mixed workloads on a single datastore and don't want virtual machines to incur excessive latency just because a single virtual machine issues a lot of I/O's, you probably shouldn't.

Is that it? No, not really. There are several questions that remain unanswered:

- What about sequential I/O in the case of Disk.SchedNumReqOutstanding?
- How does the VMkernel know when to stop using Disk.SchedNumReqOutstanding?

Let's tackle the sequential I/O question first. The VMkernel will, by default, issue up to 8 sequential commands (controlled by *Disk.SchedQuantum*) from a virtual machine in a row, even when it would normally seem more fair to take an I/O from another virtual machine. This is done in order to preserve the "sequential-ness" of virtual machine workloads because I/O's that happen to sectors nearby the previous I/O are handled an order of magnitude faster than I/O's to sectors far away – 10x is not unusual when excluding cache effects or when caches are small compared to the disk size. But, what is considered sequential? Well, if the next I/O is less than 2000 sectors away from the current one, the I/O is considered to be sequential. This distance is controlled by the advanced parameter, *Disk.SectorMaxDiff*.

Now, if one of the virtual machines becomes idle, you would more than likely prefer your active virtual machine to be able to use the full queue depth again. This is what *Disk.SchedQControlSeqReqs* is for. By default, *Disk.SchedQControlSeqReqs* is set to 128, meaning that when a virtual machine has been able to issue 128 commands without any switches, *Disk.SchedQControlVMSwitches* will be reset to 0 again and the active virtual machine can use the full queue depth of 64 again. With our previous example in mind, the idea is that, if VM-B is issuing very rare I/Os (less than 1 in every 128 from another virtual machine), then we will let VM-B pay the high penalty on latency because, presumably, it is not disk bound anyway.

Before we continue, let's be absolutely clear here as this is a general misconception that many people have; when SIOC is enabled, DSNRO is no longer applicable. SIOC applies fairness and does this based on incurred latency rather than counting VM switches. In other words, if the latency threshold is not exceeded, SIOC will not throttle the queue.

When SIOC is enabled, it will request the maximum device queue depth per device and set it to the maximum. SIOC tries to set queue depth up to 256. In most cases, however, it gets set to 32. The reason for this is that most manufacturers use this as their default value. This brings us to a design principle.

Basic design principle

As SIOC is responsible for applying fairness during contention, make use of your array's capabilities and consult your storage vendor and, when supported, set the queue depth to a minimum of 64.

If the latency threshold is exceeded (these statistics are computed every 4 seconds), SIOC dynamically throttles the hosts' queues based on their I/O slot entitlement on the array level. Note that when we talk about latency, SIOC looks at device latency. Device latency is the average latency observed on a datastore from all hosts connected to the datastore.

How does SIOC determine the entitlement for each virtual machine and ultimately each host? The PARDA whitepaper (Academic paper discussing SIOC research and development) describes it as follows:

Quote

"Resource allocations are specified by numeric shares, which are assigned to virtual machines that consume I/O resources. A virtual machine is entitled to consume storage array resources proportional to its share allocation, which specifies the relative importance of its I/O requests compared to other virtual machines. The I/O shares associated with a host are simply the total number of per-virtual machine shares summed across all of its virtual machines. Proportional share fairness is defined as providing storage array service to hosts in proportion to their shares."

The question remains, how does each host know what latency is observed by the other hosts?

Communication Mechanism?

SIOC uses a mechanism similar to HA: a shared file on a datastore. This shared file, *.iormstats.sf* (Figure 110), can be accessed by multiple hosts simultaneously. Each host periodically writes its average latency and the number of I/Os for that datastore into the file. This enables all hosts to read the file and compute the datastore-wide latency average, which in turn allows for the computation of the queue depth for each host based on the I/O slot entitlement.

Figure 110: Communication mechanism

```
/vmfs/volumes/4c6fb200-b663ac67-3b91-0022195e7f25 # ls -lah
drwxr-xr-t   1 root    root       9.8k Oct  6 17:54 .
drwxr-xr-x   1 root    root        512 Oct  7 21:47 ..
drwxr-xr-x   1 root    root        420 Aug 27 14:26 .dvsData
-r--------   1 root    root       4.8M Aug 13 10:41 .fbb.sf
-r--------   1 root    root      60.2M Aug 13 10:41 .fdc.sf
-rwxr-xr-x   1 root    root       1.0M Aug 27 15:37 .iormstats.sf
drwxr-xr-x   1 root    root        420 Aug 27 15:37 .naa.60a98000503357614e344364656f6a6d
-r--------   1 root    root     243.8M Aug 13 10:41 .pbc.sf
-r--------   1 root    root     248.3M Aug 13 10:41 .sbc.sf
-r--------   1 root    root       4.0M Aug 13 10:41 .vh.sf
```

We realize that this sounds fairly complex, so we tried visualizing how SIOC works by describing several scenarios in the following sections.

Local Disk Scheduler

The Local Disk Scheduler, sometimes referred to as SFQ (start-time fair queuing), is responsible for several things, but, as the name reveals, all of them relate to host-side scheduling. Besides assigning each virtual machine its fair share of the I/O resource in times of contention, the local disk scheduler is also responsible for limiting virtual machines when an IOPS limit has been defined.

The local disk scheduler influences the host-level prioritization for all virtual machines running on the same ESXi host. This, by itself, could be of great value when certain virtual machines need a higher priority than others, but also when all virtual machines should be treated as equals. The following diagram depicts a scenario where 3 virtual machines all have equal shares, but two of them (VM1 and VM2) receive less bandwidth because they are running on a different host.

Figure 111: Local Disk Scheduler

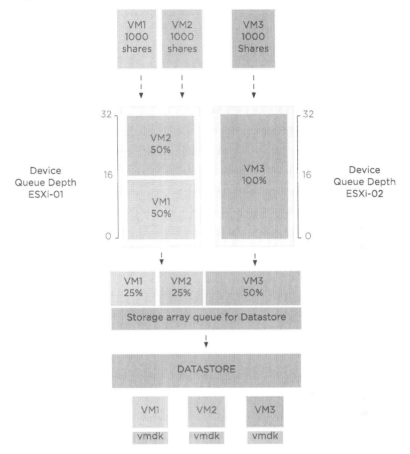

Datastore-Wide Disk Scheduler

The Datastore-wide Disk Scheduler kind of resembles the Local Disk Scheduler in that it will prioritize virtual machines over others depending on the number of shares assigned to their respective disks. It does this by calculating the I/O slot entitlement, but only when the configurable latency threshold has been exceeded.

An example would probably clarify how this works. The following diagram (Figure 112) depicts the scenario where a host is throttled as the latency threshold has been exceeded.

Figure 112: Datastore-wide Disk Scheduler

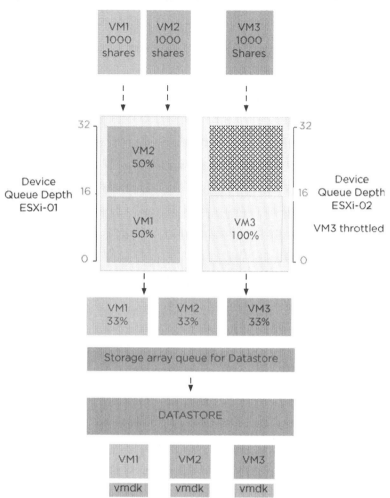

The Datastore-wide Disk Scheduler sums up the disk shares for each of the VMDKs of the virtual machines on the datastore. In the case of ESXi-01, that is 2000, and in the case of ESXi-02, it is 1000. Next, the datastore-wide disk scheduler will calculate the I/O slot entitlement based on the host-level shares and it will throttle the queue. In the example, each of the virtual machines is entitled to 33% of the storage resources. ESXi-01 will receive 66% and ESXi-02 will receive 33%. If you compare this to the scenario in Figure 111, you can understand why it is recommended to enable SIOC on all datastores, even if there is no need to prioritize.

Let it be clear that SIOC does not make latency magically dissolve. By throttling the queue, latency moves up the stack from the device to the kernel. However, this does imply that only a subset of virtual machines on a datastore incurs higher latency instead of all virtual machines on that datastore. On top of that, it is based on the entitlement of the virtual machine: a virtual machine with a lower I/O slot entitlement will incur more latency, which is how it should be.

Basic design principle

Even when there is no need to prioritize virtual machines over each other, there is a benefit to enabling Storage I/O Control as it helps prevent self-inflicted Denial of Service attacks.

Not Yet Another Example

With equal shares for all virtual machines, the example is fairly simple. However, in the case of different amounts of shares, it becomes more complex. We want to provide an additional example to make sure everyone understands the basics. In this scenario, there are 3 virtual machines (Figure 113). Two of the virtual machines (VM2 and VM3) have been assigned 500 shares each and VM1 has 1500 shares assigned. VM1 is entitled to 60% of the available I/O slots and VM2 and VM3 are entitled to 20% each. This can be calculated simply by adding up all the shares and dividing the number of shares per virtual machine by the result. In the case of VM1, the formula would be:

VM1 / (VM1 + VM2 + VM3)
or
1500 / (1500 + 500 + 500) = 60%

As shown, VM1 is entitled to 60% of the I/O slots and both VM2 and VM3 are entitled to 20%.

Figure 113: SIOC scenario 2

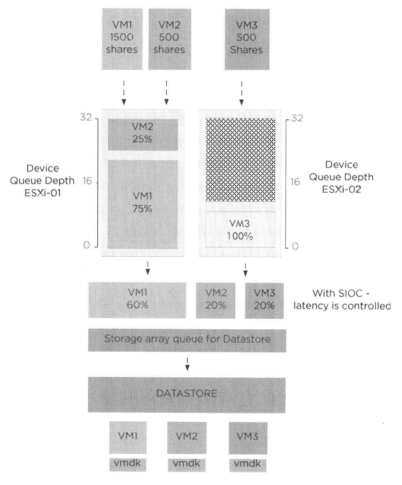

Automatic Latency Threshold Computations

The latency threshold in vSphere 5.0 is a user-specified setting, defaulting to 30 milliseconds. However this is not appropriate for all datastore types. Because SIOC supports multiple types of devices, a middle-of-the ground threshold setting is used. Certain devices such as SSD hit the natural contention point earlier than others, which requires the user to configure a lower threshold on that specific datastore. However, manually determining the correct latency can be difficult. To avoid mis-aligned latency threshold settings, SIOC in vSphere 5.1 automatically determines the latency threshold for each device.

The automatic latency threshold computation models the device throughput capabilities and sets the latency accordingly, allowing the virtual infrastructure to take advantage of the full capabilities of a device. The user interface provides controls in terms of % of Peak IOPS to influence the automatic calculations; the user interface also provides the opportunity to set the latency manually.

Figure 114: Configure Storage I/O Control

VMFS01 - Configure Storage I/O Control

Storage I/O Control is used to control the I/O usage of a virtual machine and to gradually enforce the predefined I/O share levels.

☑ Enable Storage I/O Control

Congestion Threshold: ● Percentage of peak throughput 90 ▾ %

○ Manual 30 ▾ ms

Reset to defaults

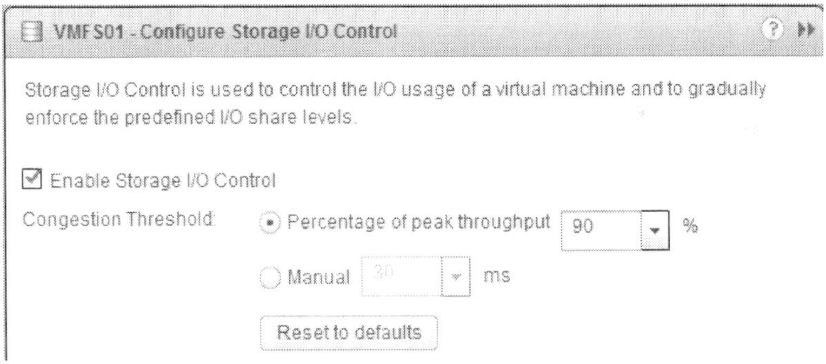

Manual Latency Threshold Recommendations

It is recommend leveraging the new automatic threshold setting provided in vSphere 5.1. If there might be occasions when there is a need to set the threshold manually, it is generally recommended to set different thresholds for different types of disks (see Table 25).

It should be pointed out, however, that when SIOC is used in conjunction with Storage DRS, the Storage DRS I/O latency threshold should be set lower than the SIOC latency threshold. Where SIOC is aimed at preventing short latency peaks by throttling the queue depth, Storage DRS aims to solve imbalances and to lower the average latency of a datastore by migrating workloads. Where SIOC looks at device latency, Storage DRS looks at overall latency, including both device and kernel latency. This means that when the SIOC latency threshold is lower than the Storage DRS I/O latency, it will not have an impact on Storage DRS recommendations because Storage DRS takes both device and kernel latency into account. As explained in the Datastore-Wide Disk Scheduler section of this chapter, latency doesn't dissolve, it moves to a different layer. We do, however, recommend setting the Storage DRS I/O latency to half of the value used for SIOC so that SIOC will mitigate latency spikes and Storage DRS will prevent hot spots.

Table 25: Recommend latency thresholds

Type of Storage Media used	Recommended Latency Threshold
SSD	10-15ms
FC	20-30ms
SAS	20-30ms
SATA	30-50ms

Injector

One of the components we haven't touched yet is the Injector. What does it do and what is it for? The Injector was introduced in vSphere 5.0 as part of SIOC to determine the performance characteristics of a datastore. We have already briefly touched on performance characteristics in Chapter 22 and made the recommendation to aggregate datastores into a datastore cluster based on availability and performance similarities. In most environments, administrators carefully define their tiers of storage, but many don't realize that the number of disks backing each datastore likely makes a difference in performance behavior. Even a small difference in the number of disks (7 vs. 9) may cause a significant difference in performance. On top of that, some arrays use large disk pools and stripe LUNs across these pools. In those scenarios, the location on the disk may even make a difference in terms of performance characteristics. Although VASA exposes some storage characteristics like RAID, it currently does not provide performance characteristics.

In order to ensure that Storage DRS I/O balancing placement logic is not only based on a threshold value and observed latency, SIOC also characterizes datastores by injecting random I/O. Before anyone gets worried that this injection might interfere with their workloads, we want to stress that the Injector only becomes active when the datastore is idle. Even when the Injector process has started, if I/O is detected from other sources, the Injector will stop characterizing and retry later. On top of that, the injected I/O is only read I/O. In order to characterize the device, different amounts of outstanding I/Os are used and latency is monitored. In other words, random read I/O is injected and every time with a different number of outstanding I/Os. The outcome can be plotted simply in a graph (Figure 115) and the slope of this graph indicates the performance of the datastore.

Quote

"In mathematics, the slope or gradient of a line describes its steepness, incline, or grade. A higher slope value indicates a steeper incline."

Figure 115: Device modeling using different numbers of disks

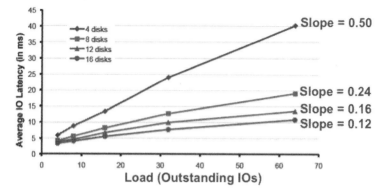

As this example demonstrates, when the number of Outstanding I/Os increases, the latency also increases for each device. The rates at which the increases occur are different, and that is exactly what helps Storage DRS make recommendations for load balancing and initial placement. We would like to refer those who want to read more on this topic to the BASIL academic paper written by the Storage DRS engineering team.

https://www.usenix.org/conference/fast-10/basil-automated-io-load-balancing-across-storage-devices

SIOC logging

Sometimes it is necessary to troubleshoot your environment and having logs
to review is helpful in determining what is actually happening. By default,
SIOC logging is disabled, but it should be enabled before collecting logs. To
enable logging:

1. Click Host Advanced Settings.
2. In the Misc section, select the Misc.SIOControlLogLevel parameter.
   Set the value to 7 for complete logging. (Min value: 0 (no logging),
   Max value: 7)
3. SIOC needs to be restarted to change the log level, to stop and
   start SIOC manually, use /etc/init.d/storageRM
   {start|stop|status|restart}
4. After changing the log level, you see the log level changes logged in
   the/var/log/vmkernel logs.

Please note that SIOC log files are saved in /var/log/vmkernel.

Exclude I/O statistics from Storage DRS

When configuring SIOC at the datastore level, vSphere 5.1 offers the
"Exclude I/O statistics from Storage DRS" option in the user interface.

Figure 116: Exclude I/O statistics from Storage DRS

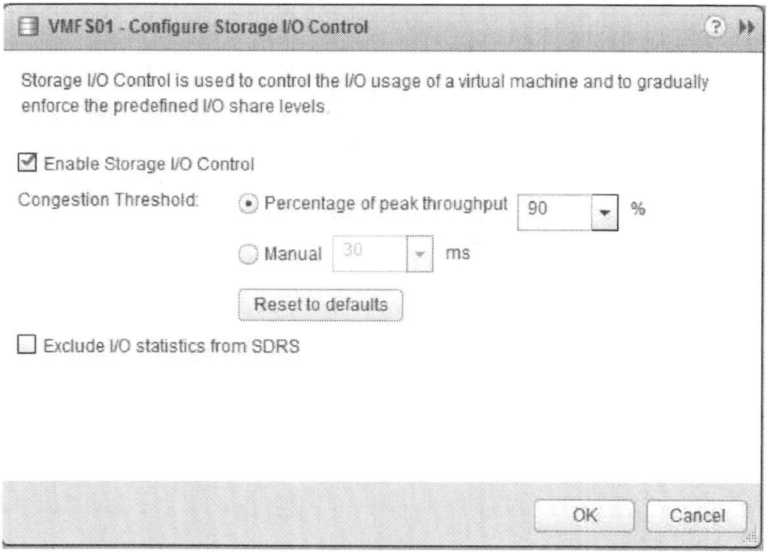

When enabled, Storage DRS stops using statistics reported by the datastore, until this option is disabled again. This allows an administrator to manually introduce a storage maintenance window for a period when reported I/O stats are abnormal and should not be taken into account for Storage DRS load balancing. Workloads that introduce abnormal stats are for example an atypical backup operation or the migration of a large group of virtual machines into the datastore cluster.

Chapter 23

Datastore Cluster Configuration

Datastore clusters form the basis of Storage DRS and can best be described as a collection of datastores aggregated (Figure 117) into a single object. Once configured, datastore clusters are managed rather than individual datastores. Please be aware that datastore clusters are referred to as "storage pods" in the vSphere API.

Figure 117: Datastore Cluster ecosystem architecture

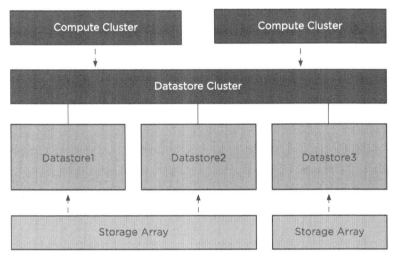

A datastore cluster is used as the storage destination during the provisioning process. The provisioning process not only refers to the creation of a virtual machine, but also to adding a disk to an existing virtual machine, cloning a virtual machine or moving a virtual machine by Storage vMotion operation into the datastore cluster.

The datastore cluster becomes a load-balancing domain once Storage DRS is enabled. Initial placement will select the datastore with the lowest space utilization and I/O load and the load balancing algorithms issue migration recommendations when thresholds have been exceeded AND there is a significant I/O or space imbalance.

The workflow for creating a datastore cluster is straightforward.

Creating a Datastore Cluster

Before we show the eight basic steps that need to be taken when creating a datastore cluster, we want to list some constraints and our recommendations for creating datastore clusters.

Constraints:

- VMFS and NFS cannot be part of the same datastore cluster.
- Similar disk types should be used inside a datastore cluster.
- Maximum of 64 datastores per datastore cluster.
- Maximum of 256 datastore clusters per vCenter Server.
- Maximum of 9000 VMDKs per datastore cluster

Recommendations:

- Group disks with similar characteristics (RAID-1 with RAID-1, Replicated with Replicated, 15k RPM with 15k RPM, etc.)
- Leverage information provided by vSphere Storage APIs - Storage Awareness

The Steps

1. Go to the Home screen.
2. Go to Storage
3. Select Datastore Clusters in Related Objects view.
4. Click on "Create a new datastore cluster".
5. Provide the datastore cluster with a name and leave "Turn On Storage DRS" enabled.
6. Select the virtual datacenter for the new datastore cluster.
7. Select "No Automation"(Manual Mode) or "Fully Automated".
8. Accept all default settings and click Next.

9. Select the Hosts and Clusters you wish to add this datastore cluster to.
10. Select the appropriate datastores.
11. Validate the selected configuration and click finish.

The datastore cluster will be created literally in seconds. Some of you might be wondering what all the Storage DRS Runtime Rules are for – we will discuss those in the following chapter. If "Storage DRS" is not enabled, a datastore cluster will be created which lists the datastores underneath, but Storage DRS won't recommend any placement action for provisioning or migration operations on the datastore cluster.

Name and Location
The first steps are to enable Storage DRS, specify the datastore cluster name and check if the "Turn on Storage DRS" option is enabled.

Figure 118: Turn on Storage DRS

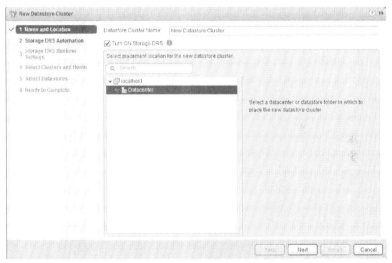

When "Turn on Storage DRS" is activated, the following functions are enabled:

- Initial placement for virtual disks based on space and I/O workload
- Space load balancing among datastores within a datastore cluster
- IO load balancing among datastores within a datastore cluster

The "Turn on Storage DRS" check box enables or disables all of these components at once. If necessary, I/O balancing functions can be disabled independently. When disabling Storage DRS by disabling the "Turn On Storage DRS" check box, all the Storage DRS settings, e.g. automation level, aggressiveness controls, thresholds, rules and Storage DRS schedules will be saved so they may be restored to the same state it was in when Storage DRS was disabled.

Storage DRS Automation

Figure 119: Storage DRS Automation levels

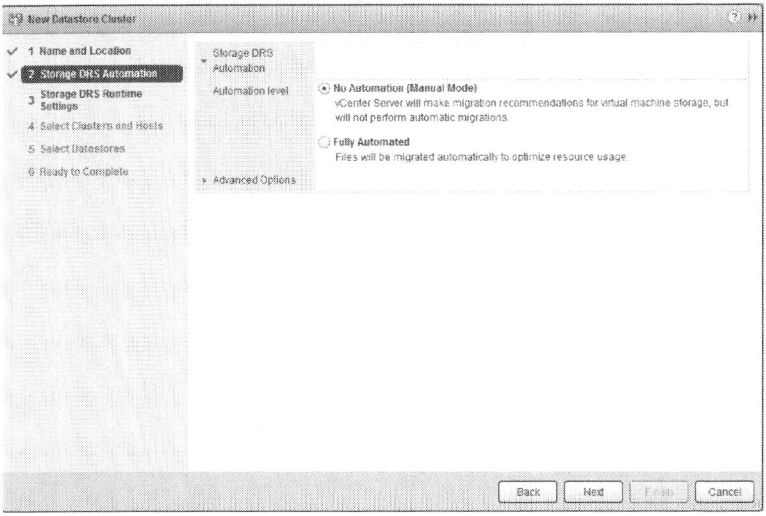

Storage DRS offers two automation levels:

No Automation (Manual Mode)
Manual mode is the default mode of operation. When the datastore cluster is operating in manual mode, placement and migration recommendations are presented to the user, but do not run until they are manually approved.

Fully Automated

Fully automated allows Storage DRS to apply space and I/O load-balance migration recommendations automatically. No user intervention is required. However, initial placement recommendations still require user approval.

Storage DRS allows virtual machines to have individual automation level settings that override datastore cluster-level automation level settings. Virtual machine level automation levels are expanded upon in chapter 21 |Storage DRS Algorithms.

Partially Automated is Missing

Storage DRS does not offer partially automated automation that provides automatic initial placement of the virtual machines. Initial placement recommendations must always be approved manually, regardless of the selected automation level. The automation level only specifies the approval-automation of space and I/O load balancing recommendations.

Storage DRS Runtime Settings

Figure 120: Storage DRS Runtime Settings

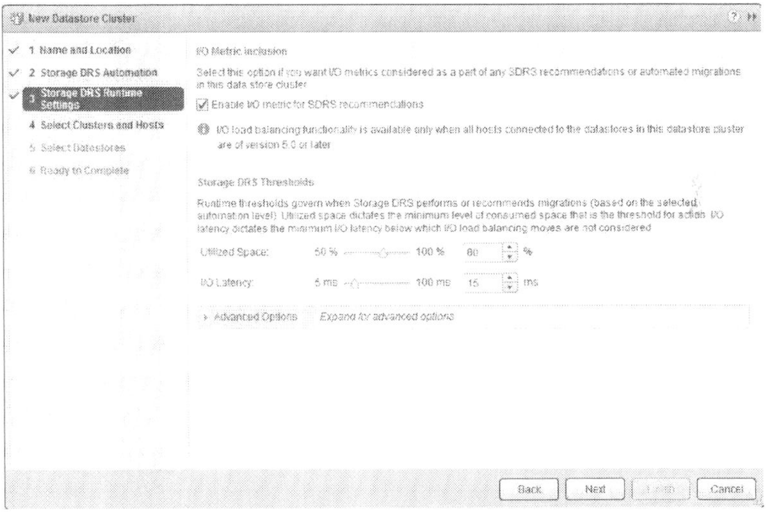

Keep the defaults for now. Chapter 21 Storage DRS Algorithms contains more information about the space and load balancing thresholds.

Select Clusters and Hosts

The "Select Hosts and Clusters" view allows the user to select one or more (DRS) clusters to work with. Only clusters within the same vSphere datacenter can be selected, as the vCenter datacenter is a storage DRS boundary

Figure 121: Select Clusters and Hosts

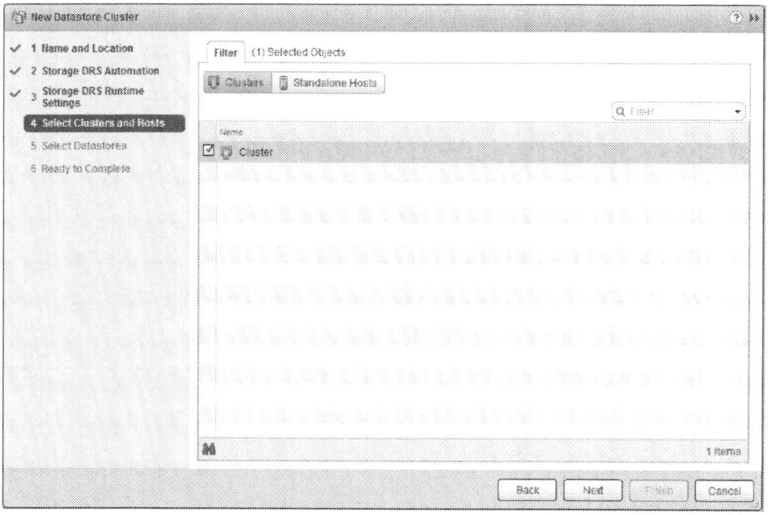

Select Datastores

By default, only datastores connected to all hosts in the selected (DRS) cluster(s) are shown. The *Show datastore* dropdown menu provides the options to show partially connected datastores. The impact of partially connected and fully connected datastores is expanded upon in the next chapter.

Figure 122: Select Datastores

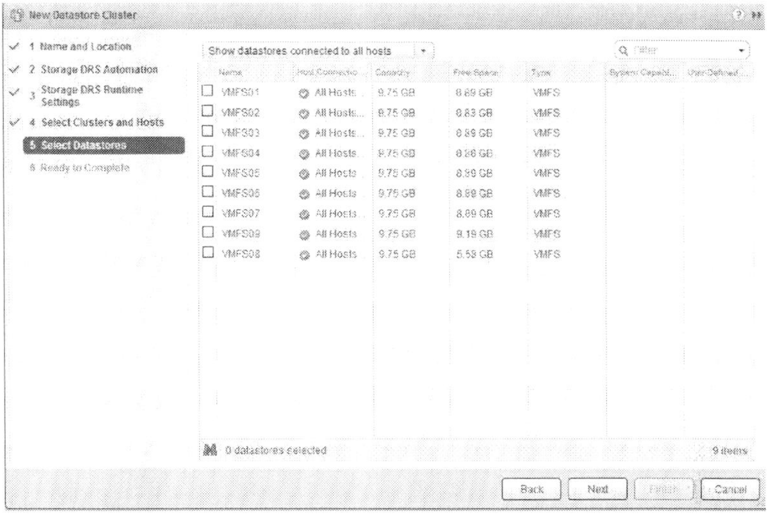

Ready to Complete

The "Ready to Complete" screen provides an overview of all the settings configured by the user.

Figure 123: New Datastore Cluster Ready to Complete

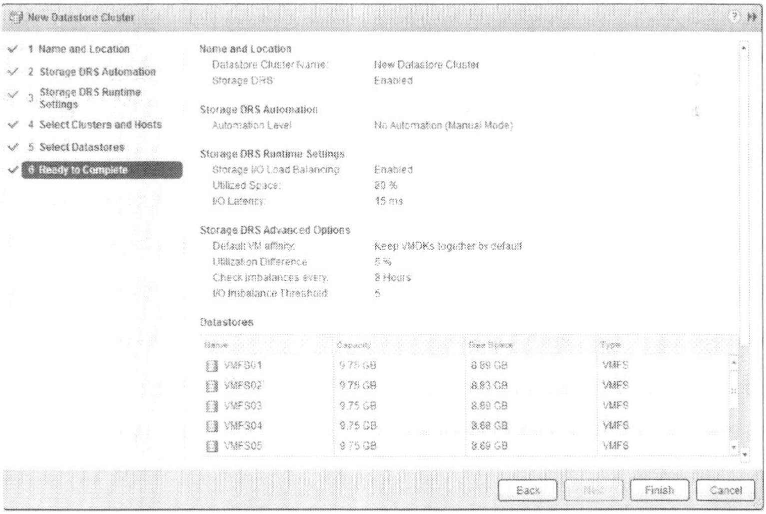

Chapter 24

Architecture and design of Datastore Clusters

Figure 124: Datastore Cluster Architecture

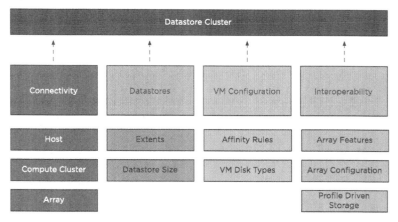

Connectivity

When introducing a datastore cluster into the infrastructure, care must be taken regarding the connectivity of the datastore cluster. There are multiple aspects of connectivity that must be considered: connectivity of a datastore cluster to hosts within a compute cluster, connectivity to multiple compute clusters, and connectivity to multiple arrays. For example, spanning a datastore cluster across multiple storage arrays is possible and supported, but what are the benefits and pitfalls of such a configuration?

Host Connectivity

Connectivity between ESXi hosts and datastores within a datastore cluster affects initial placement and load balancing decisions made by both DRS and Storage DRS. Although connecting a datastore to all ESXi hosts inside a cluster is a common practice, we still come across partially connected datastores in virtual environments. Let's start with the basic terminology.

Fully connected datastore clusters: A fully connected datastore cluster is one that contains only datastores that are available to all ESXi hosts in a DRS cluster. This is a recommendation, but it is not enforced.

Partially connected datastore clusters: If any datastore within a datastore cluster is connected to a subset of ESXi hosts inside a DRS cluster, the datastore cluster is considered a partially connected datastore cluster.

What happens if the DRS cluster is connected to partially connected datastore clusters? It is important to understand that the goal of both DRS and Storage DRS is resource availability. The key to offering resource availability is to provide as much mobility as possible. Storage DRS will not generate any migration recommendations that will reduce the compatibility (mobility) of a virtual machine regarding datastore connections. Virtual machine-to-host compatibility is calculated and captured in compatibility lists.

Compatibility list

A VM-host compatibility list is generated for each virtual machine. The compatibility list determines which ESXi hosts in the cluster have network and storage configurations that allow the virtual machine to come online successfully. The membership of a mandatory VM-to-Host affinity rule is listed in the compatibility list as well. If the virtual machine's configured network portgroup or datastore is not available on the host, or the host is not listed in the host group of a mandatory affinity rule, the ESXi server is deemed incompatible to host that virtual machine.

As mentioned, both DRS and Storage DRS focus on resource availability and resource outage avoidance. Therefore, Storage DRS prefers datastores that are connected to all hosts. Partial connectivity adversely affects the system's abilities to find a suitable initial location and load balancing becomes more challenging. During initial placement, selection of a datastore may impact the mobility of a virtual machine amongst the clustered hosts since selecting a host impacts the mobility of a virtual machines amongst the datastores in the datastore cluster.

Figure 125: Virtual machine and VMDK mobility in a partially connected architecture

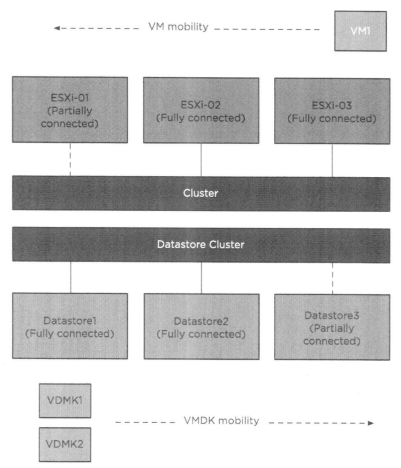

Example: During the process of generating migration recommendations, DRS selects a host that can provide enough resources to satisfy the virtual machine's dynamic entitlement, while lowering the imbalance of the cluster. DRS might come across a host with much lower utilization, than other hosts inside the cluster. If that lightly utilized host is not connected to the datastore containing the virtual machine's files, (the poor connection situation might even be the reason for the low utilization rate) DRS will not consider the host due to the incompatibility. While this host might be a very attractive option to solve resource imbalance from a DRS resource load balancing perspective, its lack of connectivity will prevent it from being more effectively utilized. Also keep in mind the impact of this behavior on VM-Host affinity rules, DRS will not migrate a virtual machine to a partially connected host inside the host group (DRS cluster). Similar imbalances can happen with Storage DRS load balancing using partially connected datastores. Partially connected datastores are not recommended when fully connected datastores are available that do not violate the space Storage DRS threshold.

Basic design principle

Connect all datastores within a datastore cluster to all ESXi host within a compute cluster

I/O load balancing

You might wonder why the space Storage DRS threshold is explicitly mentioned and not the latency threshold: that's because I/O load balancing is disabled when a partially connected datastore is detected in the datastore cluster. Not only on that single, partially connected datastore, but the *entire datastore cluster*. This effectively disables a complete feature set of your virtual infrastructure.

Partially connected datastores and the invocation period.
The connectivity status is extremely important when the Storage DRS interval expires. During the migration recommendation calculation, the connectivity state of each datastore is checked. If a partially connected datastore is detected during the check, Storage DRS disables I/O load balancing and space load balancing might not consider that datastore as a valid destination. A temporary all-paths-down status or a rezoning procedure might not have an effect on Storage DRS load-balancing behavior, but what if good old Murphy decides to give you a visit during the invocation period? Keep this in mind when scheduling maintenance on the storage platform; it might be wise to temporarily disable Storage DRS.

Benefits of partially connected datastores
We cannot identify any direct benefit of partially connecting a datastore of a cluster. Partially connected datastores impact initial placement, disable IO load-balancing and will affect both DRS load balancing and Storage DRS space balancing. Therefore a basic design decision would be to ensure that all datastores in a datastore cluster are connected to all hosts in the DRS cluster which is connected to that datastore cluster.

Increased file sharing limitations
Prior to vSphere 5.1, the maximum number of hosts that could share a read-only file on a VMFS datastore was eight. Shared files on VMFS datastores are typically linked clone virtual machines. This limits the number of hosts inside a compute cluster for VDI infrastructures and vCloud Director deployments. Storage DRS in vSphere 5.1 supports vCloud Director and its version of linked clones. Unfortunately, View's linked clones are still not supported with Storage DRS.
In vSphere 5.1, the maximum number of hosts that can share a read-only file on a VMFS has been increased to 32, allowing vCloud Director 5.1 environments to scale out to 32 fully connected hosts inside a cluster.

Note: This feature applies only to hosts running vSphere 5.1 and higher on VMFS-5.

Cluster Connectivity

A long-time best practice is to connect datastores to a single compute cluster. When introducing a new cluster, new datastores were created to contain the virtual machines provisioned onto that new cluster. This best practice was recommended primarily to reduce the number of SCSI-locks. As VAAI functionality replaces old SCSI locks, connecting datastores to multiple clusters becomes a possibility without impacting performance. With that in mind, sharing datastore clusters across multiple compute clusters is a supported configuration. Minimizing the number of datastore clusters makes initial placement of virtual machines increasingly simple. During virtual machine placement, the administrator must select the destination compute cluster and Storage DRS selects the host that can provide the most resources to the virtual machine.

A migration recommendation generated by Storage DRS does not move the virtual machine at host level. Consequently a virtual machine cannot move from one compute cluster to another compute cluster by any operation initiated by Storage DRS.

Figure 126: Load balancing domains

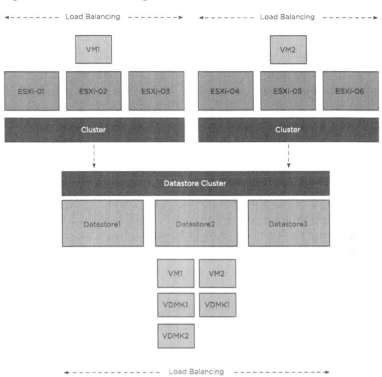

Maximums

Please remember that the maximum supported number of hosts connected to a VMFS datastore is 64. Keep this in mind when sizing compute clusters or connecting multiple compute clusters to datastore clusters using VMFS datastores. The maximum number of hosts connected to an NFS datastore depends on the maximums of the NFS filer.

The VAAI-factor

If the datastores are formatted with the VMFS, it is recommended to enable VAAI on the storage array if supported. One of the most important VAAI primitives is the hardware-assisted locking, also called Atomic Test and Set (ATS). ATS replaces the need for hosts to place a SCSI-2 disk lock on the LUN while updating the metadata or growing a file. A SCSI-2 disk lock command locks out other hosts from performing I/O on the entire LUN, while ATS enables modification of the metadata or any other sector on the disk without the use of a full SCSI-2 disk lock. This locking was the focus of many past best practices regarding datastore connectivity. To reduce the amount of locking, the best practice was to reduce the number of hosts attached to each datastore. By using newly-formatted VMFS5 volumes in combination with a VAAI-enabled storage array, SCSI-2 disk lock commands are a thing of the past. Be aware that upgraded VMFS5 volumes or VMFS3 volumes will fall back to using SCSI-2 disk locks if the ATS command fails. For more information about VAAI and ATS please read the VMware knowledge base article 1021976.

Please note that if your array doesn't support VAAI, then SCSI-2 disk lock commands can impact scaling of the architecture and performance.

Multiple compute clusters and SIOC

Virtual machines of various clusters can safely share datastores of a datastore cluster, as SIOC and its shares are datastore focused. SIOC is unaware of and unaffected by the cluster membership of a host. SIOC uses virtual disk shares to distribute storage resources fairly and these are applied on a datastore-wide level, regardless of host clustering. In short, cluster membership of the host has no impact on SIOC's abilities to detect violations of the latency threshold or manage the I/O stream to the datastore.

Array connectivity

What if multiple arrays are available to the virtual infrastructure? Are there any drawbacks to spanning the datastore cluster across multiple arrays, or would there be more benefits associated with creating a datastore cluster per array?

Combining datastores located on different storage arrays into a single datastore cluster is a supported configuration. Such a configuration could be used during a storage array data migration project where virtual machines must move from one array to another, but also when using multiple arrays on a permanent basis. The key areas to focus on are homogeneity of configurations of the arrays and datastores.

Figure 127: Array connectivity

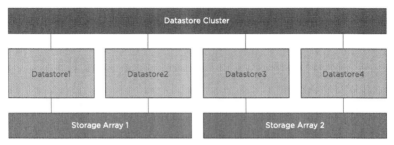

When combining datastores from multiple arrays, it is highly recommended to use datastores that are hosted on similar types of arrays, disks, and RAID levels. Using similar type of arrays implies comparable performance and redundancy features. Although RAID levels are standardized by SNIA, implementation of RAID levels by different vendors may vary from the actual RAID specifications. An implementation used by a particular vendor may affect the read and/or write performance and the degree of data redundancy compared to the same RAID level implementation of another vendor.

Would VASA and Storage profiles be any help in this configuration? VASA enables vCenter to display the capabilities of the LUN/datastore. This information could be leveraged to create a datastore cluster by selecting the datastores that report similar storage capabilities. Keep in mind that the actual capabilities surfaced by VASA are being left to the individual array storage vendors. This means that the storage capability detail and description could be similar, yet the performance or redundancy features of the datastores may differ.

Would this be harmful, or will Storage DRS stop working when aggregating datastores with different performance levels? Storage DRS will still work and will load balance virtual machines across the datastores in the datastore cluster. However, Storage DRS load balancing is focused on distributing the virtual machines in such a way that the configured thresholds are not violated and getting the best overall performance out of the datastore cluster. By mixing datastores providing different performance levels, virtual machine performance may not be consistent when migrated between datastores belonging to different arrays.

VAAI hardware offloading

Another caveat to consider is the impact of migrating virtual machines between datastores on different arrays: VAAI hardware offloading is not possible. Storage vMotion will be managed by one of the datamovers in the vSphere stack. As storage DRS does not identify "locality" of datastores, it does not incorporate the additional overhead incurred when migrating virtual machines between arrays.

Figure 128: VAAI hardware offloading

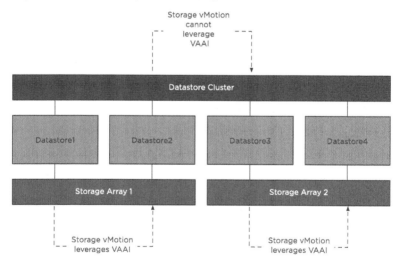

When could datastores from multiple arrays be aggregated into a single datastore cluster, if designing an environment that provides a stable and continuous level of performance, redundancy and low overhead? Datastores and array should have the following configuration:

- Identical vendor.
- Identical firmware/code.
- Identical number of spindles backing diskgroup/aggregate.
- Identical RAID Level.
- Same replication configuration.
- All datastores connected to all hosts in compute cluster.
- Equal-sized datastores.
- Equal external workload (best none at all).

We recommend creation of multiple datastore clusters, grouping of datastores belonging to each storage array into its own datastore cluster. This will reduce complexity of both the design and ongoing operations. When spanning multiple arrays, the configuration of the storage arrays need to be kept as identical, impacting the management of the storage arrays: keeping firmware versions identical across arrays in addition to maintaining array functional parity and synchronizing downtime during maintenance windows. Besides reducing operational overhead, keeping the datastore clusters confined within a storage array leverages VAAI, helping to reduce load on the storage subsystem.

Datastores

The maximum number of datastores and the disk footprint of virtual machines are usually the primary drivers of the datastore design. If a configuration standard exists within your company, be aware of the possible impact the maximum number of datastores could have on the consolidation ratio of virtual machines on a datastore cluster.

Space utilization threshold and the space safety buffer

One of the primary considerations in the consolidation ratio of the virtual machines to datastores is the space safety buffer. A common practice is to assign a big chunk of space as safety buffer to avoid an out of space situation on a datastore, which might lead to downtime of the active virtual machines. We have seen organizations using requirements of 30% free space on datastores. As Storage DRS monitors space utilization, the free space used as a safety buffer can be greatly reduced. Each ESXi host reports the virtual machine space utilization and the datastore utilization; Storage DRS will trigger an invocation if the configured space utilization threshold is violated.

By reducing slack space, a higher consolidation ratio can be achieved (if I/O performance allows this). Reclaiming slack space can provide additional space for extra datastores within the datastore cluster.

The availability of more datastores benefits Storage DRS by offering more load balancing options: more datastores increases the number of storage queues available, which benefits I/O management at the ESXi level as well as SIOC at the cluster level.

Scale up or scale out datastores

The maximum number of datastores supported in a datastore cluster is 64. If there is no predefined (company IT-standard) datastore size standard, a suitable datastore size needs to be determined. No default one-size-fits-all datastore size can be provided by us as it depends on multiple variables: consolidation ratio of virtual machines per datastore cluster, virtual machine disk footprint and storage array performance to name a few. As mentioned in the previous paragraph, more datastores means more scheduling options for storage DRS. Selecting a smaller datastore size could result in more migrations if the space utilization threshold of datastores are violated due to the disk footprint of your virtual machines.

Storage DRS supports the use of NFS, VMFS3, VMFS5 and extended VMFS datastores. Both NFS and VMFS5 allow datastores up to 64 TB. Extents are supported as well, although there are some drawbacks introduced when using extents in datastore clusters. Extending a datastore does not offer extra load balancing options to Storage DRS, just a single datastore grows in size. Storage DRS disables SIOC on an extended datastores, which in turns result in disabled I/O load balancing for that particular datastore.

Note: Storage DRS does not support combining NFS and VMFS datastores into a single datastore cluster. You need to commit to one type of file system per datastore cluster.

Virtual machine configuration

The virtual machine configurations impacts the load balancing ability of storage DRS as well as the consolidation ratio of virtual machines to datastore clusters.

Datastore Cluster Default Affinity Rule

New in vSphere 5.1 is the ability to change a default affinity rule for the datastore cluster. By default, Storage DRS recommends an Intra-VM affinity rule. If this option is deselected, the virtual machine files and VMDKs of a virtual machine are spread across different datastores.

Figure 129: Default VM affinity rule option

Default VM affinity	☑ Keep VMDKs together by default
	Specifies whether or not each virtual machine in this datastore cluster should have its virtual disks on the same datastore by default

Please note that affinity rules are covered more in detail in the next chapter. The Intra-VM affinity rule keeps the virtual machine files, such as VMX file, log files, vSwap and VMDK files together on one datastore.

Figure 130: Initial placement with default affinity rule

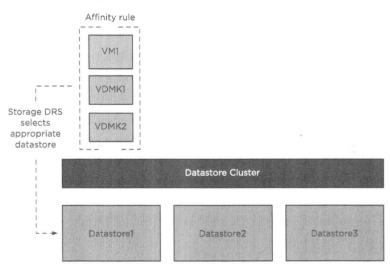

Keeping all files together on one datastore helps ease troubleshooting. However, Storage DRS load balance algorithms may benefit from the ability to distribute the virtual machine across multiple datastores. Let's zoom in how Storage DRS handles virtual machines with multiple disks when the Intra-VM affinity rule is removed from the virtual machine.

DrmDisk

Storage DRS uses the construct "DrmDisk" as the smallest entity it can migrate. A DrmDisk represents a consumer of datastore resources. This means that Storage DRS creates a DrmDisk for each VMDK belonging to the virtual machine. The interesting part is how it handles the collection of system files and swap file belonging to virtual machines: Storage DRS creates a single DrmDisk representing all of the system files. If, however, an alternate swapfile location is specified, the vSwap file is represented, as a separate DrmDisk and Storage DRS will be disabled on this swap DrmDisk. For example, for a virtual machine with two VMDK's and no alternate swapfile location configured, Storage DRS creates three DrmDisks:

- A separate DrmDisk for each Virtual Machine Disk File.
- A DrmDisk for system files (VMX, Swap, logs, etc).

Figure 131: DRMdisk overview of virtual machine

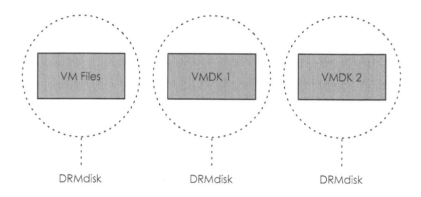

The initial placement recommendation will look similar to Figure 131 when the Intra-VM affinity rule is disabled. Notice the separate recommendation for "VM2's configuration file"? This is the DrmDisk containing the system files.

Figure 132: Storage recommendations

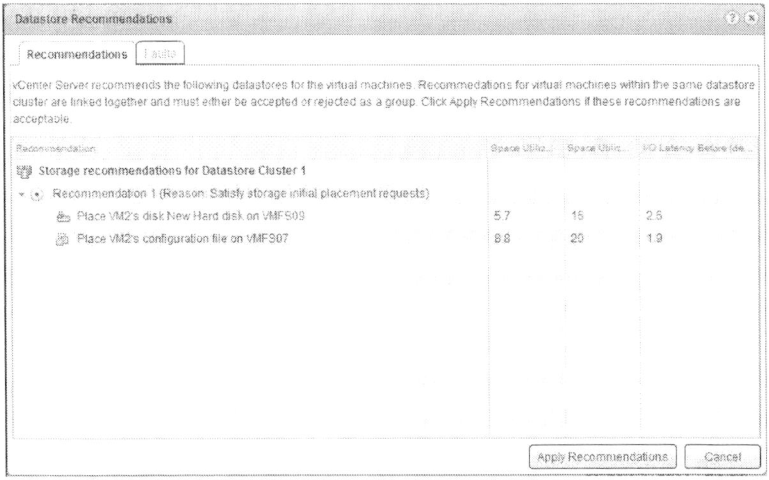

Initial placement Space load balancing

Initial placement and Space load balancing benefit tremendously from
separating virtual disks across datastores. Instead of searching for a suitable
datastore that can hold the virtual machine as a whole, Storage DRS is able
to search for appropriate datastores for each DrmDisk file separately. You
can imagine that this increased granularity means that datastore cluster
fragmentation (chapter 21) is less likely to happen and, if prerequisite
migrations are required, the number of migrations is expected to be a lot
lower.

Figure 133: Initial Placement with VMDK anti-affinity rule enabled

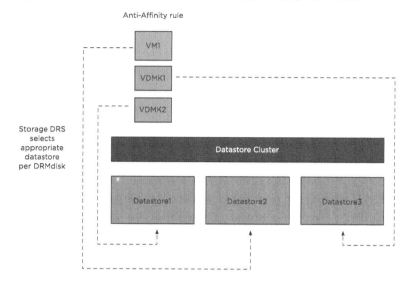

IO load balancing

Similar to initial placement and load balancing, I/O load balancing benefits from the greater granularity. Using smaller units, it can find a better fit for each workload generated by the VMDK files. The system file DrmDisk will not be migrated very often as it is small in size and does not generate a lot of I/O. Storage DRS analyzes the workload of each DrmDisk, then decides on which datastore it should place the DrmDisk to keep the load balance within the datastore cluster while also providing enough performance to each DrmDisk.

If Intra-VM affinity rules are used, Space balancing is required to find a datastore that can store the virtual machine without exceeding the space utilization threshold. If I/O load balancing is enabled, this datastore also needs to provide enough performance to keep the latency below the I/O latency threshold after placing the three DrmDisks. You can imagine it is a lot less complicated when space and I/O load balancing are allowed to place each DrmDisk on a datastore that suits their specific needs.

Disk Types

Storage DRS supports the following disk types:

- Thick
- Thin
- Independent disk
- vCloud Linked Clones
- Snapshot

Thick

By default vSphere configures a virtual machine with the thick format. During initial placement and load balancing operations, the provisioned space is used to calculate the necessary space available on the datastore. Because allocated and provisioned space are the same, the calculation is simple.

Thin provisioned disk

Storage DRS supports thin provisioned disks. As mentioned in the load-balancing algorithm chapter, it uses the committed space of a thin provisioned disk instead of the provisioned space. One caveat is that during the initial placement process, Storage DRS uses the provisioned space in its calculations. This safeguards Storage DRS from violating the space utilization threshold directly after placement.

Independent disk

By default, Storage DRS will not move virtual machines with independent disks. Independent disks can be shared or not. Determining whether the disks are shared is a very expensive operation within the algorithm, as Storage DRS needs to investigate every virtual machine and its disks in the datastore cluster. To reduce the overhead generated by Storage DRS on the virtual infrastructure, Storage DRS does not recommend such moves. When using virtual machines that have disks set to independent and are placed in a datastore cluster, attempting to enter Storage DRS maintenance mode for a datastore results in the error "Storage DRS is unable to move independent disks." An advanced parameter allows the use of non-shared independent disks in a datastore cluster.

The option sdrs.disableSDRSonIndependentDisk needs to be added to the vpxd.cfg file to use non-shared independent disks in a datastore cluster. By default this option is not listed in the vpxd.cfg and is treated as **true**. When specified and set to **false**, Storage DRS will move independent disks and the error "Storage DRS is unable to move independent disks" will not appear.

Note

Remember that adding this option to the VPXD.cfg file it automatically applies to all datastore clusters managed by that vCenter server!

Please note that this option should only be used with non-shared independent disks! Moving shared independent disks is not supported.

Virtual Machine Automation Level

Automation levels for individual virtual machines can be customized to override the Storage DRS cluster automation level. There are four automation levels for virtual machines:

- Fully Automated
- Manual
- Default (cluster automation level)
- Disabled

If the automation level of a virtual machine is set to Disabled, Storage DRS does not migrate that virtual machine or provide migration recommendations for it. By setting the automation mode of the virtual machine to Manual, Storage recommendations will be generated, but all recommendations will need to be approved by the user before any action is taken.

Impact of VM Automation Level on Load Balancing Calculation

A virtual machine set to Disabled automation level still has impact on space and I/O load balancing as both space and I/O metrics are still captured both at the datastore level and per virtual machine. With the VM automation level set to Disabled, Storage DRS will only refrain from generating migration recommendations for that virtual machine.

Interoperability

Array features

Some of you might have already thought about this and some of you might not have: what if you are using an array that offers deduplication or thin provisioning? What if you are replicating all of your datastores? Would it make sense to enable Storage DRS on datastores with those characteristics? Is there any form of integration, and what is the impact? Let's tackle these one at a time, starting with mentioning that Storage DRS is useful with ANY of these array-based features. However, it is recommended to set Storage DRS to "Manual" in all cases so that migrations must be approved and the administrator is aware of the impact. We believe that there is a lot of value in the "Initial Placement" that Storage DRS can take care of. This eliminates the operational effort normally required to find the best datastore from a capacity and latency perspective.

Basic design principle

Even when array-based features like deduplication are used, we recommend enabling Storage DRS. Its initial placement feature will help find the best location for your virtual machine.

This section might contain some bold statements, but we want to make sure everyone realizes the impact of enabling Storage DRS in a fully automated mode. We will start with our recommendation regarding how to configure Storage DRS when these array features are used and then explain our reasons.

Deduplication

Storage DRS Automation Level: Manual Mode
Load Balancing: Space + I/O

When deduplication is enabled on a LUN, it is very difficult to predict the total impact of moving a virtual machine. Depending on the amount of similar blocks on the target, migration to another datastore could have a negative impact on the efficiency of the deduplication process. When the deduplication happens out-of-band, meaning that the data must be written to disk first, there will be a period of time where the VMDK is 0% deduplicated. On top of that, the deduplication process will need to reanalyze the entire VMDK, which has an associated overhead cost.

We do, however, recommend enabling Storage DRS in Manual Mode and deciding per recommendation whether it makes sense to migrate virtual machines. In terms of space utilization, a migration may not make sense, but when there is a substantial latency imbalance, the cost of the migration (fewer deduplicated blocks) should be weighed against the potential of reduced latency after the migration.

Thin provisioning
Storage DRS Automation Level: Manual Mode
Load Balancing: Space + I/O

Prior to vSphere 5.0, there were two major challenges in dealing with thin-provisioned LUNs and frequent virtual machine migrations, deletions or provisioning. The first problem that could occur was that the migration required new blocks to be allocated to the datastore when the array did not have enough free blocks. The second problem that people ran into was that deleting or migrating a virtual machine did not free its blocks from the original datastore – we call this "dead space reclamation." As you can imagine, these scenarios imposed operational challenges.

vSphere 5.0 introduced multiple VAAI enhancements for environments using array-based thin-provisioning capabilities. The two major challenges of thin-provisioned LUNs are, as just mentioned, the reclamation of dead space and monitoring of space usage. The new VAAI Thin Provisioning primitive solves this by introducing the following:

- Dead Space Reclamation informs the array about the datastore space that is freed when files are deleted or removed from the datastore by Storage vMotion. The array can then reclaim the freed blocks and assign them to other LUNs when requested.
- Out-of-Space Conditions monitors the space usage on thin-provisioned datastores to prevent running out of physical space. A new, advanced warning has been added to vSphere 5.0 for a thin-provisioned out-of-space condition. Essentially, this surfaces the array's built-in monitoring /alerting capabilities and allows vCenter to act upon it.

Basic design principle
Validate that your array supports the Thin Provisioning primitive before migrating virtual machines.

The Out-of-Space Conditions are used by Storage DRS when making migration recommendations. Storage DRS recognizes the fact that a volume has reached its threshold and is running out of physical space because the array can't allocate more storage. Under these conditions, this specific volume will be ignored as candidate target for Storage DRS migration recommendations.

Now that we are on the topic of VAAI, we want to point out that vSphere 5.0 introduced enhanced support for INCITS T10 SCSI specifications. This allows you to leverage VAAI primitives without requiring the installation of a plug-in and enables support for many additional storage devices.

Basic design principle
Confirm with your storage vendor that they are adhering to the T10 standards to ensure VAAI offload capabilities like Full Copy, used by Storage vMotion, can be leveraged.

Replication
Storage DRS Automation Level: Manual Mode
Load Balancing: Space + I/O

Storage DRS is not aware of replication. This means that if Storage DRS initiates a migration, the replication mechanism will need to replicate all blocks that have been newly created on the target volume – in this case, every one of the VMDK's allocated blocks. The additional impact of that is that the virtual machine is "unprotected" until it has been fully re-replicated – as long as it is moved to another replicated datastore. It is recommended to check if both source and destination datastores have the same replication setup. Other solutions, that manages virtual machine replication and provides disaster recovery through replication needs to be manually reconfigured after the migration. vSphere 5.0 and 5.1 does not have full SRM + Storage DRS interoperability as SRM does not supports Storage vMotion of virtual machine it is protecting.

We recommend configuring Storage DRS in manual mode so that recommendations can be applied during a maintenance window or times of known lower utilization on the replication link.

Auto-tiering
Storage DRS Automation Level: Manual Mode
Load Balancing: I/O metric disabled

If an auto-tiering solution is enabled on the array, we recommend disabling the I/O load balancing feature of Storage DRS and only using it for space balancing and initial placement services. As mentioned in the I/O load-balancing chapter, I/O load balancing uses device modeling to understand the performance characteristics of the devices backing the datastores. In an auto-tiering solution, those characteristics may actually change based on utilization and migration of blocks within the storage array. It is important to know how Storage DRS works to realize how its behavior may cause undesirable results in this specific situation.

To understand and learn the performance of the devices backing a datastore, Storage DRS uses the Storage IO Control (SIOC) workload injector. To characterize a datastore, the SIOC injector opens and reads random blocks of the datastore. As the SIOC injector does not open every block backing the datastore, it is not guaranteed that the SIOC injector opens an identical number of blocks of each performance tier to characterize the disk. As multiple performance tiers back the datastore there is a possibility that the SIOC injector might open blocks located on similar speed disks, either slow or fast, while the datastore is primarily backed by disk with a different performance level. Let's use an example to clarify this further.

Figure 134: SIOC injector device modeling

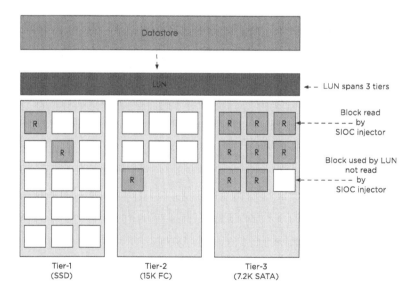

In the diagram pictured above, SIOC opens random blocks and perform its tests. Unfortunately, it doesn't open the same amount of blocks from storage at each tier. While most of the blocks backing the example datastore are located on faster performing (SSD) disks, Storage DRS device modeling will characterize this disk with performance similar to 7.2K SATA disks. This inaccurate characterization of datastore performance might lead to an incorrect performance assessment and can lead to Storage DRS withholding a migration recommendation even though there is sufficient performance available.

Segment migration triggered by auto-tiering algorithms

Using SIOC injector, Storage DRS evaluates the performance of the disks, however auto-tiering solutions migrate LUN segments (chunks) to different disk types based on the use pattern. Hot segments (frequently accessed) typically move to faster disks while cold segments move to slower disks. Depending on the array type and vendor, there are different kind of policies and thresholds for these migrations. By default, Storage DRS is invoked every 8 hours and requires performance data over more than 16 hours to generate I/O load balancing decisions. Each vendor uses different time-cycles to collect and analyze workloads before moving LUN segments: some auto-tiering solutions move chunks based on real-time workload while other arrays move chunks after collecting performance data for 24 hours. This means that auto-tiering solutions alter the landscape in which the SIOC injector performs its test. Let's turn to another scenario for clarification.

In this scenario, SIOC is primarily opening datastore blocks located in the Tier-1 diskgroup. As the datastore isn't using these segments that often (cold) the auto-tiering solution decides to migrate these segments to a lower tier. In this case, the segments are migrated to 15K disks instead of SSD devices.

Figure 135: Migrate cold segments by Auto-tiering

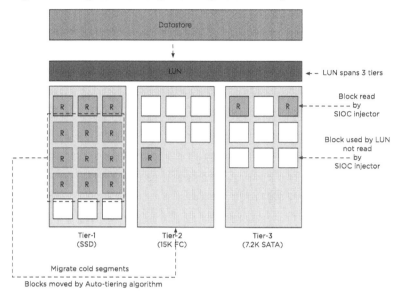

Storage DRS expects that the behavior of a LUN remains the same for at least 16 hours and it will perform its calculations using this assumption. Auto tiering solutions might change the underlying structure of the datastore based on its algorithms and timescales, conflicting with these calculations.

The possible misalignment of Storage DRS invocations and auto-tiering cycles results in unpredictability regarding when LUN segments may be moved within the array, potentially colliding with the calculations and recommendations of Storage DRS. This, together with the lack of transparency of auto-tiering algorithms to Storage DRS and the non-existing communication between Storage DRS and auto-tiering solutions creates the basis of our recommendation to disable the I/O metric on datastore clusters backed by devices managed by an auto-tiering solution. As always, be certain to verify these recommendations with your storage vendor.

Array configuration
Grouping similar type disks

As briefly mentioned, we recommend creating datastore clusters from datastores backed by similar type disks. With that meaning SATA with SATA, 15K RPM FC with 15K RPM FC and RAID-5 with RAID-5. To be clear about this, there is no check built in vCenter to prevent you from doing this. As explained in chapter 21, Storage DRS leverages the injector from Storage I/O Control (SIOC) to determine the performance characteristics of a datastore. It does this by injecting random read I/O when the datastore is idle and it uses varying amounts of outstanding I/Os. Despite the fact that Storage DRS and SIOC have this extremely smart built-in feature, we feel strongly that placement of virtual machines and virtual disks should be primarily based on the service level agreement (SLA) applicable to the respective virtual machine or virtual disk rather than just the calculated performance of the underlying physical disk.

The SLA could define the availability characteristics (RAID level, replication type) but also performance characteristics (SATA, FC, SSD). Everyone probably understands why availability characteristics are important when combining LUNs, but what about performance? Performance is not just latency, is it?

Just imagine the space utilization threshold is reached on your 15K RPM FC-backed datastore and Storage DRS migrates your virtual machine to a 7.2K RPM SATA-backed datastore. Why would this be a problem? Think about it. The number of IOPS a 15K disk can sustain (180-200) is much higher than that of a SATA drive (75-80). Although the average latency might be lower, that does not mean you are guaranteed to get the same peak performance and response. Depending on the underlying configuration, Storage DRS could even migrate the virtual machine, or virtual disk, to a different array with a different amount of cache, different disks and a different level of up-time. All of this could impact the performance of your virtual machine and result in the violation of your SLA. Maybe even worse, it could change your customer's perception of virtualization.

vSphere Storage APIs - Storage Awareness

vSphere 5.0 introduced a feature called vSphere Storage APIs - Storage Awareness. These APIs are sometimes also referred to by the short name, VASA. We will use VASA as this is the most commonly used acronym. VASA provides for communication between supported storage arrays and vCenter to allow vCenter to expose the capabilities of the storage array's LUNs that have been mapped to datastores. This makes it much easier to select appropriate datastores for virtual machine placement or the creation of datastore clusters. It can also facilitate the troubleshooting process or conversations between you (vSphere administrator) and the storage administrators by automatically providing vCenter with details such as RAID level, thin/thick provisioned, replication state and much more (Figure 136).

Figure 136: vSphere storage APIs - Storage Capability Details

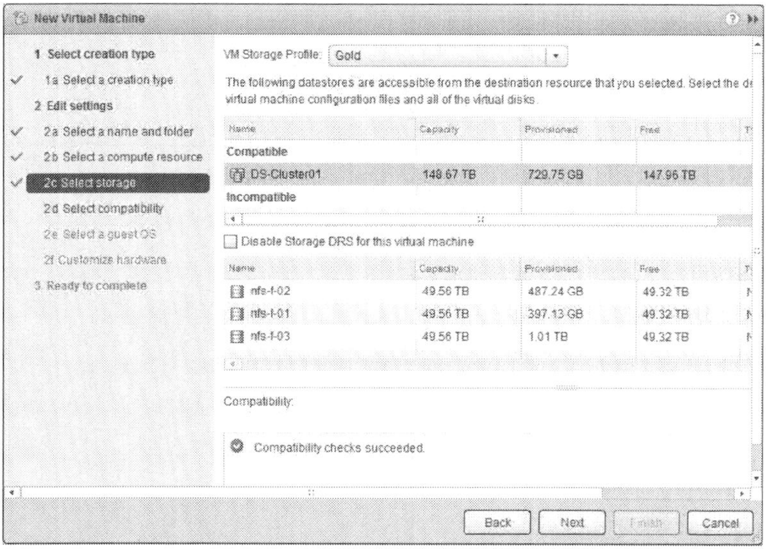

These capabilities are made visible within vCenter either via "System-defined capabilities" which are per-datastore descriptors, or via attributes that are exposed via Storage Views or the vSphere API.

Basic design principle

Leverage information provided through VASA to create your Datastore Clusters. This will help ensure that your virtual machines are provisioned on the correct storage tier.

Especially in "larger" environments where many LUNs are provisioned, storage capabilities provided through VASA will lower the amount of administration required. It aims to eliminate the need for maintaining massive spreadsheets detailing the storage capabilities of each LUN, which are often used to validate the correct tier of storage is used during virtual machine or virtual disk provisioning.

This is, however, just the beginning. Wouldn't it be nice if it was possible to create profiles per tier and assign these profiles to virtual machines or virtual disks to ensure that they remain on appropriate storage throughout their lifecycle? The good news is that you can with vSphere 5.0, and it even integrates with SDRS for the provisioning process.

Profile-Driven Storage

Prior to the availability of Profile-Driven Storage, managing datastores and matching the SLA requirements of virtual machines with the appropriate datastores was challenging, to say the least. Profile-Driven Storage allows for rapid and intelligent placement of virtual machines based on pre-defined storage profiles. These profiles usually represent a storage tier and are created through a vCenter feature called "VM Storage Profiles." Typically, characteristics like RAID level, replication, performance, deduplication and thin/thick provisioned are used to define different tiers. An example of these tiers would be:

- Gold, RAID-10, Synchronous Replication, 15K FC
- Silver, RAID-5, A-Synchronous Replication, 10K FC
- Bronze, RAID-5, Deduplication enabled, 7K SATA

Using VM Storage Profiles, different storage characteristics, provided through the Storage APIs (system defined) or manually entered (user defined), can be specified in a VM Storage Profile. These VM Storage Profiles are used during provisioning, cloning and Storage vMotion to ensure that only those datastores or datastore clusters compliant with the VM Storage Profile are made available. This is shown in Figure 137 where the VM Storage Profile "Bronze" is selected and the datastore cluster "dsc-nonrep-rp-001" is presented as compliant with this VM Storage Profile.

Figure 137: Selecting a datastore using a VM Storage Profile

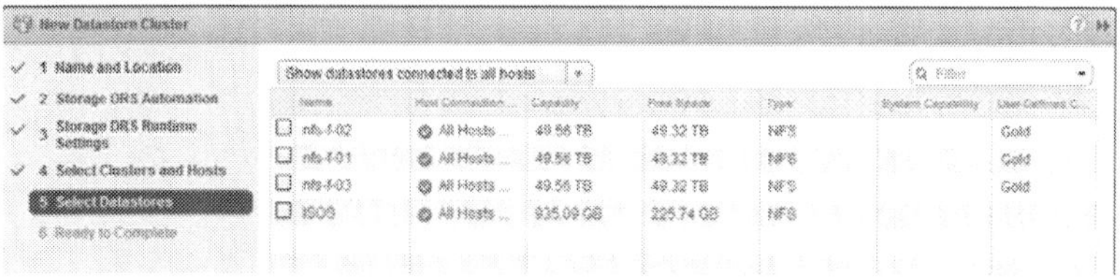

The reason we are discussing this feature is because Profile-Driven Storage helps select the correct datastore cluster. Only datastore clusters that are compliant with the VM Storage Profile will be presented. A requirement for this to work, however, is that similar type datastores are selected during the creation of the datastore cluster.

Unfortunately, today it is not possible to use VM Storage Profiles to select the correct datastores within a datastore cluster, however System Capabilities (VASA) are shown within the Storage DRS "Datastore Cluster creation" workflow as shown in Figure 138.

Figure 138: System capabilities visible during datastore cluster creation

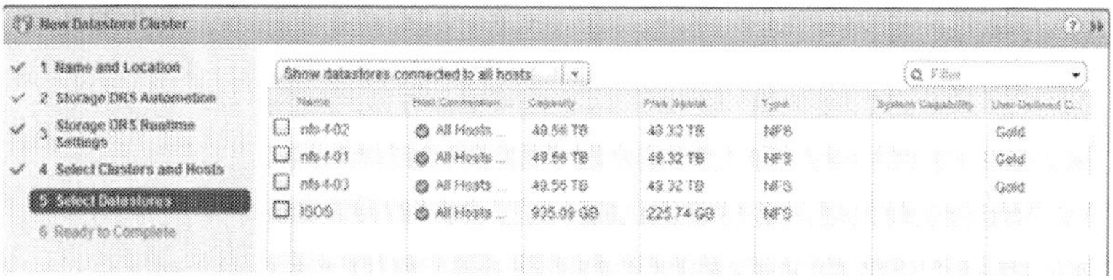

In many environments, this will lead to a decrease in administration. It will also decrease the chances of human errors when it comes to virtual machine or virtual disk placement.

Basic design principle

Define VM Storage Profiles to ease provisioning of virtual machines and the associated virtual disks. Define tiers of storage based on your SLAs with your (internal) customers.

Probably the most adopted storage tiering model is the "Gold, Silver" Bronze" approach. Keep in mind that VM Storage Profiles do not limit you to this approach. In many cases, taking a per-use-case approach could ease the provisioning process: rather than defining a rank-name for the tier ("Gold"), the use case for the datastore is specified ("Web Servers" or "Databases"). Although the traditional approach might make sense for many vSphere Administrators, this use case or even a "line-of-business" approach could make more sense in larger environments where provisioning is done by a different team (2nd line support).

A profile by itself is great, but fairly useless when it is impossible to validate compliancy of a virtual machine and the associated disks against the profile. Fortunately, Profile-Driven Storage also allows for this. Figure 139 depicts this process.

Figure 139: VM Storage Profile compliancy

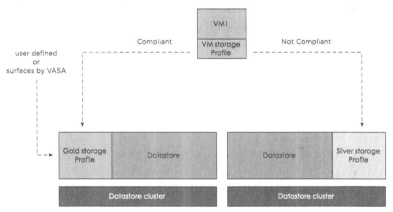

As mentioned before, Profile-Driven Storage can leverage capabilities surfaced through the VASA. If, for whatever reason, your storage vendor does not have a VASA provider, keep in mind that Datastores can be provided manually with information ("user-defined") regarding storage capabilities manually.

Virtual machine compliance status

VM Storage Profiles enable you to validate compliance of virtual machines and their associated virtual disks in a single pane of glass (Figure 140) but it also allows you to see this on a per-virtual machine basis, ensuring that even "virtual machine administrators" who don't necessarily have access on all the different layers can validate compliance on the virtual machine's Summary tab (Figure 141).

Figure 140: Single pane of glass for compliance

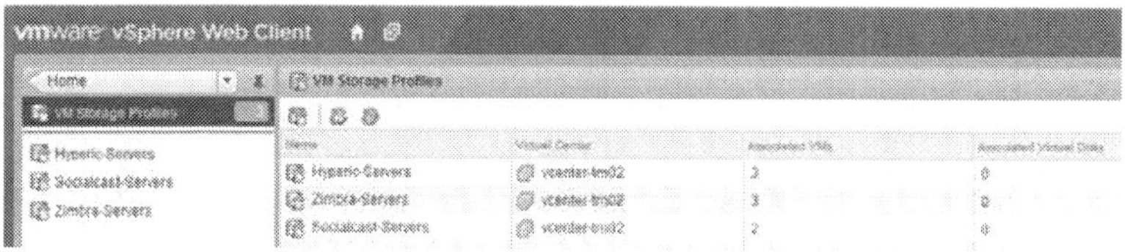

Figure 141: Per virtual machine profile compliance

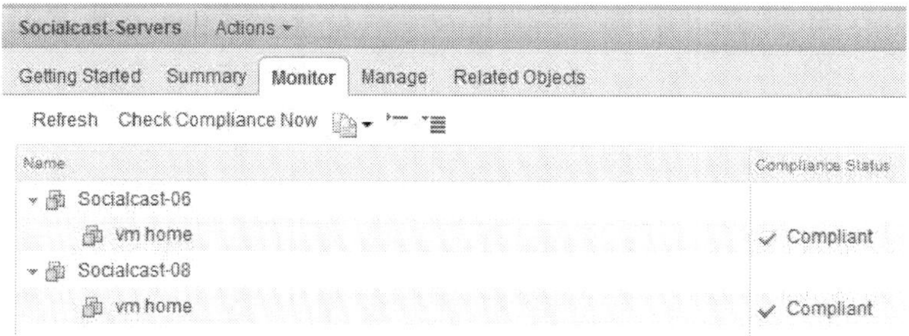

Profile-Driven Storage will make managing storage tiers, provisioning, migrating, cloning virtual machines and correct virtual machine placement in vSphere deployments easier and more user-friendly. More importantly, with regards to the topic of this book, it will enable you to create datastore clusters based on pre-defined profiles which will result in more efficient usage of your storage.

Basic design principle

Use the tools provided to make the right decisions during the creation of your datastore clusters and the provisioning process. This will reduce the chances of human error and unexpected behavior.

Chapter 25

Impact on Storage vMotion Efficiency

In this section we will explain the process and some enhancements in Storage vMotion. Storage vMotion has been around ever since ESX 3.0 when it was called DMotion and used to enable the upgrade from 2.5.x to 3.x. With VI 3.5, Storage vMotion was released as a command line feature for day-to-day use. As of vSphere 4.0, it was officially integrated into the UI and people started widely adopting it for storage migrations. Today, it is heavily used by Storage DRS.

Many aspects of Storage vMotion appear to be generally misunderstood, and having a better understanding of the process it uses will help you make design decisions around the configurable thresholds of Storage DRS. It will also help during troubleshooting and understanding the overall impact both Storage vMotion and Storage DRS can have on your environment.

The Process

The Storage vMotion process is fairly straightforward and not as complex as one might expect.

1. The virtual machine working directory is copied by VPXA to the destination datastore.
2. A "shadow" virtual machine is started on the destination datastore using the copied files. The "shadow" virtual machine idles, waiting for the copying of the virtual machine disk file(s) to complete.
3. Storage vMotion enables the Storage vMotion Mirror driver to mirror writes of already copied blocks to the destination.
4. In a single pass, a copy of the virtual machine disk file(s) is completed to the target datastore while mirroring I/O.
5. Storage vMotion invokes a Fast Suspend and Resume of the virtual machine (similar to vMotion) to transfer the running virtual machine over to the idling shadow virtual machine.
6. After the Fast Suspend and Resume completes, the old home directory and virtual machine disk files are deleted from the source datastore.

It should be noted that the shadow virtual machine is only created in the case that the virtual machine home directory is moved. If and when it is a "disk-only Storage vMotion, the virtual machine will simply be stunned and un-stunned.

Just 6 steps that enable you to live migrate any virtual machine or virtual disk from one datastore to another. Changed Block Tracking, which was part of Storage vMotion in previous versions of vSphere, was removed when redesigning the Storage vMotion process for vSphere 5. Let's dive a little bit deeper in the Storage vMotion process.

Mirror Mode

We have briefly touched on this already, and some might wonder what happened to *Change Block Tracking* (CBT). CBT is no longer leveraged by Storage vMotion. Although CBT was efficient compared to legacy storage migration mechanisms, the Storage vMotion engineers came up with an even more elegant and efficient solution, which is called Mirror Mode. Mirror Mode does exactly what you would expect it to do; it mirrors the I/O. In other words, when a virtual machine that is being Storage vMotioned writes to disk, the write will be committed to both the source and the destination disk. The write will only be acknowledged to the virtual machine when both the source and the destination have acknowledged the write. Because of this, it is unnecessary to perform repeated iterative copies to ensure all blocks are synchronized prior to completing the switchover.

A few questions remain: How does this work? Where does Mirror Mode reside? Is this something that happens inside or outside of the guest? A diagram will make this more obvious.

Figure 142: Data flow with Mirror Mode driver

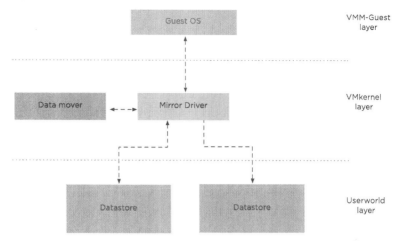

By leveraging certain APIs, the Mirror Driver can be enabled for the virtual machine that needs to be Storage vMotioned. Before this driver can be enabled, the virtual machine will need to be stunned and of course unstunned after it has been enabled. The new driver leverages one of the datamovers to do a single-pass block copy of the source disk to the destination disk. Additionally, the Mirror Driver will ensure synchronization by mirroroging any writes that occur to the source and destination VMDKs. Not only has efficiency increased but also migration time predictability, making it easier to plan migrations.

There is one caveat though when it comes to Storage vMotion. Storage vMotion leverages a datamover to migrate data from A to B. Migration throughput is dependent on which datamover used.

Upgraded VMFS Volumes?

The hypervisor uses a component called the datamover for copying data during Storage vMotion and when provisioning new virtual machines. The datamover was first introduced with ESX 3.0 and is utilized by Storage vMotion as blocks will need to be copied between datastores. There are currently three types of datamovers:

- fsdm – This is the legacy 3.0 datamover which is the most basic version and the slowest as the data moves all the way up the stack and down again.

- fs3dm – This datamover was introduced with vSphere 4.0 and contained some substantial optimizations so that data does not need to traverse the entire stack.
- fs3dm – hardware offload – This datamover, introduced with vSphere 4.1, leverages the VAAI Full Copy hardware offload mechanism and provides maximum performance with minimal host CPU/Memory overhead.

We realize that it is difficult to understand the impact of using different types of datamovers. The following diagram, however, clearly demonstrates the efficiencies gained by using the HW Offload feature from the fs3dm datamover, as data does not flow through the host or storage fabric, but remains within the array:

Figure 143: Data flow per datamover

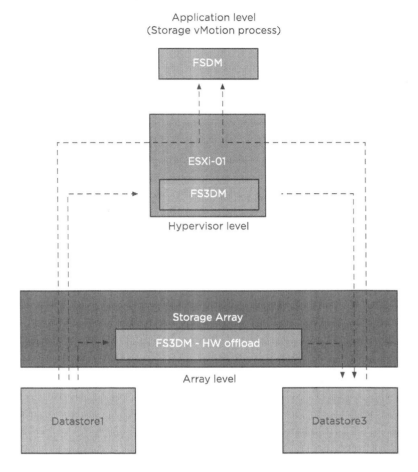

Higher up in the stack in this case means less efficient, increased overhead, and more than likely slower. Note that with 'application' we are not referring to an application within the virtual machine but for instance, to vmkfstools or Storage vMotion. When the application "Storage vMotion" leverages the fsdm datamover, it reads blocks into a buffer and writes them out again. This is a fairly expensive task as it passes through multiple layers without awareness of the underlying file system. So, when is each datamover used?

When a destination VMFS volume is selected that is hosted on a different array or has a different block size from the source VMFS volume, ESXi reverts to the legacy datamover (*fsdm*). If the same block sizes are used and the VMFS volumes are on the same array, the new datamover (*fs3dm*) will be utilized. Depending on the capabilities of the array, the task will be performed via the software stack (depicted in the diagram as "fs3dm") or offloaded through the use of VAAI (depicted in the diagram as "HW offload") to the array. That leads us to a design and operational consideration.

Basic design principle

Design for performance and efficiency by using a single blocksize for all volumes. It is true that new VMFS-5 volumes all use 1 MB blocks, but remember that VMFS-3 volumes which are upgraded will retain their original block size.

Why would you care about this and will it really make a difference in your environment? It depends is the answer. As stated previously, when upgrading a VMFS-3 volume to VMFS-5, it will retain the original block size. When mixed with newly created VMFS-5 volumes, which may have a different block size, this could lead to a potential loss in efficiency and it will increase the time needed for Storage vMotion operations to complete.

Basic design principle

When acquiring new Storage Hardware, verify the device is VAAI capable or will be in the near future. Leveraging VAAI will increase efficiency and decrease overall time to complete storage tasks.

Storage I/O Control

The rules change when a datastore is nearing saturation. If SIOC is enabled on the datastore, the default when Storage DRS I/O load balancing is enabled, Storage vMotion operations can be throttled by SIOC. Depending on its share value, a virtual machine is given an I/O quota that specifies a certain number of concurrent I/Os. If Storage DRS triggers a Storage vMotion for a virtual machine, the I/O generated by this process is billed to the virtual machine. This means that the I/O quota of the virtual machine is divided between the normal I/O traffic and the Storage vMotion traffic. If the virtual machine performs a lot of I/O, the quota is evenly split up between the virtual machine's I/O stream and Storage vMotion process. If the I/O activity of the virtual machine is low, the Storage vMotion can use up the rest of the virtual machine's quota. SIOC is expanded upon in chapter 22.

VAAI

But what if the storage is VAAI compatible? If the Storage vMotion process is initiated, the VMkernel issues a request to the storage array to initiate the copy on behalf of the ESXi host. In this case, the I/O traffic remains inside the storage array and informs the ESXi host once the copy is completed.

Note

Please note that the Storage vMotion is completely transparent to the local scheduler (SFQ) and is not impacted by SIOC.

If Storage vMotion migrates a virtual machine between datastores with different block sizes, VAAI hardware assistance is disabled and requires the VMkernel to revert to legacy datamovers.

Parallel disk migrations

vSphere 5.1 allows up to 4 parallel disk copies per Storage vMotion operation, where previous versions of vSphere copied disks serially. When you migrate a virtual machine with five VMDK files, Storage vMotion copies of the first four disks in parallel, then starts the next disk copy as soon as one of the first four finishes.

Figure 144: Parallel disk copies during the Storage vMotion process

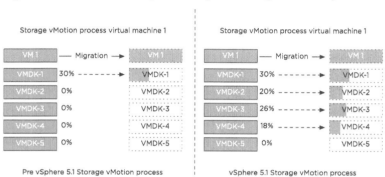

To reduce performance impact on other virtual machines sharing the datastores, Parallel disk copies only apply to disk copies between distinct datastores. This means that if a virtual machine has multiple VMDK files on datastore A and B, parallel disk copies will only happen if destination datastores are C and D.

Figure 145: Parallel migration of VMDKs on distinct datastores

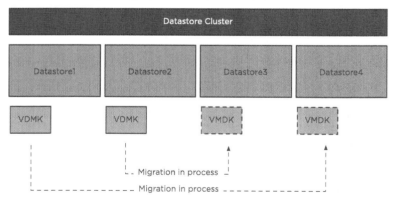

Let's use an example to clarify the process. Virtual machine VM1 has four vmdk files. VMDK1 and VMDK2 are on Datastore1, VMDK3 and VMDK4 are on Datastore2. The VMDK files are moved from Datastore1 to Datastore4 and from Datastore2 to Datastore3. VMDK1 and VMDK3 are migrated in parallel, while VMDK2 and VMDK4 are queued. The migration process of VMDK2 is started the moment the migration of VMDK1 is complete, similar for VMDK4 as it will be started when the migration of VMDK3 is complete.

Figure 146: Multiple migrations to select distinct datastores

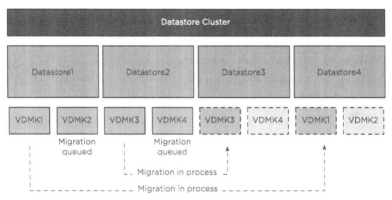

A fan out disk copy, in other words copying two VMDK files on datastore A to datastores B and C, will not have parallel disk copies. The common use case of parallel disk copies is the migration of a virtual machine configured with an anti-affinity rule inside a datastore cluster.

Different VMFS Block Sizes
Datastores with different block sizes can exist in a datastore cluster. If VMFS-3 datastores are upgraded to VMFS-5, the block size is retained. As VMFS-5 uses a standard block size of 1 MB, upgrading VMFS-3 datastores, which use larger block sizes, may result in block size mismatching within a datastore cluster. This block size mismatch forces the VMkernel to use the old legacy datamover (FSDM), reducing the benefit of using a VAAI capable storage array.

As a result, mixing migrated VMFS-5 datastores with new VMFS-5 datastores within the same datastore cluster may lead to performance degradation of Storage vMotion and can result in longer Storage DRS lead times to reach the steady state where maximum resource availability is being offered.

If datastores with different block sizes exist in a datastore cluster, we recommend replacing the current datastores with native VMFS-5 datastores for optimum performance. After upgrading VMFS-3 datastores, migrate the virtual machines to new VMFS-5 datastores and reformat the evacuated datastores with a fresh coat of VMFS-5. We are aware that this procedure will increase the migration time to VMFS-5 and datastore clusters, but the return on investment is well worth it. Storage DRS will be able to reach a balanced steady state faster and VAAI migration offloads will be enabled, impacting I/O performance of virtual machines in a positive manner.

Basic design principle
Avoid mixing datastores with different block sizes.

As mentioned in the previous chapter, the cost-benefit risk analysis of Storage DRS takes the duration of the average Storage vMotion into account when identifying suitable migration candidates. Reducing Storage vMotion duration will have a positive effect on Storage DRS and its capabilities to more quickly reach a steady and balanced state.

Thin Disks

Thin provisioned VMDK files are treated by Storage DRS in the same way as thick-provisioned disks. As ever, there are a few exceptions to the rule. One exception is applied when addressing space imbalance. When Storage DRS recommends a migration, it will take the space growth rate of the thin provisioned disk into account. When the placement of the virtual machine files and the estimated growth rate will exceed the threshold, Storage DRS will refrain from recommending this move.

Another exception is the input for cost calculation. When estimating the costs of the migration, the allocated amount of space is used in the calculation instead of the provisioned space.

VMFS-5

We are not going to do a full deep dive on VMware's file system as that is not the topic of this book. However, some of the changes in VMFS-5 are important to understand, as they will impact your ability to make the right decisions for your environment. On top of that, you will have a better understanding of the end-to-end solution and will, when the right decisions are made, achieve a faster return on investment. We have listed the most significant changes below:

- Unified blocksize
- Improved sub-block mechanism
- 64TB Device Support

One of the most controversial topics when it comes to storage has always been block sizes. VMFS-3, used 4 different block sizes each with their own limitations:

- 1MB Blocksize – Maximum file size 256GB
- 2MB Blocksize – Maximum file size 512GB
- 4MB Blocksize – Maximum file size 1024GB
- 8MB Blocksize – Maximum file size 2048GB-512B

It was believed by many that a larger block size would result in better performance. This is an urban myth. The VMFS block is primarily used to allocate disk space to a virtual machine. VMFS blocks are not used when it comes to Guest-OS I/O. For newly created VMFS-5, there is a single block size: 1MB. However, the maximum file size for VMFS-5 is 2048GB-512B. This should simplify the decisions required during datastore creation. Another important difference is that GPT is used for new VMFS-5 volumes where VMFS-3 volumes use MBR. Although it is possible to upgrade VMFS-3 volumes non-disruptively to VMFS-5, it should be noted that the block size that was once chosen for the VMFS-3 volume will not change and MBR will remain. As also pointed out in the different VMFS block sizes paragraph, having different block sizes in your environment could have an impact. As such, when different block sizes are used throughout the environment, a "rip and replace" approach should be considered as the best solution for optimal performance.

Basic design principle

Understand the possible impact of upgrading VMFS-3 volumes to VMFS-5. In the case where various block sizes were used, migration to newly-created VMFS-5 datastores should be considered.

One of the most criticized maximum values has always been the maximum supported LUN size: 2TB. As of VMFS-5, this has been increased to 64TB without the need to resort to extents. It is good to realize that this also applies to pass-through RDMs, enabling the virtualization of large fileservers or databases. Just think for a second about the possibilities you will have for creating a single, but huge, storage object. What about those "sub-block" limitations that VMFS-3 had? When small files needed to be stored, VMFS-3 used 64KB sub-blocks, regardless of the VMFS block size, and had a limit of 3000. Although large blocks would be allocated beyond that as needed, there was a perception that this imposed some kind of limitation. With VMFS-5, this has been enhanced as the sub-block size has been decreased to 8KB, ensuring that even less space is wasted for small files. On top of that, the maximum number of sub-blocks has been increased to ~30K and the maximum number of files per datastore to ~130K (versus ~30K with VMFS-3), enabling greater scalability within a datastore.

Chapter 26

Affinity rules

By default, Storage DRS will apply an Intra-VM affinity rule (VMDK affinity) that specifies storing all files belonging to a virtual machine on one datastore.
After configuring a datastore cluster, the advanced options allows you to change this default VM affinity rule.

Figure 147: Advanced options

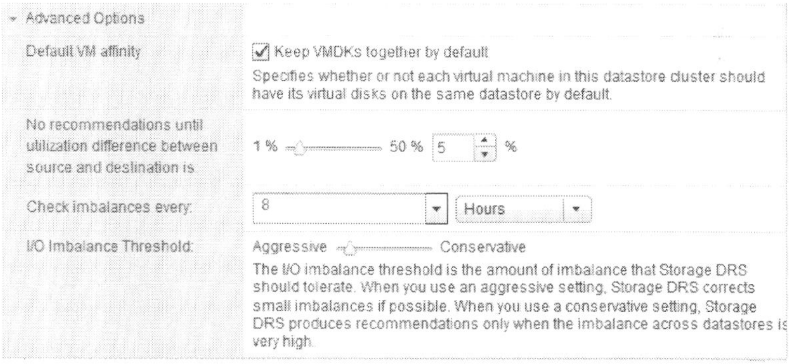

By deselecting the Default VM affinity section's "Keep VMDKs together by default" option, all new virtual machines are configured with an anti-affinity rule, meaning that Storage DRS initial placement and load balancing keeps the VM files and VDMK files stored on separate datastores. This chapter takes a closer look at the affinity rules provided by Storage DRS, how they can impact initial placement and load balancing operations and how to configure them.

Intra-VM and Inter-VM affinity rules

Storage DRS provides the option to control the placement of virtual disks. The affinity rule keeps virtual disks of a virtual machine together on the same datastore and this rule is considered to be an Intra-VM rule. Anti-Affinity rules can be specified on an Intra-VM level as well as an Inter-VM level.

Figure 148: Intra-VM and Inter-VM affinity rules

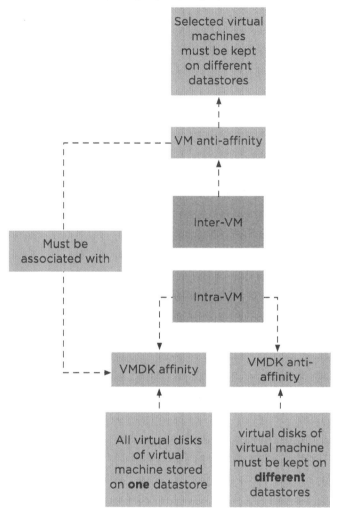

Note that all rules are enforced during initial placement and Storage DRS-recommended Storage vMotions, but they are not enforced on user-initiated Storage vMotions.

Intra-VM VMDK Affinity Rule

Storage DRS applies a VMDK affinity rule to each virtual machine by default. This default rule is commonly referred to as the Intra-VM affinity rule (Figure 149). The Intra-VM affinity rule keeps the VMDKs belonging to a virtual machine stored together on the same datastore.

Figure 149: Intra VM-VMDK affinity rule

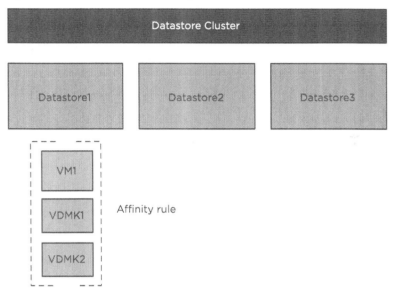

Intra-VM VMDK Anti-Affinity Rule

The Intra-VM VMDK anti-affinity rule keeps the specified VMDKs belonging to a virtual machine on separate datastores.

Figure 150: Intra-VM anti-affinity rule

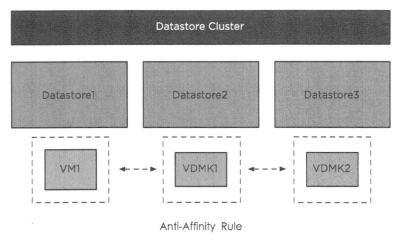

Anti-Affinity Rule

When the default VM affinity rule option at datastore cluster level is deselected, Storage DRS places each virtual machine disk file on a separate datastore. During the creation of a new virtual machine, Storage DRS recommends placing the VMDK files on distinct datastores.

Figure 151: New virtual machine with default cluster-wide anti-affinity rule

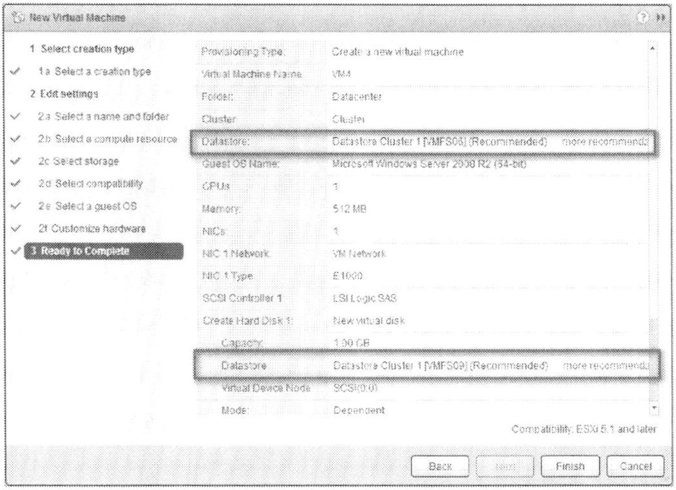

Inter-VM VM Anti-Affinity Rule

The Inter-VM VM anti-affinity rule keeps the specified virtual machines on different datastores. This rule can help maximize the availability of a collection of related virtual machines. The availability of the set of virtual machines is increased by not allowing Storage DRS to place the virtual machines on the same datastore. For example, web servers in a load-balance cluster or domain controllers.

Figure 152: Inter-VM anti-affinity rule

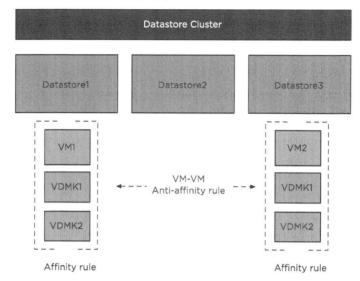

Storage DRS VM anti-affinity rules can contain two or more virtual machines. We recommend applying VM anti-affinity rules sparingly. Anti-Affinity rules place limitations on Storage DRS initial placement, maintenance mode and load-balancing operations by reducing the possibilities it has to reach a steady and balanced state.

Virtual machines that are associated with an Inter-VM VM anti-affinity rule must be configured with an Intra-VM affinity rule. If a virtual machine is configured with an Intra-VM anti-affinity rule, this could be due to the cluster-wide default anti-affinity rule, vCenter displays the following warning and the user is required to fix the violation manually.

Figure 153: Intra-VM anti-affinity violation

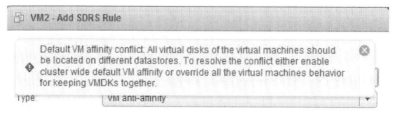

Violate Anti-Affinity Rules

Initial placement, I/O and space load balancing do not violate anti-affinity rules; however, when generating migration recommendations for datastore maintenance mode, Storage DRS may provide recommendations that potentially violate the affinity and anti-affinity rules.

Storage DRS will generate migration recommendations with the rules intact and will provide these recommendations to the user if no faults are generated. If Fully Automatic mode is selected, maintenance mode does not require manual approval unless there is a fault.

Configuring a complex and elaborate set of rules in a datastore cluster with a small number of datastores may lead Storage DRS to generate faults. If there are faults, Storage DRS runs the algorithm again but drops the affinity and anti-affinity rules, which may lead to recommendations that violate the affinity rule set.

Anti-Affinity rules with datastore correlation
Datastore correlation typically indicates resource sharing. It is best to avoid using two correlated datastores to enforce an anti-affinity rule (VM-VM or VMDK-VMDK). vSphere 5.1 allows controlling affinity rules when performance correlation is detected. Set the EnforceCorrelationForAffinity in the advanced options of the datastore cluster:

- Value=0: No consideration for correlations.
- Value=1: soft enforcement: Do not use any correlated datastores unless it is absolutely necessary when fixing an anti-affinity rule violation.
- Value=2: hard enforcement: Do not use correlated datastores. If the rule can't be fixed without using correlated datastores, generate faults.

Overriding Datastore Cluster Default

Storage DRS provides the ability to override the default datastore cluster affinity rule at the virtual machine level. This can be done during the creation of a virtual machine or when the virtual machine is placed inside the datastore cluster. When the virtual machine is created, the affinity rule can be changed via the VM override option of the datastore cluster settings page or by editing the settings of the virtual machine directly.

During virtual machine creation

Step 2F of the "create new virtual machine" process provides the option to change the default affinity rule. Select the SDRS option in the top menu and click on the Add button. The "Add SDRS rule" window provides the ability to change the default rule.

Figure 154: New virtual machine - Add Storage DRS rule

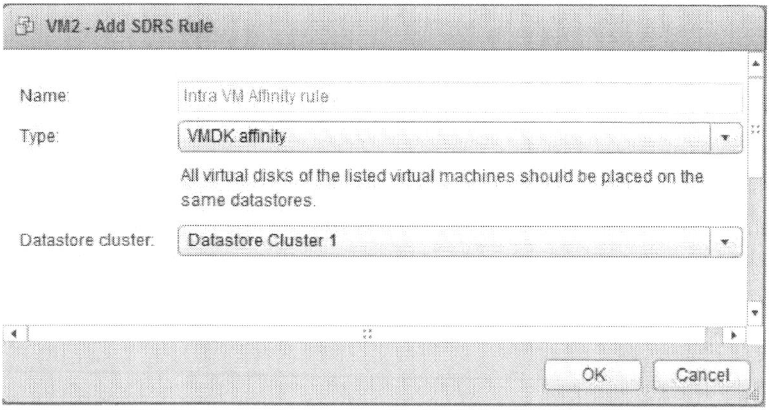

Existing virtual machine

Select the virtual machine and click on "edit settings" in the sub menu. Select the option "SDRS Rules" in the top menu. This provides an overview of the configured rules for the virtual machine. A virtual machine can be assigned more than one rule. This occurs when the virtual machine is a part of a VM-VM affinity rule.

Figure 155: Manage Storage DRS rules at virtual machine level

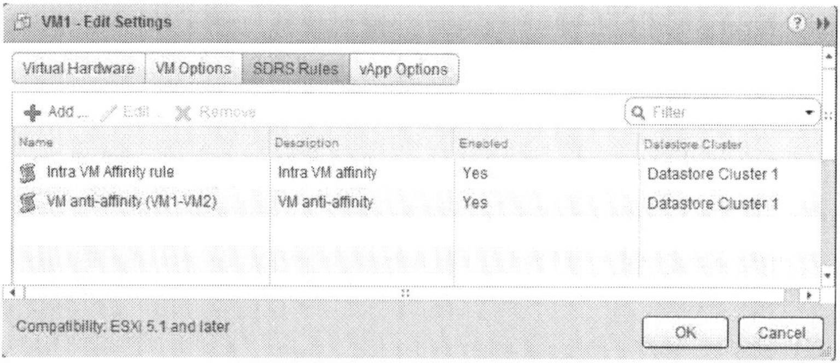

When selecting the default cluster-wide rule, the edit button remains grayed out. This rule needs to be removed before adding a VMDK anti-affinity rule. vCenter will report the following fault when creating an VMDK anti-affinity rule while the cluster wide default rule is still active on the virtual machine:

Figure 156: VM override conflict

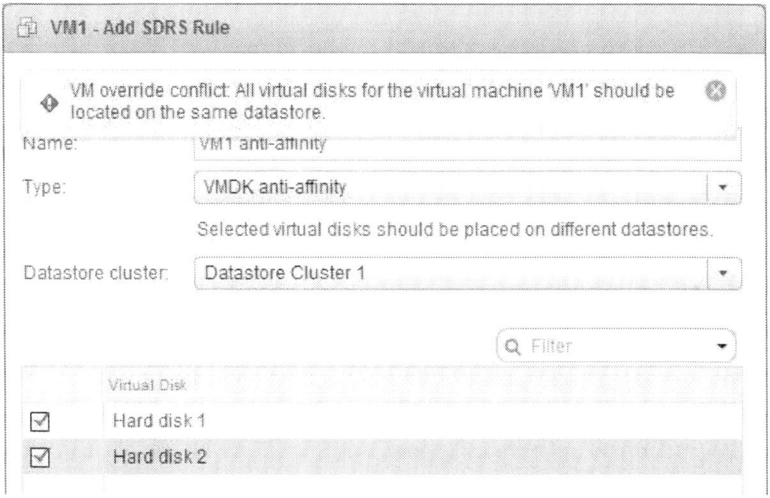

Note: a VMDK anti-affinity rule can only be created manually if the virtual machine contains 2 or more hard disks.

Changing Storage DRS rules at Datastore cluster level
Affinity rules can be changed at datastore cluster level. The advantage of changing rules at the datastore cluster level is that multiple virtual machines can be selected and changed at once.

Figure 157: Add virtual machine overrides

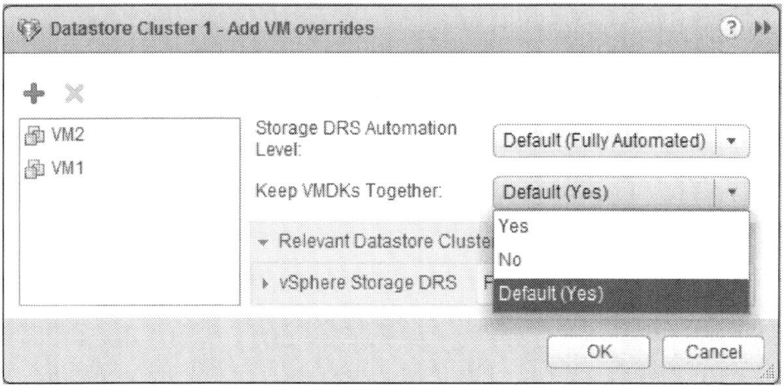

The VM overrides option can be found in the manage tab of the datastore cluster settings. Please note that only Intra-VM rules can be configured in this section.

Moving a virtual machine into a datastore cluster

If an existing virtual machine is moved into a datastore cluster, the application of an Intra-VM affinity rule depends on the disk layout configuration of the virtual machine and the method of introduction. A virtual machine can be moved into a datastore cluster by either Storage vMotion or by adding the datastore(s) containing its disks to a datastore cluster.

Table 26: Applying the Intra-VM affinity rule

Disk layout source	Method	Rule activate	Disk layout destination
All VMDKs on single DS	SvMotion	Yes	All VMDKs on single DS
VMDKs on multiple DS	SvMotion	Yes	All VMDKs on single DS
All VMDKs on single DS	Add storage	Yes	All VMDKs on single DS
VMDKs on multiple DS	Add storage	No	VMDKs on multiple DS

Be aware of the result of these actions when migrating to a datastore cluster. When a virtual machine is moved into a datastore cluster by Storage vMotion, placement of the VMDKs associated with the virtual machine is made in accordance of the cluster wide default affinity rule. If a VMDK affinity rule is configured as cluster wide default rule, Storage DRS will consolidate all of the VMDKs onto a single datastore, regardless of the original layout.

When adding datastores to the cluster, Storage DRS configures the existing virtual machines with VMDKs stored on a single datastore. If the VMDK files associated with a virtual machine span multiple datastores, Storage DRS disables the default affinity rule (if there is one) for the virtual machine configuration. This is done to avoid an SvMotion storm when moving a datastore into a datastore cluster if the datastore contains existing VMDKs that are not kept together.

Chapter 27

Datastore Maintenance Mode

Datastore maintenance mode is similar to Host Maintenance Mode. When a datastore is placed in Maintenance Mode, all registered virtual machines on that datastore are migrated to other datastores in the datastore cluster. By using the vCenter datastore API, Storage DRS learns which registered virtual machines are using the datastore. This list is used as input for generating migration recommendations. Because Storage DRS depends on vCenter's inventory, virtual machines that are not registered in vCenter will not be migrated off the datastore. The same is true for any other files on the datastore that are not related to registered virtual machines. Such as ISO files and FLP image files.

Automation mode

Depending on the Storage DRS automation mode, vCenter automatically executes Storage vMotions for the virtual machines if Storage DRS is configured in *Fully Automated* mode. Otherwise, vCenter generates a recommendation list and presents this to the user for validation.

Using Datastore maintenance mode for migration purposes

Datastore maintenance mode can be used to safely migrate virtual machines out of the datastore for storage array related maintenance operations such as migrating a LUN to another RAID group, however it is also an excellent feature that can help you during a storage migration project migrating virtual machines from standalone VMFS-3 datastores to VMFS-5 datastores aggregated in a datastore cluster.

Moving virtual machines manually out of a VMFS-3 datastore to a datastore in a datastore cluster is a time-consuming operation. Fortunately, by selecting the datastore cluster as the migration target, Initial placement will help you select the appropriate datastore, however you still need to manually start a Storage vMotion process for each virtual machine and manage the migrations until the last virtual machine is migrated.

Datastore maintenance mode on a VMFS3 datastore

By adding a VMFS-3 datastore to a datastore cluster and placing the datastore in maintenance mode, Storage DRS will take care of the tedious process described above. When the VMFS-3 datastore inside a datastore cluster is placed into maintenance mode, migration recommendations are generated to empty the datastore. Storage DRS reviews the virtual machines on the datastores and distributes them across the other datastores in the datastore cluster. Storage DRS finds an optimal placement based on the space and I/O utilization of the virtual machines and moves them to selected datastores while keeping the datastore cluster as balanced as possible in terms of space and I/O load.

Depending on the Storage DRS automation mode, it will generate a list of recommendations (Manual mode) or will automatically execute migrations of the virtual machines (Fully Automated).

After all the virtual machines have been migrated, Storage DRS will indicate that the datastore is in maintenance mode. At this point you can remove the datastore from the datastore cluster. If the datastore is going to be reused, we recommend reformatting the empty datastore to VMFS-5 file system. Please note that SIOC needs to be disabled on the datastore first, before a reformat can begin. By reformatting the datastore instead of upgrading, the datastore is using the unified blocksize. One of the advantages of having datastores configured with a unified blocksize is the possible improvement of storage vMotion times. If your storage array is VAAI-enabled, and the datastores use the same blocksize, Storage vMotion can leverage the FS3DM datamover's hardware offload capability. Using hardware offload will offer maximum performance while creating the least host CPU and memory overhead. Hardware offload will decrease the time required for the Storage vMotion process, allowing datastore clusters to reach a balanced steady state faster and impacting I/O performance of virtual machines in the datastore cluster in a positive manner.

After giving the datastore a fresh coat of VMFS-5, add it to the datastore cluster, add another VMFS-3 datastore, rinse and repeat the datastore maintenance mode operation on another loaded VMFS-3 datastore.

How to throttle the number of Storage vMotion operations

When enabling datastore maintenance mode, Storage DRS will move virtual machines out of the datastore as fast as it can. As indicated in the previous section, the number of virtual machines that can be migrated into or out of a datastore is 8 and is controlled by the operation costs and limits defined at various levels. This is related to the concurrent migration limits of hosts, network and datastores. To manage and limit the number of concurrent migrations, either by vMotion or Storage vMotion, a cost and limit factor is applied. Although the term "limit" is used, a better description would be "maximum cost." In order for a migration operation to be able to start, the cost of the operation cannot exceed the maximum cost (limit) configured on the resources. In this case, vMotion and Storage vMotion are considered operations and the ESXi host, network and datastore are considered resources. A resource has both a maximum and an in-use cost. When an operation is requested, the in-use cost plus the new operation cost cannot exceed the maximum cost.

Figure 158: Resource max cost and operation cost

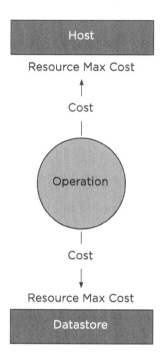

The operation cost of a storage vMotion on a host is "4", the max cost of a host is "8". If one Storage vMotion operation is running, the in-use cost of the host resource is "4", allowing one more Storage vMotion process to start without exceeding the host limit.

As a storage vMotion operation also hits the storage resource cost, the max cost and in-use cost of the datastore needs to be factored in as well. The operation cost of a Storage vMotion for datastores is set to 16, the max cost of a datastore is 128. This means that 8 concurrent Storage vMotion operations can be executed on a datastore. These operations can be started on multiple hosts, not more than 2 storage vMotion from the same host due to the max cost of a Storage vMotion operation on the host level.

Figure 159: Storage vMotion in progress

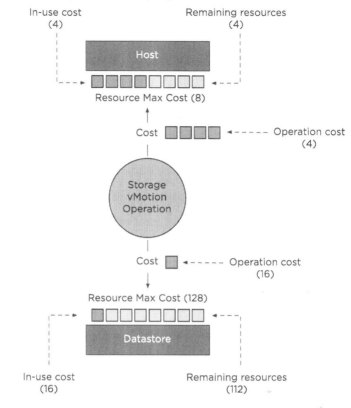

How do you throttle the number of Storage vMotion operations?

You may want to throttle the number of storage vMotion operations in order to reduce the IO hit on a datastore during maintenance mode. The preferred method for doing so is to reduce the max cost for provisioning operations to the datastore. Adjusting host costs is strongly discouraged. Host costs are defined according to host resource limitation issues and adjusting host costs can impact other host functionality that is unrelated to vMotion or Storage vMotion processes.

Adjusting the max cost per datastore can be done by editing the vpxd.cfg or via the advanced settings of the vCenter Server Settings in the administration view.

If done via the vpxd.cfg, the value
vpxd.ResourceManager.MaxCostPerEsx41DS should be added as follows:

< config >
< vpxd >
< ResourceManager >
< MaxCostPerEsx41DS > new value < /MaxCostPerEsx41DS >
< /ResourceManager >
< /vpxd >
< /config >

As the max costs have not been increased since ESX 4.1, the value-name
remains the same and is valid for all ESX 4.1 or higher hosts.
Please remember to leave some room for vMotion when resizing the max
cost of a datastore since the vMotion process has a datastore cost as well.
During the stun/unstun of a virtual machine, the vMotion process hits the
datastore, and the cost involved with this process is 1.

As an example, changing the MaxCostPerEsx41DS to 112, allows 7
concurrent Storage vMotions against a given datastore in the vCenter
inventory. If 7 concurrent Storage vMotions are started on this datastore, a
vMotion process of a virtual machine using this datastore will be queued as
the vMotion process would violate the max cost of the datastore. 7 x 16 = 112
+ 1 vMotion = 113. The moment a Storage vMotion is completed, the
vMotion process will resume as resources become available.

Please note that cost and max values are applied to each migration process,
impact normal day-to-day DRS and Storage DRS load balancing operations
as well as the manual vMotion and Storage vMotion operations occurring in
the virtual infrastructure managed by the vCenter server.
As mentioned before, adjusting the cost at the host side can be tricky as the
costs of operations and limits are relative to each other and can even harm
other host processes unrelated to migration processes. Think about the
impact on DRS if you adjust the cost at the host side! When increasing the
cost of a Storage vMotion operation on the host, the available "slots" for
vMotion operations are reduced. This might impact DRS load balancing
efficiency when a storage vMotion process is active and should be avoided at
all times.

Chapter 28

Summarizing

Hopefully we have succeeded in giving you a better understanding of the internal workings of Storage DRS and how you can benefit from this feature. Introducing Storage DRS to your virtual infrastructure impacts the architectural and operational perspective and we hope that this book has handed you the tools needed to update your vSphere design and ultimately to decrease the operational effort associated with monitoring and provisioning storage and virtual machines.

We have tried to simplify some of the concepts to make it easier to understand; yet we acknowledge that some concepts are difficult to grasp. We hope that after reading this section of the book, everyone is confident enough to make the required or recommended changes.

If there are any questions please do not hesitate to reach out to either of the authors. We will we do our best to answer your questions.

Part IV

Stretched Cluster Architecture Study

Chapter 29

Stretched Cluster Architecture Study

In this part we will be discussing a specific infrastructure architecture and how HA, DRS and Storage DRS can be leveraged and should be deployed to increase availability. Be it availability of your workload or the resources provided to your workload, we will guide you through some of the design considerations and decision points along the way. Of course, a full understanding of your environment will be required in order to make appropriate decisions regarding specific implementation details. Nevertheless, we hope that this section will provide a proper understanding of how certain features play together and how these can be used to meet the requirements of your environment and build the desired architecture.

Scenario

The scenario we have chosen is a stretched cluster also referred to as a VMware vSphere Metro Storage Cluster solution. We have chosen this specific scenario as it allows us to explain a multitude of design and architectural considerations. Although this scenario has been tested and validated in our lab, every environment is unique and our recommendations are based on our experience and your mileage may vary.

A VMware vSphere Metro Storage Cluster (vMSC) configuration is a VMware vSphere 5 certified solution that combines synchronous replication with storage array based clustering. These solutions are typically deployed in environments where the distance between datacenters is limited, often metropolitan or campus environments.

The primary benefit of a stretched cluster model is to enable fully active and workload-balanced datacenters to be used to their full potential. Many customers find this architecture attractive due to the capability of migrating virtual machines with vMotion and Storage vMotion between sites. This enables on-demand and non-intrusive cross-site mobility of workloads. The capability of a stretched cluster to provide this active balancing of resources should always be the primary design and implementation goal.

Stretched cluster solutions offer the benefit of:
- Workload mobility
- Cross-site automated load balancing
- Enhanced downtime avoidance
- Disaster avoidance

Technical requirements and constraints

Due to the technical constraints of an online migration of virtual machines, there are specific requirements that must be met prior to consideration of a stretched cluster implementation. These requirements are listed in the Storage section of the VMware Hardware Compatibility Guide, and are included below for your convenience:

- Storage connectivity using Fibre Channel, iSCSI, SVD (Storage Virtualization Device), and FCoE is supported
- Storage connectivity using NAS (NFS protocol) is not supported with vMSC configurations at the time of writing (August 2012)
- The maximum supported network latency between sites for ESXi management networks is 10 ms Round Trip Time (RTT)
    - Note that 10ms of latency for vMotion is only supported with Enterprise+ licenses (Metro vMotion)
- The maximum supported latency for synchronous storage replication links is 5 milliseconds RTT, always validate with your storage vendor what their maximum allowed RTT is
- Minimum of 622Mbps redundant network links for the ESXi vMotion network

The storage requirements are slightly more complex than typical synchronous storage replication solutions. A vSphere Metro Storage Cluster requires what is in effect a single storage subsystem that spans both sites. In this design, a given datastore must be accessible (able to be read **and** written to), simultaneously from both sites. Further, when problems occur, the ESXi hosts must be able to continue to access datastores from either site transparently with no impact to ongoing storage operations.

This precludes traditional synchronous replication solutions, as they create a primary/secondary relationship between the active (primary) LUN where data is being accessed and the secondary LUN that is receiving replication. In these solutions, in order to access the secondary LUN, replication must be stopped (or reversed) and the LUN made visible to hosts. This now "promoted" secondary LUN typically has a completely different LUN ID and is essentially a newly available copy of a former primary. This type of solution works for traditional disaster recovery configurations, as it is expected that virtual machines would need to be started up on the secondary site. The vMSC configuration requires simultaneous, uninterrupted access so as to allow live migration of running virtual machines between sites; a normal vMotion does not relocate a virtual machine's disk files.

The storage subsystem for a vMSC must be able to be read from and write to both locations simultaneously, and all disk writes are committed synchronously at both locations to ensure that data is always consistent regardless of the location from which it is being read. This storage architecture requires significant bandwidth and very low latency between the sites involved in the cluster. Increased distances or latencies will cause delays to writing to disk, making performance suffer dramatically, and will disallow successful vMotion between the cluster nodes that reside in different locations.

Uniform versus Non-Uniform

vMSC solutions are classified in two distinct categories. These categories are based on a fundamental difference in how hosts access storage. It is important to understand the different types of stretched storage solutions, as this will influence your design. The two main categories are as described on the VMware Hardware Compatibility List as follows:

- Uniform host access configuration - ESXi hosts from both sites are all connected to a storage node in the storage cluster across all sites. Paths presented to ESXi hosts are stretched across distance.
- Non-Uniform host access configuration - ESXi hosts in each site are connected only to storage node(s) in the same site. Paths presented to ESXi hosts from storage nodes are limited to local site.

Let us describe both more in-depth to ensure it is absolutely clear what either means from an architecture / implementation perspective.

Uniform, is where hosts in Datacenter-A and Datacenter-B have access to the storage systems in both Datacenter-A and Datacenter-B. In effect, the storage area network is stretched between the sites and all hosts can access all LUNs. In this configuration, read-write access to a LUN takes place on one of the two arrays, and a synchronous mirror is maintained in a hidden, read only state on the second array. For example, if a LUN containing a datastore is read-write on the array at Datacenter-A, all ESXi hosts would access that datastore via the array in Datacenter-A. For ESXi hosts in Datacenter-A, this would be a local access. ESXi hosts in Datacenter-B that are running virtual machines hosted on this datastore would be sending read-write traffic across the network between datacenters. In case of an outage, or operator-controlled shift of control of the LUN to Datacenter-B, all ESXi hosts would continue to see the identical LUN being presented, except it is now being accessed via the array in Datacenter-B.

Figure 160: Uniform Storage Architecture

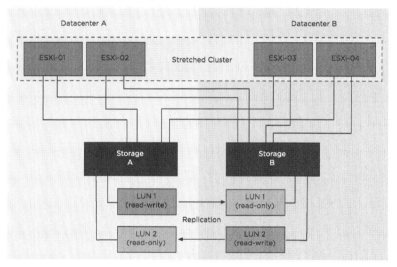

As you can see, the ideal situation is one where virtual machines access a datastore which is controlled (read-write) by the array in the same datacenter. This minimizes traffic between datacenters and avoids performance impact of reads going across the interconnect.

The notion of "site affinity" for a virtual machine is dictated by the read-write copy of the datastore, "site affinity" is also sometimes referred to as "site bias" or "LUN locality". Meaning that when a virtual machine has site affinity with Datacenter-A, its read-write copy of the datastore is located in Datacenter-A. This will be explained in more detail in the DRS section of this chapter.

Non-uniform, is where hosts in Datacenter-A only have access to the array within the local datacenter, and the array (and its peer array in the opposite data center) is responsible for providing access to all datastores. In most cases the concept of a "virtual LUN" is used. This allows ESXi hosts in each data center to read and write to the same datastore/LUN.

It is good to know that even in the case where two virtual machines reside on the same datastore but are both located in a different datacenter they will write locally. A key point in this configuration is that each of the LUNs / datastores have "site affinity" defined; this is also sometimes referred to as "site bias" or "LUN locality". In other words, if anything happens to the link in between sites then the storage system on the preferred site for a given datastore will be the only one left who can access it in a read-write manner. This is of course to avoid data corruption in the case of a failure scenario.

Figure 161: Non-uniform Storage Architecture

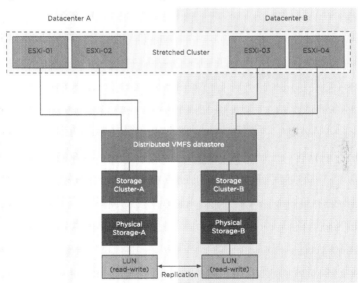

As uniform solutions are today most commonly deployed our test case will use Uniform storage. It should be noted that many of the design considerations will also apply to non-uniform configurations and we will call out when this is not the case.

Scenario Architecture

In this section we will describe the architecture deployed for this scenario. We will also discuss some of the basic configuration and behavior of the various vSphere features. For an in-depth explanation of each respective feature, refer to the HA and the DRS section of this book. We will make specific recommendations based on VMware best practices and provide operational guidance where applicable. In our failure scenarios it will be explained how these practices prevent or limit downtime.

Infrastructure

The infrastructure used for this scenario consists of a single vSphere 5.1 cluster with 4 ESXi hosts. These hosts are managed by a vSphere vCenter Server, revision 5.1. It was decided to use vSphere 5.1 to allow testing the improved handling of "Permanent Device Loss" (PDL) scenarios that were introduced in vSphere 5.0 Update 1. These enhancements have been introduced primarily for Stretched Cluster environments. We will discuss this in more detail in the vSphere HA sub-section of this chapter. It should be noted that there are no changes with regards to PDL behavior in vSphere 5.1.

For the purpose of our tests, we have simulated a customer environment with two sites. Our first site is called Frimley and our second site is called Bluefin. (Referring to the names of the cities in which VMware has offices in the United Kingdom and the location of our lab environment.) The network between the Frimley datacenter and the Bluefin datacenter is a stretched Layer 2 network with a minimal distance in between as is typical in campus cluster scenarios. vCenter Server is installed on a virtual machine running within the same cluster.

Each site holds two ESXi hosts, and the vCenter Server is configured with vSphere DRS affinity (should rule) to the hosts in Bluefin datacenter. Note that in a stretched cluster environment only a single vCenter Server instance is used. This is different from a traditional VMware Site Recovery Manager configuration in which a dual vCenter Server configuration is required. The configuration of VM-Host affinity rules is discussed in more detail in chapter 15. In our scenario iSCSI is the main protocol.

The vSphere 5.1 cluster is connected to a NetApp MetroCluster in a fabric configuration according to a uniform device access model. This configuration is described in-depth in NetApp's Technology Report "TR-

3548". This means that every host in the cluster is connected to both storage nodes. Each of the nodes is connected locally to two Brocade switches, which are connected to two similar switches in the secondary location. For any given LUN, one of the two storage nodes is presenting the LUN as Read/Write via iSCSI. The opposite storage node is maintaining the replicated, read only copy that is effectively hidden from the ESXi hosts until it is needed.

When using a NetApp MetroCluster, an iSCSI connection is bound to a particular virtual IP address. This virtual IP-Address enables ESXi hosts to connect to a given storage controller. I In the case of a failure, this IP-Address shifts to the opposite storage controller, allowing seamless access to storage without requiring reconfiguration of the target storage IP address.

A total of 8 LUNs were created: four of these were accessed through the virtual iSCSI IP address active in the Frimley datacenter and four were accessed through the virtual iSCSI IP address active in the Bluefin datacenter.

Figure 162: Infrastructure architecture

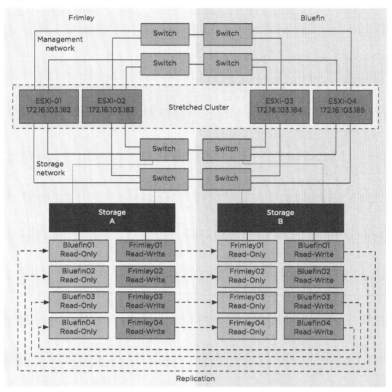

Table 27: Infrastructure details

Location	Hosts	Datastores	Local isolation address
Bluefin	172.16.103.184	Bluefin01	172.16.103.10
	172.16.103.185	Bluefin02	
		Bluefin03	
		Bluefin04	
Frimley	172.16.103.182	Frimley01	172.16.103.11
	172.16.103.183	Frimley02	
		Frimley03	
		Frimley04	

Chapter 30

vSphere Configuration

Our focus for this scenario will be on vSphere HA, vSphere DRS and Storage DRS in relationship to stretched cluster environments as design and operational considerations around these vSphere components are commonly overlooked and underestimated. A lot of emphasis has traditionally been placed on the storage layer with little thought being applied as to how the workloads will be provisioned and managed.

As we mentioned previously, the key drivers for using a stretched cluster are typically workload balancing and disaster avoidance. How do we ensure our environment is properly balanced without impacting availability or severely increasing the operational expenditure? How do we build the requirements into our provisioning and ongoing management processes and how do we validate periodically that we still meet our requirements? Failure to define and adhere to these requirements will make the environment confusing to administer and less predictable during the various failure scenarios you are hoping it will assist you with. In fact, ignoring this part of the process may lead to *additional* downtime in the event of a failure.

Each of these three VMware vSphere features has very specific configuration requirements and can enhance the resiliency of your environment and availability of your workload. Throughout this section, architectural recommendations will be made. These recommendations are based on our findings during the testing of the various failure scenarios. Each of the failure scenarios tested are documented in one of the following sections. Keep in mind that these failure scenarios apply directly to this example configuration and that your environment may be subject to additional failure scenarios based on your implementation and configuration options.

vSphere HA specifics

Our example environment has 4 hosts and a uniform stretched storage solution. As a full site failure is one scenario that needs to be taken into account in a resilient architecture, we recommend enabling Admission

Control. As availability of workloads is the primary driver for most stretched cluster environments, it is recommended to allow sufficient capacity for a full site failure. As such, hosts will be equally divided between both sites, and to ensure all workloads can be restarted by HA it is recommended to configure the admission control policy for 50 percent.

We recommend using the percentage-based policy as it offers the most flexibility and reduces operational overhead. Even when new hosts are introduced to the environment there is no need to change the percentage and there is no risk of skewed consolidation ratios due to the possible use of virtual machine-level reservations. For more details please read chapter 6.

HA uses heartbeat mechanisms to validate the state of a host. As explained in chapter 3 there are two heartbeat mechanisms; namely network and datastore heartbeats. Network heartbeating is the primary mechanism for HA to validate availability of the hosts. Datastore heartbeating is the secondary mechanism used by HA to determine the exact state of the host once network heartbeating has failed.

If a host is not receiving any heartbeats, it uses a mechanism to detect whether it is merely isolated from other hosts or completely isolated from the network. This process involves pinging the host's default gateway. In addition or in place of the default gateway, one or more isolation addresses can be specified manually to enhance reliability of isolation validation. We recommend specifying at a minimum two additional isolation addresses and each of these addresses to be site-local. This enables HA to validate for complete network isolation even in case of a connection failure between sites, and provides redundancy in case one IP endpoint should fail.

However, if a host is isolated, vSphere HA can trigger a response. This is, as explained earlier, called an *isolation response*. An isolation response is triggered to ensure that virtual machines are handled appropriately when the host has lost connection with the management network. Isolation response has been discussed in-depth in chapter 3. Depending on the type of storage used and the physical network implemented, a decision will need to be made around which isolation response will be used. We would like to refer to chapter 4, table 3 to support this decision.

In our test-bed, one of these addresses would physically reside in the Frimley datacenter and the other would physically reside in the Bluefin datacenter. The screenshot below shows an example of how to configure multiple isolation addresses. The vSphere HA advanced setting used is *das.isolationaddress* and more details on how to configure this can be found in KB article 1002117.

In order for vSphere HA datastore heartbeating to function correctly in any type of failure scenario, we recommend increasing the number of heartbeat datastores from two to four. The minimum number of heartbeat datastores is two and the maximum is five, where four is recommended in a stretched cluster environment as this would provide full redundancy in either location. It is also recommended to define four specific datastores as preferred heartbeat datastores and in doing so select two from one site and two from the other. This will allow vSphere HA to heartbeat to a datastore even in the event of a connection failure between sites. These datastores would be useful if a network partition should occur within a site after the connection between sites fails.

The number of heartbeat datastores can be increased by adding an advanced HA setting called *das.heartbeatDsPerHost*.

We recommend using "Select any of the cluster datastores taking into account my preferences" as this will allow vSphere HA to select any other datastore should the four designated datastores, which we have manually selected, become unavailable. The reason that we recommend four is that if the inter-site connection fails, vCenter will end up on one site, and so there will be no opportunity for HA to change the datastores used for heartbeats by the hosts in the other site. This setting is shown in the screenshot below.

Figure 163: Heartbeat Datastores

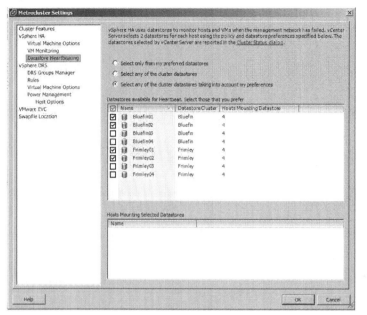

vSphere 5.0 Update 1 Permanent Device Loss enhancements

As of vSphere 5.0 Update 1, enhancements have been introduced to allow for an automated fail-over of virtual machines residing on a datastore that has a "Permanent Device Loss" (PDL) condition. A PDL condition, as will be shown in one of our failure scenarios, is a condition that is communicated by the array controller to ESXi via a specific SCSI sense code. This condition indicates that a device (LUN) has become unavailable and is likely permanently unavailable. An example scenario in which this condition would be communicated by the array would be when a LUN is set offline by a storage administrator. This condition is used in non-uniform models during a failure scenario to ensure ESXi takes appropriate action when access to a LUN is revoked. It should be noted that when a full storage failure occurs, it is impossible to generate the Permanent Device Loss condition as there is no communication possible between the array and the ESXi host. This state will be identified by the ESXi host as an All Paths Down (APD) condition.

It is important to recognize that the following settings only apply to a PDL condition and not to an APD condition. In our failure scenarios, we will demonstrate the difference in behavior for these two conditions.

In order to allow vSphere HA to respond to a PDL condition, two advanced settings have been introduced in vSphere Update 1. The first setting is configured at the host level and is *disk.terminateVMOnPDLDefault*. This setting can be configured in /etc/vmware/settings and should be set to "True" by default. Note that this is a per-host setting and the host requires a reboot for this setting to take effect. This setting ensures that a virtual machine is killed when the datastore on which it resides enters a PDL state. The virtual machine is killed as soon as it initiates disk I/O on a datastore which is in a PDL condition. If a virtual machine's files do not all reside on the same datastore and a PDL condition exists on one of its datastores, the virtual machine may not get restarted by HA. This issue was fixed in vSphere 5.1. To ensure that PDL conditions can be mitigated by HA, we recommend setting *disk.terminateVMonPDLDefault* to "True" and placing all virtual machine files for a given virtual machine on a single datastore. Please note that virtual machines are only killed when they attempt to issue I/O to the datastore, not before. If the virtual machine is not issuing I/O to the datastore, the virtual machine remains alive. Virtual machines that are running memory-intensive workloads without issuing I/O to the datastore may remain active in such situations.

The second setting is a vSphere HA advanced setting called *das.maskCleanShutdownEnabled*. This setting was introduced in vSphere 5.0 Update 1 and is not enabled by default. It will need to be set to "True" on your HA cluster(s). This setting allows HA to trigger a restart response for a virtual machine which has been killed automatically due to a PDL condition. HA cannot differentiate between a virtual machine that was killed due to the PDL state and a virtual machine that has been powered off by an administrator. Setting this flag to "True" tells HA to assume the former. Note that a VM powered off during an APD by a user will be subject to the behavior enabled by this flag.

We recommend setting *das.maskCleanShutdownEnabled* to "True" in order to limit downtime for virtual machines residing on datastores in a PDL condition. When *das.maskCleanShutdownEnabled* is not set to "True" and a PDL condition exists while *disk.terminateVMonPDLDefault* has been set to "True," virtual machine restart will **not** occur after virtual machines have been killed as HA will assume these virtual machines were powered off (or shutdown) manually by the administatrator.

vSphere DRS

vSphere DRS is used in many environments to distribute load within a cluster. vSphere DRS offers many other features which can be very helpful in stretched environments. We recommend enabling vSphere DRS to allow for load balancing across hosts in the cluster. The vSphere DRS load balancing calculation is based only on CPU and memory use. As such, care must be taken with regards to both storage and networking resource utilization and traffic flow. In order to avoid unintended storage and network traffic overhead in a stretched cluster environment, we recommend implementing vSphere DRS affinity rules to allow for a logical and predictable separation of virtual machines. This will subsequently help improve availability, and for virtual machines that are responsible for infrastructure services like Active Directory and DNS, it will assist by ensuring separation of these services across sites.

vSphere DRS affinity rules also help prevent unnecessary downtime or storage and network traffic flow overhead by enforcing desired site affinity. We recommend aligning vSphere VM-Host affinity rules with the storage configuration. Here we mean setting VM-Host affinity rules so that a virtual machine prefers to run on a host at the same site as the array that is configured as the primary read/write node for a its datastore. For example, in our test configuration, virtual machines stored on the Frimley-01 datastore are set with VM-Host affinity to prefer hosts in the Frimley datacenter. This ensures that in the case of a network connection failure between sites, virtual machines will not lose connection with the storage system that is primary for their datastore. VM-Host affinity rules configured according to this recommendation will try to ensure that virtual machines stay local to the storage primary for that datastore. This coincidentally results in all read I/O from the virtual machines staying local to their sites as well. Note: Different storage vendors use different terminology to describe the relationship of a LUN to a particular array or controller. In this chapter we will use the generic term "Storage Site Affinity." Storage Site Affinity means the preferred location for read-write access to a given LUN.

We recommend implementing "should rules" as these are able to be violated by HA in the event of a failure. Availability of services should always prevail over performance. In the case of "must rules," HA will not violate the rule-set, and this could potentially lead to service outages during site or host failures. In the scenario where a complete datacenter fails, "must rules" will make it impossible for vSphere HA to restart the virtual machines as they will not have the required affinity to be allowed to start on hosts in the other datacenter. vSphere DRS communicates these rules to vSphere HA, and these are stored in a "compatibility list" that governs allowed startup. It should be noted that vSphere DRS, under certain circumstances such as massive host imbalance coupled with aggressive recommendation settings, can also violate "should" rules. Although this is very rare, we do recommended monitoring for violation of these rules as a violation could possibly impact availability and performance of your workload.

We recommend manually defining "sites" by creating a group of hosts that belong to a site, and adding virtual machines to these sites based on the affinity of the datastore on which they are provisioned. In our scenario only a limited number of virtual machines were provisioned. We recommend automating the process of defining site affinity using tools like vCenter Orchestrator or PowerCLI. If automating the process is not an option, we recommend using a generic naming convention to simplify the creation of these groups. We recommend that these groups are validated on a regular basis to ensure all virtual machines belong to the group with the correct site affinity.

The following screenshots depict the configuration used for this scenario. In the first screenshot, all the VMs that should remain local to the Bluefin location have been added to the Bluefin VMs group.

Figure 164: DRS Groups –virtual machines

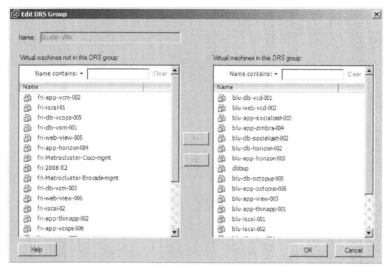

Next, a Bluefin Hosts group is created containing all hosts residing in this location.

Figure 165: DRS Groups - hosts

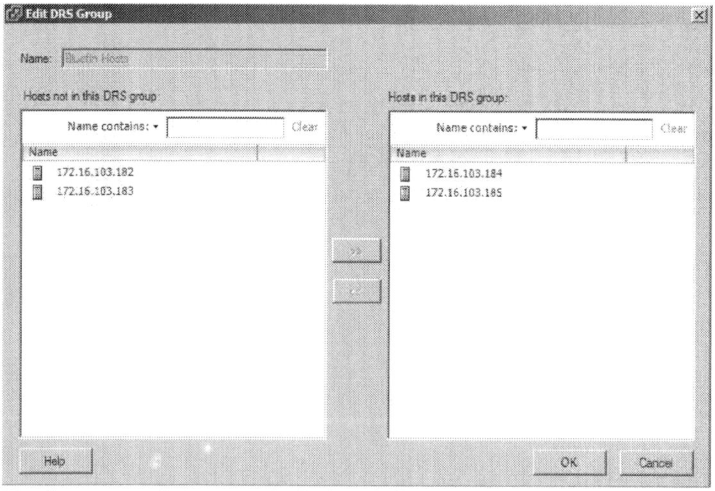

Finally, a new rule is created which is defined as "should run on" rule linking the host group and the VM group for the Bluefin location.

Figure 166: VM-Host rules

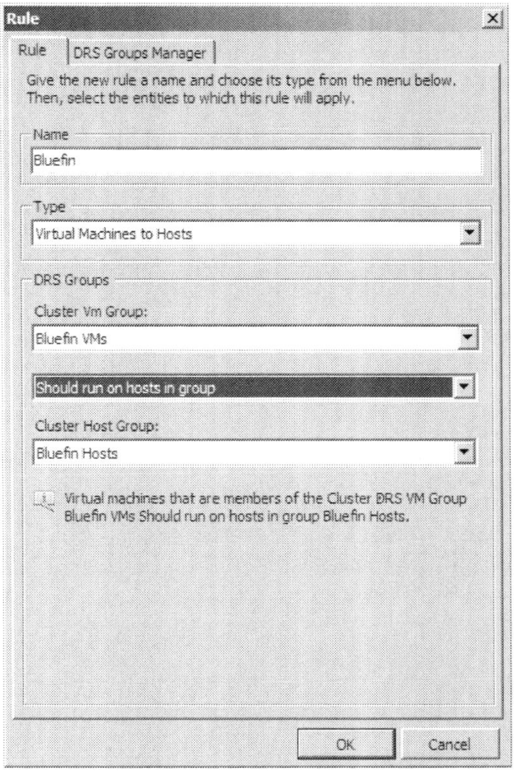

This should be done for both locations, which should result in four groups and two rules.

Figure 167: End result - affinity rules

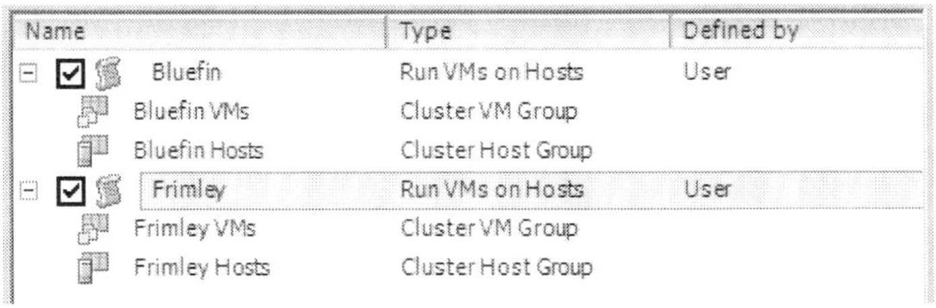

Name	Type	Defined by
☑ 🖥 Bluefin	Run VMs on Hosts	User
🖥 Bluefin VMs	Cluster VM Group	
🖥 Bluefin Hosts	Cluster Host Group	
☑ 🖥 Frimley	Run VMs on Hosts	User
🖥 Frimley VMs	Cluster VM Group	
🖥 Frimley Hosts	Cluster Host Group	

Correcting Affinity Rule Violation

DRS assigns a high priority to correcting affinity rule violations. During invocation, the primary goal of DRS is to correct any violations and generate recommendations that migrate virtual machines to the hosts listed in the Cluster Host Group. These moves have a higher priority than load-balancing moves and will be started before load balancing moves.

DRS is invoked every 5 minutes by default, but DRS is also triggered if the cluster detects changes. For instance, when a host reconnects to the cluster, DRS is invoked and generates recommendations to correct any identified violations. Our testing has shown that DRS generates recommendations to correct affinity rule violations within 30 seconds after a host reconnects to the cluster. Note that DRS is limited by the overall capacity of the vMotion network, which means that it might take multiple invocations before all affinity rule violations are corrected.

vSphere Storage DRS

Storage DRS enables aggregation of datastores in to a single unit of consumption from an administrative perspective and balances virtual machines' disks when defined performance or capacity thresholds are exceeded. Storage DRS ensures sufficient disk resources are available to your workload. We recommend enabling Storage DRS.

Storage DRS uses Storage vMotion to migrate virtual machine disks between datastores within a datastore cluster. As the underlying stretched storage systems use synchronous replication, a migration or series of migrations will have an impact on replication traffic and could cause the virtual machines to become temporarily unavailable due to contention for network resources during the movement of disks. Migration to random datastores could also potentially lead to additional I/O latency in Uniform Access configurations if virtual machines are not migrated along with their virtual disks, from a site perspective. For example, if a virtual machine resident on a host in Frimley has its disk migrated to a datastore in Bluefin, it will continue operating but with potentially degraded performance. The virtual machine's disk reads will now be subject to the increased latency associated with reading from the virtual iSCSI IP at Site B and reads will be subject to inter-site latency instead of being satisfied by a local target.

In order to control when and if migrations occur, we recommend configuring Storage DRS in manual mode. This allows for human validation per recommendation and allows for recommendations to be applied during off-peak hours while gaining the operational benefit and efficiency of the Initial Placement functionality.

We recommend creating datastore clusters based on the storage configuration with respect to Storage Site Affinity. Datastores with a site affinity for Site A should not be mixed in datastore clusters with datastores with a site affinity for Site B. This will allow for operational consistency and ease the creation and on-going management of DRS VM-Host affinity rules. It is recommended to ensure that all vSphere DRS VM-Host affinity rules are updated accordingly when virtual machines are migrated (Storage vMotion) between datastore clusters and crossing defined storage site affinity boundaries. We recommend aligning naming conventions for datastore clusters and VM-Host affinity rules to simplify the provisioning and management processes.

The naming convention used in our testing gave both datastores and datastore clusters a site-specific name to simplify alignment of DRS host-affinity with virtual machine deployment in the correct site. See the graphic below for our site-specific storage layout in our sites "Bluefin" and "Frimley". Please note that vCenter map functionality cannot be used to view site affinity with regards to storage as currently it does not display datastore cluster objects.

Figure 168: Datastore cluster architecture

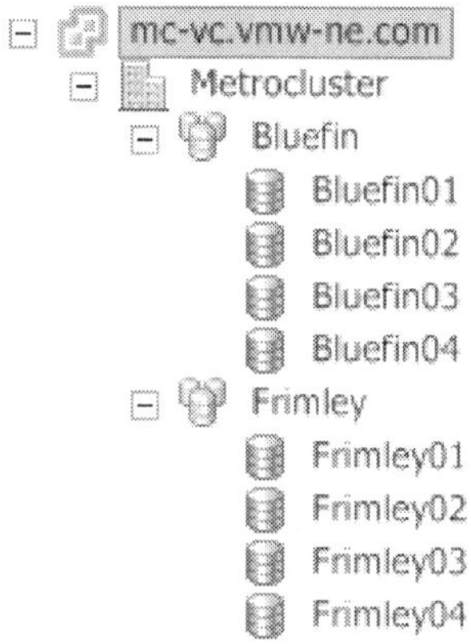

Chapter 31

Failure scenarios

There are many failures that can be introduced in clustered systems, but in a properly architected environment, HA, DRS and the storage subsystem will be unaware of many of these. We will not address the zero-impact failures, like the failure of a single network cable, as they are explained in-depth in the documentation provided by the storage vendor of your chosen solution. We will discuss the following "common" failure scenarios:

- Single host failure in Frimley datacenter (DC)
- Single host isolation in Frimley DC
- Storage partition
- Datacenter partition
- Disk shelf failure in Frimley DC
- Full storage failure in Frimley DC
- Full compute failure in Frimley DC
- Full compute failure in Frimley DC and full storage failure in Bluefin DC
- Loss of complete Frimley DC

We will also examine scenarios wherein specific settings are incorrectly configured. These settings will determine the availability and recoverability of your virtual machines in a failure scenario and hence it is important to understand the impact of misconfiguration such as:

- Incorrectly configured VM-Host affinity rules
- Incorrectly configured Heartbeat Datastores
- Isolation address incorrectly configured
- Incorrectly configured Permanent Device Loss handling
- vCenter Server split brain scenario

All of these scenarios have been extensively tested. Below are our findings per scenario and possible recommendations where applicable.

Single host failure in Frimley DC

In this scenario, we simulated the complete failure of a host in Frimley datacenter by pulling the power cables on a live system. This scenario is depicted in the following diagram.

Figure 169: Single host failure

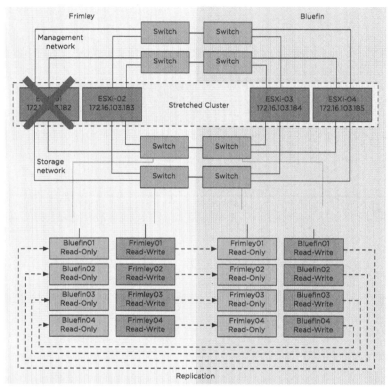

Result

All virtual machines successfully restarted by vSphere HA, however not in accordance with VM-Host affinity rules.

Explanation

If a host fails, the failure is detected by the cluster's HA master node, as network heartbeats from it are no longer being received. After the master has detected network heartbeats are missing, it will start monitoring for datastore heartbeats. Since the host has failed completely, it cannot generate datastore heartbeats, and these too will be detected as missing by the HA master node. During this time a third availability check is done, which is to ping the management addresses of the failed hosts. If all of these checks return as unsuccessful, the master will declare the missing host as dead, and will attempt to restart all the protected virtual machines that were running on the host before the master lost contact with the host.

The vSphere DRS VM-Host affinity rules defined on a cluster level are "should rules," meaning that the virtual machines could potentially be restarted on a host in the other datacenter. In our testing we witnessed this behavior multiple times, where virtual machines started on any available host in the cluster including hosts at Bluefin datacenter. vSphere DRS will attempt to correct any violated affinity rules at the first invocation and will automatically migrate virtual machines in accordance with their affinity rules to bring virtual machine placement into alignment. We recommend manually invoking vSphere DRS to ensure all virtual machines are placed on hosts in the correct location to avoid possible performance degradation and reduced availability should a second failure occur. In our scenario, misplacement would lead to increased latency, as the virtual machine would be accessing storage in the other location. The below screenshot depicts how to manually run DRS from the DRS tab on a vCenter cluster object within the vSphere client.

Figure 170: Manually trigger DRS

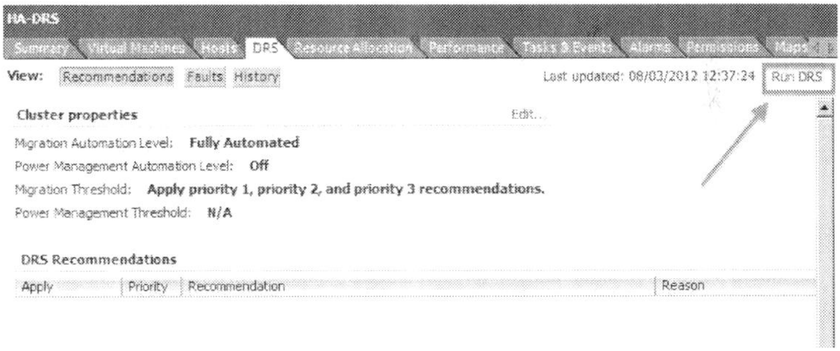

Single host isolation in Frimley DC

In this scenario, we isolated a single host in Frimley datacenter from the rest of the network by disconnecting all network links. The storage network was not impacted.

Figure 171: Single host isolation

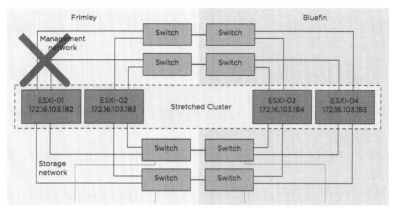

Result
Virtual machines remained running, as isolation response was configured to "Leave Powered On".

Explanation
When a host is isolated, the isolation is detected by the HA master node, as network heartbeats from it are not received any longer. When the master has detected network heartbeats are missing, it will start monitoring for datastore heartbeats. Since the host is isolated, it will generate datastore heartbeats for the secondary HA detection mechanism. Detection of valid host heartbeats will allow the HA master node to determine that the host is running but isolated from the network. Depending on the isolation response configured, the impacted host might choose to power off or shut down virtual machines or alternately leave the virtual machines powered on. The isolation response is triggered approximately 30 seconds after the host has detected it is isolated.

We recommend aligning the isolation response to business requirements and physical constraints. From a best practices perspective, "Leave Powered On" is the recommended isolation response setting for the majority of environments. Isolated hosts are a rare event in a properly architected environment, given the built-in redundancy of most modern designs. In environments that use network-based storage protocols, such as iSCSI and NFS, the recommended isolation response is "Power Off". With these environments, it is more likely that a network outage that causes a host to become isolated will also affect the host's ability to communicate with the datastores.

If a different isolation response than the recommended "Leave Powered On" is selected and a power off or shut down isolation response is triggered, virtual machines will be restarted by the HA master on the remaining nodes in the cluster. The vSphere DRS VM-Host affinity rules defined on a cluster level are "should rules," meaning that the virtual machines could potentially be restarted on a host in the other datacenter. In our testing, we have witnessed this behavior multiple times. Following host isolation and the associated cluster response, we recommend manually invoking vSphere DRS to ensure all virtual machines are placed on hosts in the correct location to avoid possible performance degradation due to misplacement. In our scenario, misplacement would lead to increased latency, as the virtual machine would be accessing storage in the other location.

Storage Partition

In this scenario, a failure was simulated on the storage network between datacenters, as depicted in the below diagram.

Figure 172: Storage partition

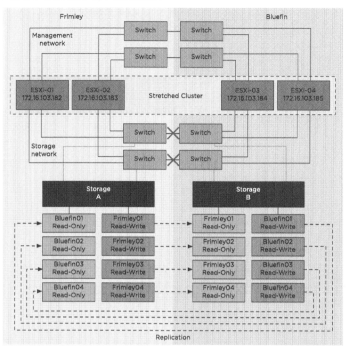

Result
Virtual machines remained running with no impact.

Explanation
Each LUN has storage site affinity defined and vSphere DRS rules aligned with this affinity. Due to this configuration, none of the virtual machines were impacted as their storage remained available within the site where they were running.

If for any reason the affinity rule for a virtual machine has been violated and the virtual machine is running on a host in the Frimley datacenter while its disk resides on a datastore that has affinity with Bluefin datacenter, it will not be able to successfully issue I/O following a inter-site storage partition as the datastore will be in an All Paths Down (APD) condition. As the HA master is still receiving network heartbeats from all hosts in the cluster it would not take any action: Any virtual machines which have violated their site affinity **will not** be restarted by HA unless these virtual machines are manually powered off.

We recommend monitoring compliance of vSphere DRS rules to avoid unnecessary downtime in an APD scenario. Although vSphere DRS is invoked every five minutes, it does not guarantee all affinity rule violations will be resolved during each invocation. Therefore, rigid monitoring is recommended to allow for quick identification of anomalies while preventing unnecessary downtime.

Datacenter Partition

In this scenario, we fully isolated Frimley datacenter from Bluefin datacenter, as depicted in the diagram below.

Figure 173: Datacenter partition

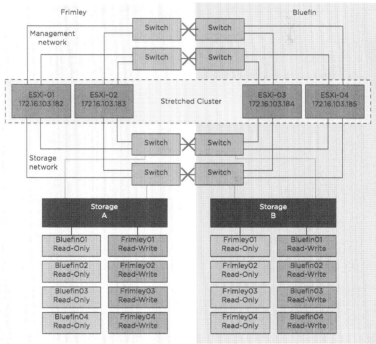

Result
Virtual machines remained running with no impact

Explanation
In this scenario, both Datacenters were fully isolated from each other. This scenario is similar to both the storage partition and host isolation scenarios.

Virtual machines were not impacted by this failure, as vSphere DRS rules were correctly implemented and no rules were violated. HA follows a logical process to determine which virtual machines require restarting during a cluster partition:

The HA master node running in the Frimley datacenter will detect that all hosts in Bluefin datacenter are unreachable. The HA master will first detect that there are no network heartbeats received. After that it will validate if there are any storage heartbeats being generated; this check will not detect storage heartbeats, as the storage connection between sites has also failed and the heartbeat datastores will only be updated "locally" at each site. As the virtual machines with affinity to the remaining hosts are still running, no action is needed for them. Next, HA will validate if a restart can be attempted. Because the read-write versions of the datastores located in Bluefin are not accessible by the hosts in Frimley, so no attempt will be made to start the missing virtual machines at either site.

Likewise, the ESXi hosts in the Bluefin datacenter will detect there is no master available and initiate a master election process. After the new master has been elected, it will try to discover which virtual machines were running before the failure and attempt to restart them. As all virtual machines with affinity to Bluefin are still running in the Bluefin datacenter, there is no need for a restart. Only the virtual machines with affinity to Frimley are unavailable (according to the master at Bluefin), and vSphere HA will not be able to restart these virtual machines because the datastores on which they are stored have affinity to Frimley and are unavailable in the Bluefin datacenter.

If host affinity rules were violated, i.e. virtual machines were running in a location where its storage was not defined as read-write by default, the behavior changes. We purposely violated the configured affinity rules to document this behavior: we manually moved a virtual machine from Frimley to Bluefin. In doing so, we created a situation in which the virtual machine was running on a host in the Bluefin datacenter but was accessing a datastore in the Frimley datacenter. The following sequence is what was witnessed when the datacenters were isolated from each other:

1. The virtual machine with affinity to Frimley but residing in Bluefin was unable to reach its datastore. This resulted in the virtual machine being unable to write to or read from its disk.
2. In the Frimley datacenter, this virtual machine was restarted by vSphere HA as the master in Frimley datacenter was not aware of the instance running in Bluefin datacenter.

3. Since the datastore was only available to hosts within the Frimley datacenter, one of the hosts in the Frimley datacenter could acquire locks on the VM's files and was able to power-on this virtual machine.

4. This created a scenario in which the same virtual machine was powered on and running in both datacenters.

Figure 174: Power-on sequence

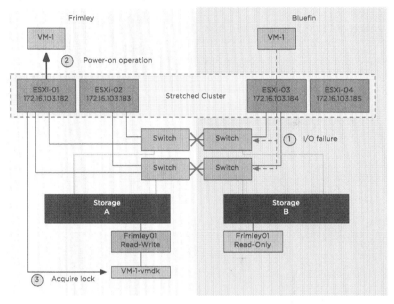

Why is this possible?

- The network heartbeat from the host that is running this virtual machine is missing because there is no Management network connection between sites.

- The datastore heartbeat is missing because there is no storage network connection between sites.

- A ping to the management address of the host which was running the virtual machine fails because there is no Management network connection between sites.

- The master located in the Frimley datacenter knows the virtual machine was powered on before the failure, and since it is unable to communicate with the virtual machine's host in the Bluefin datacenter after the failure, it will attempt to restart the virtual machine.

- The datastore is determined as All Paths Down by hosts in the Bluefin datacenter. As such, no action was taken. As explained earlier, only with a PDL condition will the virtual machine be automatically killed.

When the connection between sites is restored, a classic "virtual machine split brain scenario" will exist. For a short period of time, two copies of the virtual machine will be active on the network with the same MAC address. Only one copy, however, will have access to the virtual machine files, and HA will recognize this. As soon as this is detected, all processes belonging to the virtual machine copy that has no access to the virtual machine files will be killed as depicted in the screenshot below.

Figure 175: Locking problems log messages

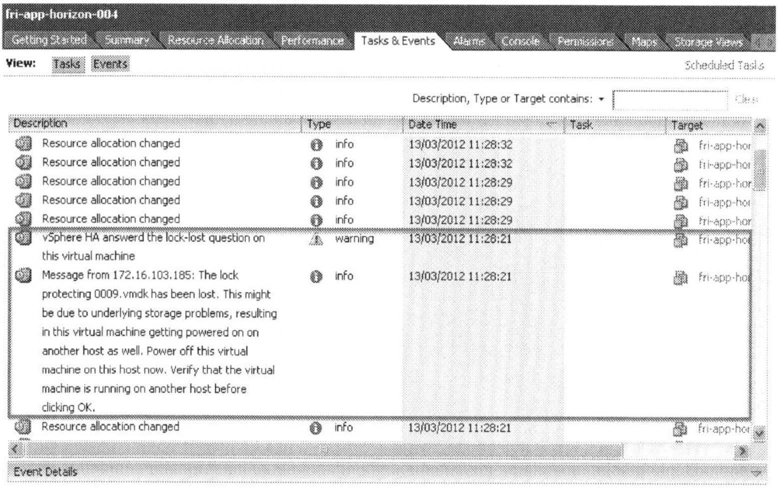

In this example the unnecessary downtime equates to a virtual machine having to be restarted when in reality it shouldn't have been that way if site affinity was maintained correctly. As such we recommend closely monitoring that vSphere DRS rules align with datastore site affinity to prevent unnecessary down time.

Disk shelf failure in Frimley DC

In this scenario, one of the disk-shelves in the Frimley datacenter failed. Both Frimley01 and Frimley02 on Storage A are impacted.

Figure 176: Disk shelf failure

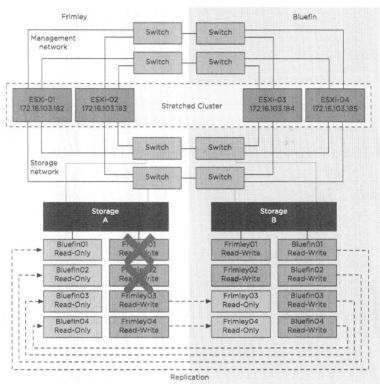

Result

Virtual machines remained running but possibly with increased storage latency.

Explanation

In this scenario, only a disk shelf in the Frimley datacenter failed. The storage processor recognized the failure and instantly switched from the primary disk shelf in the Frimley datacenter to the mirror copy in the Bluefin datacenter. During our tests there was no noticeable impact to any of the virtual machines except for a short spike in terms of "I/O response" time, this was due to the low latency connection between Frimley and Bluefin. This scenario is fully recognized and handled by the stretched storage solution. There is no need for a rescan of the datastores or the HBAs, as the switchover is seamless, and from the ESXi perspective, the LUNs are identical.

Full storage failure in Frimley DC

In this scenario, we tested a full storage system failure in the Frimley datacenter, as depicted in the diagram below.

Figure 177: Full storage failure

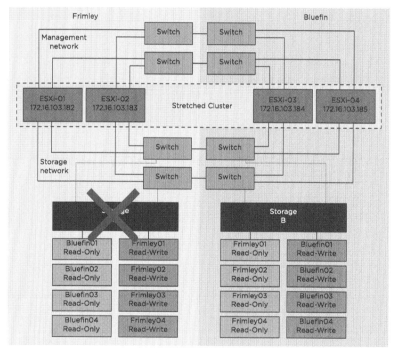

Result
Virtual machines remained running with no impact.

Explanation
When the full storage system failed in the Frimley datacenter, a "take over"

command **had to be initiated manually**. As described above, we used a NetApp MetroCluster configuration. This "take over" command is particular to NetApp environments, but similar commands or processes would be expected to exist in stretched storage solutions from other vendors. After the command was initiated, the mirrored, read-only copy of each of the failed datastores was promoted to read-write and was instantly accessible. Please note we are describing this process on an extremely high level. For more details please refer to the storage vendor's documentation.

From a virtual machine's perspective, this failover is seamless, meaning the storage controllers will handle this and no action is required from the vSphere or Storage administrator. (Note that this is seamless when the take over command is initiated by the Storage Admin!) It should be noted that all I/O will now pass across the intra-site connection to the other Datacenter, as virtual machines will remain running in the Frimley datacenter while their datastores are accessible only in the Bluefin datacenter.

vSphere HA is not aware of this type of failure. Although the datastore heartbeat might be lost briefly, HA will not take action as the HA master agent only checks for the datastore heartbeat when the network heartbeat has not been received for three seconds. Since the network heartbeat remained available throughout the storage failure, HA was not required to initiate any restarts.

Permanent Device Loss

In this scenario, we tested a permanent device loss condition. As this scenario is uncommon in uniform configurations, we forced this by setting a LUN to "offline". Permanent Device Loss conditions are more common in non-uniform vMSC configurations.

Figure 178: Permanent device loss

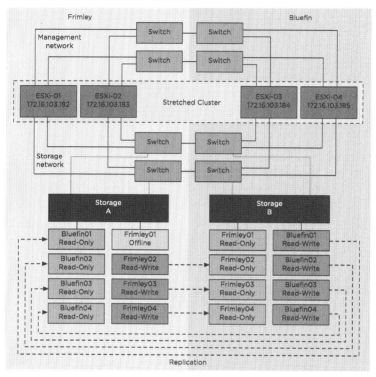

Result
Virtual machines were killed by ESXi and restarted by HA.

Explanation
When the Permanent Device Loss condition was simulated, the virtual machines residing on the datastore were killed instantly. After being killed, the virtual machines were restarted by vSphere HA. The permanent device loss and killing of the virtual machine world group can be witnessed by following the vmkernel.log file located in /var/log/ on the ESXi host. The following is an outtake of the vmkernel.log file where a PDL is recognized and appropriate action is taken.

```
2012-03-14T13:39:25.085Z cpu7:4499)WARNING: VSCSI:
4055: handle 8198(vscsi4:0):opened by wid 4499
(vmm0:fri-iscsi-02) has Permanent Device Loss.
Killing world group leader 4491
```

We recommend setting advanced options *disk.terminateVMOnPDLDefault* and *das.maskCleanShutdownEnabled* to "True". If these are not configured (by default *das.maskCleanShutdownEnabled* is set to "False"), then vSphere HA will not take any action and the virtual machines affected by a PDL would possibly not be restarted.

Full Compute Failure in Frimley DC

In this scenario, we tested a full compute failure in the Frimley datacenter by simultaneously removing power from all hosts within the site.

Figure 179: Full compute failure

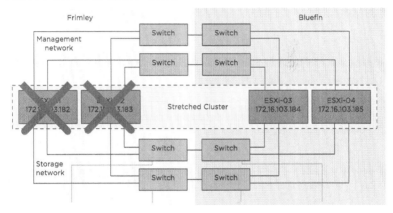

Result

All virtual machines were successfully restarted on hosts in the Bluefin datacenter. Note that the storage used is in Frimley.

Explanation

The vSphere HA master was located in Frimley at the time of the full compute failure in the Frimley datacenter. Once the hosts in the Bluefin datacenter detected that no network heartbeats were being received, an election process was started. Within ~20 seconds, a new vSphere HA master was elected from the remaining hosts after which the new master determined which hosts had failed and which virtual machines were impacted by this failure. As all hosts at the other site had failed and all virtual machines they held were impacted, vSphere HA initiated the restart of all of these virtual machines. vSphere HA can initiate 32 concurrent restarts on a single host, providing a low restart latency for most environments. The only sequencing of start order comes from the broad categories of *High, Medium* and *Low* categories for HA, which is a policy that must be set on a per-virtual machine basis. These policies were seen to be adhered to, and high priority virtual machines were started first, followed by the medium and low priority virtual machines.

As part of the test, we powered on the hosts in Frimley datacenter again. As soon as vSphere DRS detected these hosts were again available, a vSphere DRS run was invoked. This initial DRS execution only solved the violated vSphere DRS affinity rules. As expected, the resulting resource imbalance was not corrected until the next full invocation of vSphere DRS. DRS is invoked by default every 5 minutes, or when virtual machines are powered off / on through the use of the vCenter client.

Loss of Frimley datacenter

In this scenario, a full failure of the Frimley datacenter is simulated.

Figure 180: Loss of datacenter

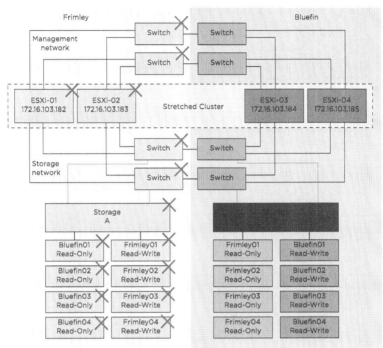

Result

All Frimley virtual machines were successfully restarted in the Bluefin datacenter.

Explanation

In this scenario, the hosts in the Bluefin datacenter lost contact with the vSphere HA master and elected a new vSphere HA master. As the storage system had failed, a "take over" command needed to be initiated on the surviving site, again due to NetApp specific process. After the "take over" command had been initiated, the new vSphere HA master accessed the per-datastore files that HA uses to record the set of protected virtual machines. The vSphere HA master then attempted to restart those virtual machines that were not running on the surviving hosts in the Bluefin datacenter. In our scenario, all virtual machines were restarted within two minutes after failure and fully accessible and functional again. Note: vSphere HA might stop attempting to start a virtual machine after 30 minutes by default. If the storage team had not issued the take over command within that timeframe, the vSphere administrator would need to manually start up virtual machines once the storage is available.

There is a slight variance if the newly elected master is still connected to vCenter. Although highly unlikely in most environments, if this happens vCenter will tell the new master that the failed virtual machines are initially not compatible with any host in the surviving datacenter, and will then tell it when they are compatible again. If the master knows the virtual machines are incompatible, it will not keep trying to restart them. The master will not initiate the restart but will wait for the hosts to become compatible and then attempt the restarts.

Chapter 32

Summarizing

Hopefully we have succeeded in giving you a better understanding of all the clustering features vSphere offers and how these integrate with each other in a specific scenario. All of these have one common goal: increase availability. Whether it is uptime, compute or storage resource availability, vSphere 5.1 offers a solution for all.

We have tried to simplify some of the concepts to make it easier to understand; yet we acknowledge that some of these concepts are difficult to grasp. We hope though that after reading this book everyone is confident enough to make the required or recommended changes to increase availability of their virtual machines.

If there are any questions please do not hesitate to reach out to either of the authors. We will we do our best to answer your questions.

Thanks for reading,

Duncan and Frank

Made in the USA
Lexington, KY
28 May 2013